COMPANY SECRETARY'S CHECKLISTS

CW01034391

Eleventh edition

Douglas Armour FCG

icsa
The Chartered
Governance
Institute

First published 1992

Published by
ICSA Publishing Limited
Saffron House, 6–10 Kirby Street
London ECIN 8TS

© ICSA Publishing Limited, 2019

All rights reserved. No part of this publication may be reproduced, stored
in a retrieval system, or transmitted, in any form, or by any means,
electronic, mechanical, photocopying, recording or otherwise, without prior
permission, in writing, from the publisher.

The right of Douglas Armour to be identified as author of this Work has
been asserted by him/her in accordance with sections 77 and 78 of the
Copyright, Designs and Patents Act 1988.

Typeset by Paul Barrett Book Production, Cambridge
Edited by Sheida Heidari
Cover designed by Anthony Kearney

British Library Cataloguing in Publication Data
A catalogue record for this book is available from the British Library.

ISBN 978-1-86072-775-7

As with all legislation, the provisions of the Companies Acts and related
legislation are open to interpretation and must be assessed in the context
of the particular circumstances at hand, the articles of association of the
company in question, and any relevant shareholders' agreement or other
pertinent ancillary agreements. While every effort has been made to ensure
the accuracy of the content of this book, neither the author nor the publisher
can accept any responsibility for any loss arising to anyone relying on the
information contained herein.

Table of Contents

About the author

Douglas Armour FCG had a career spanning more than 31 years at David Venus & Company, including a period as managing director following the acquisition of the company by the Equiniti Group. Douglas was group company secretary at Equiniti Group PLC during its transition from private equity ownership through its IPO and Listing on the London Stock Exchange in 2015. Douglas left the Equiniti Group at the end of 2016 and after a short career break joined Intertrust's capital markets governance team as a senior manager and team leader.

Douglas has more than 30 years' experience in all aspects of company secretarial procedures for companies of all sizes from owner-managed private companies to FTSE 100 companies.

Over the course of those 30 years, Douglas has accumulated a wealth of practical experience and has drawn on this to include in this book those procedures that company secretaries, directors and practitioners will find most useful.

Foreword

I am delighted to introduce this new edition of the Company Secretary's Checklists.

Governance is everywhere. It seems that more days than not there is an article in the press about some aspect of governance. That makes it a great time to be a company secretary or governance professional because, for every negative story that we see, there are countless other organisations where good governance, well done, benefits both business and society.

Over the last decade or so, the role of the company secretary has changed beyond all recognition. As expectations of governance standards have grown across all organisations, not just in the corporate sector, company secretaries are increasingly visible and our role has grown in scope from that of technical expert to one of adviser and counsellor to the board.

We are seeing a shift from the simple mastery of specialist knowledge to an increasing focus on the development of the so-called softer skills and values essential to a governance role; the ability to influence and guide. Beyond a certain level, employers take technical ability as read, but they know that without the ability to communicate, support others and connect legal and regulatory knowledge for commercial purpose, growth potential is limited.

The core focus of our profession, that technical ability, is fundamental to what we do and who we are. It gives us access to the boardroom where our knowledge and expertise are tested. Without a sound basis of technical knowledge our ability to deliver at the highest levels of our organisation will be limited.

Just to challenge us that little bit more, we have also seen in recent years a constant stream of revisions from Government and from regulators of the rules underpinning our specialist knowledge. We have also witnessed constant development and restatement of good practice in our market, be it guidance from our Institute or, more often, statements from investors, their advisers and commentators. A few examples of these changes, which you can find in this new edition, include the 2018 UK Corporate Governance Code, the Wates Principles for governance in large private companies and new disclosure requirements covering the gender pay gap, Modern Slavery Act, payment policies and the PSC Register.

That is why these checklists are so helpful – they provide a quick reference guide to the latest statutory and regulatory requirements. You can be forgiven for missing a new opinion piece from a consultancy, however helpful or sensible it may be, but not for a legal or regulatory mis-step. This book is now in its 11th edition and I am sure that it will soon become one of the most thumbed items on your team bookshelf.

Victoria Whyte, FCG
(Victoria has been a practicing Company Secretary for over 15 years and GlaxoSmithKline plc's Company Secretary since 2011).

Preface

The *Company Secretary's Checklists* provides a handy, quick reference guide to the more common company secretarial procedures. The book is not intended to be a legal reference book, and accordingly little explanation of the relevant legislation is made. As more detailed information will often be required, the book has been cross-referenced to the relevant legislation, the *Company Secretary's Handbook* (12th edition).

Each topic comprises a general commentary on the particular matter, a checklist of items to be considered, procedural steps to be taken, Companies House filing requirements, as well as general notes and cross-references. All section number references are to the Companies Act 2006 unless stated otherwise.

The Companies House references are to their series of guidance booklets which are available on request by post or may be downloaded from the Companies House website (www.gov.uk/government/organisations/companies-house).

These checklists should not be regarded as exhaustive, to be followed in all circumstances, but should serve as a guide to the reader indicating procedures that should be considered in the context of the matter at hand.

Although, overall, the checklists have been prepared with private or non-traded public companies in mind, many of the procedures are equally applicable, and in some cases only applicable, to public or listed companies.

The book will be of particular interest to the following:

▶ *Accountant/auditors*. Many private company directors will turn to their accountant for advice on company secretarial matters. This book sets out answers to the majority of procedural queries likely to be raised.

▶ *Solicitors/chartered secretary practices*. While most solicitors and chartered secretaries will have access to extensive libraries of legal reference books, these are often too detailed for quick reference. This book is intended to complement rather than duplicate existing reference sources.

▶ *Company secretaries/directors*. Company secretaries will find this book of particular use when advising their directors on particular matters, even if advice will ultimately be sought from the company's professional advisers.

An understanding of the practical issues for any particular matter will facilitate proper discussion at board level, collation of relevant information and the issuing of coherent instructions to professional advisers.

Douglas Armour

September 2019

Acronyms

ABI	Association of British Insurers
AGM	annual general meeting
BEIS	Department of Business, Energy and Industrial Strategy
CA2006	Companies Act 2006
CGC	UK Corporate Governance Code
CIC	Community Interest Companies
EEA	European Economic Area
EEIG	European Economic Interest Grouping
EES	European Employment Strategy
EU	European Union
FCA	Financial Conduct Authority
FRC	Financial Reporting Council
FSMA2000	Financial Services and Markets Act 2000
HMRC	Her Majesty's Revenue & Customs
HR	human resources
LLP	limited liability partnership
LPA	lasting power of attorney
LPDTR	Listing, Prospectus, Disclosure and Transparency Rules
LTIP	Long-term Incentive Plan
MCA2005	Mental Capacity Act 2005
MiFID	Markets in Financial Instruments Directive
NAPF	National Association of Pension Funds
NE RFI	NEX Exchange Rules for Issuers
NI	National Insurance
OCR	Overseas Companies Regulations (2009)
PAYE	pay as you earn
PLC	public limited company
PROOF	PROtected Online Filing
PSC	person with significant control
RIS	Regulatory Inspection Service
SAIL	single alternative inspection location
SAYE	save as you earn
SBEE2015	Small Business Enterprise and Employment Act 2015
SIC	Standard Industrial Classification
UCITS	Undertakings for Collective Investment in Transferable Securities
UKLA	United Kingdom Listing Authority
VAT	value added tax

Accounting reference date

All companies other than dormant companies, whether trading or not, must prepare accounts and file a copy with the Registrar of Companies. The accounts are prepared in respect of each accounting period. Accounting periods begin at the conclusion of the previous period, or the date of incorporation, and end on the accounting reference date. Companies may choose an accounting reference date. If no alternative date is chosen, the company's accounting reference date will default to the last day of the month of its incorporation.

s.394

s.391(4)

A company may change its accounting reference date at any time, provided the filing date for the existing period has not expired. An accounting reference period may not exceed 18 months and, except in the circumstances set out below, a company may not extend its accounting period twice in any five-year period.

s.392

A company may only extend its accounting period more than once in any five-year period if it is changing to fall in line with the accounting reference date of a holding or subsidiary company, or if the company is in administration.

s.392(3)

Provided the filing date for the period being shortened has not expired, a company may shorten its current or immediately preceding accounting period as often as it wishes and there is no minimum period. Where the accounting period is shortened, the new filing date will be nine months (private company) or six months (public company) from the end of the new accounting period or, if later, three months after the notice to shorten.

s.442(4)

Checklist

▷ The filing period for the financial year being changed must not have expired.

s.392(4)

▷ The filing period for the proposed new period must not have expired.

s.392(5)

▷ The new period must not be longer than 18 months, unless an administration order is in force.

s.392(5)

▷ If extending the period, the company must not previously have extended its accounting year-end in the previous five years, or if it has, can the change be justified?

s.392(3)

▷ If the new year-end has already passed, can accounts to that date be prepared (e.g. stocktakes, asset valuation)?

▶ Directors' resolution is required either at a meeting or by written resolution.

▶ File form AA01.   s.392(1)

Procedure

▶ Convene a directors' meeting to authorise the change in accounting year.

▶ Form AA01 must be filed at Companies House.

Filing requirement

▶ Form AA01.

Notes

▶ The company's first accounting period must be longer than six
months, but not longer than 18 months, starting from the date of   s.391(5)
incorporation. The first accounting period begins with the date of
incorporation even if the company does not immediately commence   s.390(2)
trading.

▶ The second and subsequent accounting periods may be as short as the
directors wish, but may not exceed 18 months.   s.392(5)

▶ A company can extend its accounting year only once in any five-year
period, unless the accounting period is being changed to coincide   s.392(3)
with that of its holding company or any subsidiary. The accounting
period can be shortened as many times as required.

▶ The length of any accounting period, even one that has ended, can
be altered, provided that the relevant form is received by the Registrar
before the end of the period in which the accounts for that current or   s.392(1)
proposed period must be filed. The change in year-end will become
effective once the Registrar of Companies has received and accepted
the appropriate form.

▶ Directors wishing to extend the accounting period must first confirm
that the accounting year-end has not been extended in the previous
five years.

▶ The date by which accounts must be submitted to the Registrar may
be lengthened when the accounting period is for a period of less than
12 months, as the filing period is the usual period after the accounting
reference date or three months after the date of receipt of the form
AA01, if longer (see page 12).

▶ Normally a private company has nine months from its accounting   s.442(4)
reference date to file its accounts; for a public company the period is   s.442
six months.

▷ Companies can make their accounts up to any date within seven days
of the actual accounting reference date. This is to enable companies to
undertake a stocktake outside normal business hours without needing
to change their year-end. **s.390(2)(b)**

▷ Companies may apply for an extension to the filing deadline provided
this is received by the Registrar prior to the filing deadline; however,
there need to be exceptional circumstances in order to be granted an
extension. **s.442(5)**

▷ In addition to notifying the Registrar of Companies, the directors may
also consider notifying the following: bankers, auditors, accountants,
HM Revenue & Customs, subsidiaries, joint venture partners, London
Stock Exchange (if listed).

▷ The change in accounting reference date is only effective once the
form AA01 is accepted and registered by Companies House.

More information

▷ *Company Secretary's Handbook*, Chapter 11

▷ Companies House Guidance – Filing accounts

Accounts – approval

Accounts, whether audited or not, must be prepared and approved by the board of directors and issued to the company's members, any debenture holders and anyone else entitled to receive notice of general meetings.

ss.394,414,423

Although members of a public company consider and receive the accounts in general meetings and can vote on whether or not to accept them, they do not, strictly speaking, approve them. If the members reject them, the directors are not obliged to amend the accounts unless they contain a factual error. However, non-acceptance of accounts will be regarded as a vote of no confidence in the board.

s.437

Checklist

▶ Convene a directors' meeting for directors to approve the accounts. Ensure valid quorum present.

s.414(1)

▶ The strategic report and directors' report must be signed by a director or by the company secretary, as required.

ss.414D(1),419(1)
s.433

▶ Quoted companies must prepare a directors' remuneration report which must be signed by a director or the company secretary (see page 7). Companies defined as large under the Act must prepare a separate, clearly identifiable statement describing how the directors have had regard to the matters set out in CA2006 s. 172(1)(a) to (f) when performing their duty under s. 172 [s.172(1)].

ss.420,422

▶ The balance sheet must be signed by at least one director.

s.414(2)

▶ The name of the person(s) signing the directors' report, strategic report, remuneration report (if any) and balance sheet must be stated.

s.433

▶ If audited, the audit report must be signed by the auditor, if an individual, or by the senior statutory auditor, in the case of a firm, and the person's name and the date of approval shown.

ss.503–505

▶ The name of the senior statutory auditor may be omitted if there are concerns over safety.

s.506

▶ Small companies must issue to their members the accounts in the same format as those placed on the public record. In the case of a private company it must send out its accounts to members before the end of

ss.423,424,444

the period allowed for filing the accounts (usually nine months (see page 12)). In the case of a public company, the accounts must be sent out at least 21 days before the date of the meeting to receive them.

▷ Full or abridged accounts must be filed at Companies House by the due date (see page 12). **ss.441,442**

Procedure

▷ Convene a directors' meeting to consider the accounts and to convene a general meeting. Ensure valid quorum present.

▷ Final draft of the accounts to be approved by the directors.

▷ The directors' report, strategic report and the balance sheet must be signed. The directors' report and strategic report can be signed by the company secretary or a director; however, the balance sheet must be signed by at least one director. The published accounts must include the names of the director and/or company secretary who have signed the balance sheet and directors' report.

▷ A quoted company must prepare a directors' remuneration report, which must be signed by a director or the company secretary.

▷ The same director can sign the directors' report, strategic report, directors' remuneration report (if any) and the balance sheet.

▷ If the accounts are audited, signed copies must be returned to the auditors so that the audit report can be signed.

▷ Once signed, a copy of the accounts must be filed with the Registrar of Companies within the appropriate period (see below).

▷ Copies of the accounts must be sent to the members and public companies must convene a general meeting of the members, for the shareholders to consider the accounts, within six months. Private companies are exempted from the obligation to convene a members' meeting unless required to do so by their articles of association. **s.442**

▷ Companies, if authorised to do so by individual members, may issue the strategic report and supplemental material to the members in place of the full accounts, provided that the full accounts are made available on request. This replaces the option to issue a summary financial statement which has been withdrawn. **s.426**

▷ Certain companies may file abridged accounts with the Registrar of Companies (see pages 17 and 21).

▷ Full accounts will be required for submission to HM Revenue & Customs.

▷ Additional copies will normally be sent to the company's bankers.

▷ The usual period for delivery of accounts to the Registrar is nine months from the end of the accounting period for a private company, and six months for a public company. However, if the accounts are **s.441,442** the first accounts and are for a period of more than 12 months, the accounts must be submitted no later than nine months (six months for a public company) from the first anniversary of incorporation, or three months from the end of the period – whichever expires later. **s.442(3)**

▷ Where the accounting period has been shortened, the period for delivery of the accounts is nine months for private companies and six months for public companies from the end of the period, or three months from the date of notice – whichever expires later. **s.442(4)**

▷ The Registrar of Companies imposes penalties for late submission of accounts. When setting the accounting reference date, care must be taken to ensure that the accounts can be prepared in time to submit them to the Registrar of Companies (see page 12). **s.453**

Filing requirement

▷ Full or abridged copy of the accounts within 21 months of the start of the accounting period for a private company (usually nine months after the year-end) and within 18 months of the start of the accounting period for a public company (usually six months after the year-end).

Notes

▷ Accounts must have original signatures on the directors' report, strategic report, directors' remuneration report, audit report (if audited) and balance sheet. **s.414(1)**

▷ The name of the person signing must be shown.

▷ The company registration number must be shown on the first page.

▷ As the Registrar will unbind and discard any folder, an unbound copy of the accounts should be filed.

▷ The accounts must be legible and be capable of being digitally scanned. Accordingly, it is best to file typed accounts printed on plain paper. Accounts printed on coloured or glossy paper or with graphics are likely to be rejected as illegible.

▷ As the accounts are not subject to member approval, it is not necessary to wait until after the general meeting at which the accounts are received by members before filing a copy of the accounts with the Registrar of Companies. The s. 172 statement applies to financial years beginning on or after 1 January 2019.

More information

▷ *Company Secretary's Handbook*, Chapter 10

▷ Companies House Guidance – Filing accounts

Accounts – directors' remuneration report

Directors of listed companies are required to include a remuneration report in the annual report and accounts. The report must also comply with the Listing Rules and the UK Corporate Governance Code. Where the provisions of the UK Corporate Governance Code are not complied with, a statement of those provisions not complied with and the explanation for such departure must be included.

s.420(1)

The requirements of the Large and Medium-sized Companies and Groups (Accounts and Reports) (Amendment) Regulations 2013 came into force on 1 October 2013 and, in particular, replaced schedule 8 of the Large and Medium-sized Companies and Groups (Accounts and Reports) Regulations 2008. References here to schedule 8 are to the 2008 regulations as amended by the 2013 regulations and as further amended by the Companies, Partnerships and Groups (Accounts and Reports) Regulations 2015.

In addition to these regulations, provisions of the Enterprise and Regulatory Reform Act 2013 ss. 79–82 made changes to the Companies Act 2006 regarding the payments to directors of quoted companies, and these will also need to be considered.

The Directors' Remuneration Report now comprises two parts: an annual Statement and Report on Remuneration (the Implementation Report) and the Directors' Remuneration Policy (the Remuneration Policy).

Checklist

Annual statement

▷ Annual statement by the chairperson of the committee of any major decisions or substantial changes on directors' remuneration during the year.

Para. 3 sch. 8,
SI 2008/410
(as amended)

Remuneration

▷ Single total figure of remuneration for each director, broken down into:

▷ salary and fees;

Para. 4–12 sch. 8,
SI 2008/410
(as amended)

▷ all taxable benefits;

▷ money or other assets received/receivable for more than one financial year;

▷ pension-related benefits; and

▷ total (aggregate of the above).

▶ Total pension entitlements.

▶ Scheme interests awarded during the financial year.

▶ Payments to past directors.

▶ Payments for loss of office.

▶ Statement of directors' shareholding and share interests.

▶ Performance graph and table.

▶ Percentage change in remuneration of CEO.

▶ Relative importance of spend on pay.

▶ Statement of implementation of remuneration policy in the following financial year.

▶ Consideration by the directors of matters relating to directors' remuneration.

▶ Statement of voting at general meeting.

▶ Details of the unexpired term of any service contract of a director proposed for election or re-election at the AGM, and if any director does not have a directors' service contract, a statement to that effect.

Para. 13 sch. 8, SI 2008/410 (as amended)
Para. 14 sch. 8, SI 2008/410 (as amended)
Para. 15 sch. 8, SI 2008/410 (as amended)
Para. 16 sch. 8, SI 2008/410 (as amended)
Para. 17 sch. 8, SI 2008/410 (as amended)
Para. 18 sch. 8, SI 2008/410 (as amended)
Para. 19 sch. 8, SI 2008/410 (as amended)
Para. 20 sch. 8, SI 2008/410 (as amended)
Para. 21 sch. 8, SI 2008/410 (as amended)
Para. 22 sch. 8, SI 2008/410 (as amended)
Para. 23 sch. 8, SI 2008/410 (as amended)

Procedure

▶ The contents of the remuneration report must be approved by the board at a board meeting.

s. 422

▶ A resolution to approve the remuneration report (advisory, not binding) must be put to shareholders at the same meeting at which the accounts are received.

s. 439

More information

▶ *Company Secretary's Handbook*, Chapter 10

▶ FCA Listing Rules

Accounts – exemption from audit

Small private companies and dormant public companies qualify for exemption from audit if they satisfy certain criteria. These companies do not need to apply for the exemption; they are automatically exempt if they qualify.

ss. 477, 480, 482

For accounting years beginning on or after 1 January 2016, qualifying subsidiary companies can claim exemption from audit. Subsidiary companies that are public (unless they are dormant), regulated under FSMA and members of ineligible groups cannot take advantage of the new exemption.

s. 476

Shareholders holding between them at least 10% of the company's issued share capital, or 10% of the members in the case of a company without share capital, may give notice to the company requiring that the accounts be audited, provided that the notice is given no later than one month prior to the end of the financial year.

s. 477

Checklist

▶ Total exemption is available to companies:

  ▷ that qualify as a small company in relation to that year (see page 21) by meeting any two of the following:

s. 477, 479, 480

    – whose turnover does not exceed £10.2 million in that year; or

    – whose balance sheet total for that year does not exceed £5.1 million; or

    – whose average number of employees is not more than 50.

▶ A company is not entitled to exemption from audit if at any time during the financial year:

s. 478, 479B, 481

  ▷ it was a public company, unless it was dormant; or

  ▷ it was a banking or insurance company, e-money issuer, a MiFID investment firm, a UCITS management company or carried on insurance market activities; or

  ▷ it was a special register body or an employers' association as defined in the Trade Union and Labour Relations (Consolidation) Act 1992 or the Industrial Relations (Northern Ireland) Order 1992.

▶ A company that is a parent or subsidiary undertaking at any time during the financial year is not entitled to exemption from audit unless:

   ▷ the group qualifies as small (see page 21) and was not at any time during that year an ineligible group (see below);

   ▷ turnover of the whole group does not exceed £10.2 million net or £12.2 million gross; and

   ▷ the group's continued balance sheet total does not exceed £5.1 million net or £6.1 million gross.

s.479 (A)

▶ A company that is a dormant subsidiary throughout the period is not excluded from qualifying as small under s. 479(2).

s.479(3)

▶ A group is ineligible if any member of the group is:

s.384

   ▷ a traded company;

   ▷ a corporate body whose shares are admitted to trading on a regulated market in an EES State;

   ▷ a person authorised under FSMA2000 to carry on a regulated activity;

   ▷ a small company that is an authorised insurance company, banking company, e-money issuer, MiFID investment firm or a UCITS management company; or

   ▷ a person who carries on insurance market activity.

Procedure

▶ There is no procedure; exemption is automatic if the criteria are met.

▶ To qualify for the subsidiary company exemption, the following must be filed prior to the expiry of the period allowed for filing accounts. In practice these are usually submitted at the same time as the subsidiary's accounts are filed at Companies House:

   ▷ Written notice that all members agree to the exemption.

   ▷ Form AA06 – statement from parent undertaking that it guarantees the subsidiary.

s.479C

   ▷ Copy of parent undertaking's consolidated accounts, including a copy of the auditor's report and annual report on these accounts.

Filing requirement

▶ Copy of the accounts within the appropriate timescale, usually six months for a public company or nine months for a private company (see page 12).

s.442

▶ Copies of the accounts are still required to be circulated to members within the appropriate timescale: six months for a public company and nine months for a private company.

s.423

For subsidiary exemption

▷ Written notice that all members agree to the exemption.

▷ Form AA06 – statement from parent undertaking that it guarantees the subsidiary.

▷ Copy of parent undertaking's consolidated accounts, including a copy of the auditor's report and annual report on these accounts.

Notes

▷ A company that qualifies for exemption from audit is also exempt from the obligation to appoint auditors.

ss. 475, 485

More information

▷ *Company Secretary's Handbook*, Chapter 10

▷ Companies House Guidance – Filing accounts

Accounts – filing period

All companies except dormant subsidiaries, whether trading or not, must prepare accounts and file a copy with the Registrar of Companies. Dormant subsidiaries may take an advantage not to file accounts with Companies House provided those accounts are consolidated in their parent company accounts, all the members consent, the parent company guarantees the liabilities of the subsidiary and relevant notifications are made to the Registrar. The accounts are prepared in respect of each accounting period. Accounting periods begin at the conclusion of the previous period, or the date of incorporation, and end on the accounting reference date.

s.390, 448A

There are strict timescales for the filing of accounts and financial penalties imposed when accounts are filed late (see page 14).

s.390(2)

Accounts must be filed even where the company does not or has never traded.

Checklist

▶ Accounts for a private company must be filed within nine months of the accounting reference period ending, unless:

s.442(2)(a)

  ▷ it is the first accounting period and is for a period of greater than 12 months – the deadline is three months after the period end or 21 months from the date of incorporation, whichever is later; or

s.442(3)

  ▷ the company has shortened its accounting period – the deadline is nine months from the end of the new period or three months after the change was registered at Companies House, whichever expires last.

s.442(4)

▶ Accounts for a public company must be filed within six months of the accounting reference period ending, unless:

s.442(2)(b)

  ▷ it is the first accounting period and is for a period of greater than 12 months – the deadline is three months after the period end or 18 months from the date of incorporation, whichever is later; or

s.442(3)

  ▷ the company has shortened its accounting period – the deadline is six months from the end of the new period or three months after the change was registered at Companies House, whichever expires last.

s.442(4)

▶ Whether the filing period follows the period allowed for a private or public company is determined by the company's status immediately before the end of the relevant period.   **s.442(6)**

▶ When calculating the filing deadline, it should be noted that the date of the month is the same date in the appropriate month corresponding to the accounting reference date. Thus a private company with an accounting reference date of 10 January must file its accounts no later than 10 October following.   **s.443(2)**

▶ If the accounting reference date is the last date of the month, the filing period ends on the last day of the appropriate month. Thus a private company with an accounting reference date of 30 April must file its accounts no later than 31 January.   **s.443(3)**

▶ If the accounting reference date is the 29th or 30th (and not the last day of that month) and the appropriate deadline month is February, the filing period ends on the last day of February in that year.   **s.443(4)**

More information

▶ *Company Secretary's Handbook*, Chapter 10

▶ Companies House Guidance – Filing accounts

Accounts – late filing penalties

If accounts, whether audited or dormant, are received by the Registrar of Companies after the due date for filing has passed, the company will be fined according to a sliding scale.

s.453

It should be noted that the onus is on directors to deliver accounts to the Registrar of Companies within the specified time. It is not sufficient to show that they were posted within the specified time. Late filing penalties do not apply to annual returns.

s.441(1)

The scale of penalties is as follows:

	Private companies	Public companies
Up to one month late	£150	£750
Up to three months late	£375	£1,500
Up to six months late	£750	£3,000
More than six months late	£1,500	£7,500

Notes

▶ The penalties are imposed on the company, not the directors, and are a civil matter. However, under certain circumstances, the directors may also be prosecuted for failure to submit accounts on time. This is a criminal offence, and on conviction a maximum fine of £2,000 may be imposed by the court for each separate offence.

s.453
s.451

▶ Unlimited companies do not need to file copies of their accounts with the Registrar of Companies.

s.448

▶ The penalties are doubled if a company files its accounts late in two successive financial years beginning on or after 6 April 2008.

More information

▶ *Company Secretary's Handbook*, Chapter 10

▶ Companies House Guidance – Filing accountss

Accounts – medium-sized companies

Companies qualifying as medium-sized can prepare accounts under special provisions applicable to medium-sized companies and can choose to submit reduced information to Companies House.

ss.441(1), 445

Checklist

▶ In order to qualify or to be treated as qualifying as a medium-sized company in respect of any particular financial year, the company must be or have been medium-sized during one or more of the following periods:

s.465(1)

  ▷ in its first financial year;

s.465(2)(a)

  ▷ in that year and in the year before;

s.465(2)(b)

  ▷ in that year and if the company qualified in the year before; or

s.465(2)(c)

  ▷ in the preceding year and if the company qualified as medium-sized in respect of that year.

s.465(3)

▶ A medium-sized company is one that meets at least two of the following requirements:

  ▷ turnover not exceeding £36 million;

s.467(1)

  ▷ balance sheet total not exceeding £18 million; and

s.467(2)

  ▷ average number of employees not exceeding 250.

▶ A company does not qualify if at any time during the financial year it was:

  ▷ a public company;

s.467(1)

  ▷ authorised under Part 4 FSMA2000 to carry on a regulated activity or carry on insurance market activities; or

  ▷ a member of an ineligible group.

▶ A group is ineligible if any of its members is:

  ▷ a public company;

  ▷ a corporate body whose shares are admitted to trading on a regulated market in an EES State;

▷ a person (other than a small company) authorised under FSMA2000 to carry on a regulated activity;

▷ a small company that is an authorised insurance company, banking company, e-money issuer, MiFID investment firm or a UCITS management company; or

▷ a person who carries on insurance market activity.

Procedure

▶ The information required for medium-sized accounts must include:

▷ full balance sheet;   **s.445(1)**

▷ profit and loss account;   **s.445(3)(a)**

▷ special auditors' report unless exempt from audit;   **ss.449(2),(5)**

▷ directors' and strategic reports; and   **s.445(1)**

▷ full notes.

Filing requirement

▶ Copy of the medium-sized accounts within the appropriate timescale,   **s.442**
usually six months for a public company and nine months for a private
company (see page 12).

Notes

▶ As with the exception of the profit and loss account and the omission of an analysis of non-financial key performance, medium-sized accounts are the same as full accounts; there may be little practical benefit from utilising the exemption.

▶ Copies of the full statutory accounts, omitting, if desired, disclosures   **s.423**
relating to compliance with accounting standards and related party
transactions, are still required to be circulated to members within the
appropriate timescale: six months for a public company and nine
months for a private company.

More information

▶ *Company Secretary's Handbook*, Chapter 10

▶ Companies House Guidance – Filing accounts

Accounts – micro-sized companies

Within the category of small companies is a sub-set for extremely small or micro companies.

s.384A

Checklist

▶ In order to qualify or to be treated as qualifying as a micro-sized company in respect of any particular financial year, the company must be or have been micro-sized during one or more of the following periods:

  ▷ in its first financial year;   s.384A(1)

  ▷ in that year and in the year before; or   s.384A(2)

  ▷ if it fails to qualify in that year but the company qualified in the year before.   s.384A(3)

▶ A micro-sized company is one that meets at least two of the following requirements:

  ▷ turnover not exceeding £632,000;

  ▷ balance sheet total not exceeding £316,000; and   s.384A(4)

  ▷ average number of employees not exceeding 10.

▶ A company does not qualify if at any time during the financial year it was:

  ▷ a company excluded from the small companies regime by virtue of s. 384;

  ▷ an investment undertaking;   s.384B(1)

  ▷ a financial holding undertaking;

  ▷ a credit or insurance institution; or

  ▷ a charity.

▶ A company does not qualify if:

  ▷ it is a parent company which prepared group accounts; or

  ▷ the company is not a parent but its accounts are included in consolidated group accounts for that year.

Procedure

▶ The information required for micro-sized accounts is:

  ▷ balance sheet;   **ss. 444, 444A**

  ▷ special auditors' report unless exempt from audit; and

  ▷ relevant notes.

▶ Additionally there must be the following note to the accounts: **s. 444**

  ▷ a statement above the director's signature on the balance sheet that the directors have relied on the exemptions the company is entitled to benefit from as a micro-sized company.

Filing requirement

▶ Copy of the micro-entity accounts within the appropriate timescale, usually six months for a public company and nine months for a private company (see page 12).   **s. 442**

Notes

▶ As with the exception of the profit and loss account, abbreviated micro-sized accounts are the same as full accounts; there is little practical benefit from utilising the exemption.

▶ Small companies must now place on public record the same set of accounts and reports as circulated to its members. Previously, companies circulated full accounts to their members and could opt to file abbreviated accounts for the public record.   **s. 444(3)**

More information

▶ *Company Secretary's Handbook*, Chapter 10

▶ Companies House Guidance – Filing accounts

Accounts – overseas company

The obligation for an overseas company, registered in the UK, to file accounting information depends on whether it is required to prepare, disclose and deliver accounting information under its parent law and if it is, whether it is an EEA company.

reg. 34 SI 2009/1801

An EEA company that is required to prepare, disclose and deliver accounting documents under its parent law must deliver the same documents to Companies House within three months of the deadline for disclosure in its home country.

reg. 40 SI 2009/1801

An EEA company that is required to prepare and disclose but not deliver accounts under its parent law is not required to deliver accounts to Companies House.

A non-EEA overseas company that is required to prepare and disclose accounting documents under its parent law must deliver these to Companies House within three months of the deadline for disclosure in its home country.

A non-EEA company that is not required to prepare and disclose accounting documents under its parent law is required to prepare, sign and deliver accounts to Companies House. The accounting provisions are set out in the Overseas Companies Regulations 2009.

An overseas company that is not required to prepare and disclose accounts under its parent law is required to prepare accounts as if it were a company incorporated under the Companies Act, and ss. 390–392, 394–397, 399, 402–406, 441, 442, 451, 471–474 apply as modified by regs. 37–42 SI 2009/1801. The period allowed for filing those accounts is 13 months from the end of the relevant accounting reference period.

Checklist

▷ Is the company an EEA company?

   ▷ If yes and disclosure of accounts is required in its home state, file a copy of the same accounts within three months of the filing deadline in the parent country.

   ▷ If yes and disclosure of accounts is not required in its home state, no accounts need to be filed in the UK.

▶ If not an EEA company, does the legislation in its country of incorporation require the delivery of accounts?
Regs. 36 and 37
SI 2009/1801

▷ If yes, file a copy of the accounts under reg. 34 SI 2009/1801 within three months of publication together with certified translation if required; or reg. 31 SI 2009/1801.

▷ If no, prepare audited accounts in accordance with regs 37–42 SI 2009/1801.
Reg 31
SI 2009/1801

▶ Accounts must be for the whole company, not just the UK establishment.

Filing requirement

▶ Copy of accounts under reg. 34 SI 2009/1801 within three months of publication together with certified translation if required; or

▶ Copy of accounts under reg. 40 SI 2009/1801 within 13 months of year-end. These need not include directors' or auditors' reports, information relating to turnover, UK taxation, subsidiaries, directors' emoluments and loans to directors.
Reg 40
SI 2009/1801

▶ Filing fee £20.

Notes

▶ Different rules (not dealt with here) apply to overseas credit or financial institutions.

▶ The exemptions available to small- and medium-sized companies and dormant companies are not available to overseas companies.

▶ Although overseas companies that are required to prepare accounts are subject to the same rules regarding accounting reference dates (see page 1), as non-overseas companies they may extend their year-ends as many times as they wish.

More information

▶ *Company Secretary's Handbook*, Chapter 24

▶ Companies House Guidance booklet CP01

Accounts – small-sized companies

Companies qualifying as small-sized may file small company abridged accounts with the Registrar of Companies and circulate these to their members.

ss.441(1),444,444(a)

Checklist

▶ In order to qualify or to be treated as qualifying as a small-sized company in respect of any particular financial year, the company must be or have been small-sized during one or more of the following periods:

    ▷ in its first financial year;   **s.382(1)**

    ▷ in that year and in the year before;   **s.382(2)(a)**

    ▷ in that year and if the company qualified in the year before; or   **s.382(2)(b)**

    ▷ if the qualifying conditions were met in the preceding year and the company qualified as small-sized in respect of that year.   **s.382(2)(c)**

▶ A small-sized company is one that meets at least two of the following requirements: **s.382(3)**

    ▷ turnover not exceeding £10.2 million;

    ▷ balance sheet total not exceeding £5.1 million; and

    ▷ average number of employees not exceeding 50.   **s.384(1)**

▶ A company does not qualify if at any time during the financial year it was:

    ▷ a public company;

    ▷ an authorised insurance company, banking company, e-money issuer, MiFID investment firm or a UCITS management company; or   **s.384(1)**

    ▷ a member of an ineligible group.   **s.384(2)**

▶ A group is ineligible if any of its members is:

    ▷ a public company;

▷ a corporate body whose shares are admitted to trading on a regulated market in an EES State;

▷ a person (other than a small company) authorised under FSMA2000 to carry on a regulated activity;

▷ a small company that is an authorised insurance company, banking company, e-money issuer, MiFID investment firm or a UCITS management company; or

▷ a person who carries on insurance market activity.

Procedure

▶ The information required for abridged accounts of a small-sized company is:

▷ full balance sheet;

▷ a statement above the director's signature on the balance sheet that the accounts have been prepared in accordance with the special provisions applicable to companies subject to the small companies regime; and   **s.444(5)**

▷ an audit report unless the company qualifies for and takes advantage of exemption from audit.   **s.442(2)**

Filing requirement

▶ Copy of the abbreviated accounts within the appropriate timescale – usually six months for a public company and nine months for a private company (see page 12).   **s.444(3)**

Notes

▶ Small companies must now place on public record the same set of accounts and reports as circulated to its members. Previously, companies circulated full accounts to their members and could opt to file abbreviated accounts for the public record.

More information

▶ *Company Secretary's Handbook*, Chapter 10

▶ Companies House Guidance – Filing accounts

Acquisition of non-cash assets from members in initial period

Special requirements apply where a public company proposes to acquire non-cash assets from its subscribers within the period of two years commencing on the date of the issue of its trading certificate, or in circumstances where a private company is re-registered as a public company and the company wishes to acquire certain non-cash assets from the members of the company, either at that time or within a period of two years from the re-registration.

s.598

s.603

s.598(3)

In either circumstance the company may only acquire non-cash assets from its subscribers or members provided the assets are independently valued and approval is obtained from the members. These provisions do not apply where it is part of the company's ordinary business to acquire such assets and the transaction is entered into in the normal course of its business.

s.598(4)

These provisions should not be confused with the provisions relating to the issue of shares for non-cash consideration, which are subject to s. 593.

ss.598(1),603(a)

s.598(1)(c)

Checklist

▷ Is the asset being transferred from a subscriber or from a person who was a member at the date of re-registration as a public company?

ss.598(2),603(b)

▷ Is the value of the asset equal to 10% or more of the company's issued share capital?

s.599

▷ Is the transfer taking place within two years of issue of the company's s. 761 trading certificate for transfers from a subscriber or within two years of re-registration as a public company in respect of transfers from a member?

▷ Appoint an independent valuer to value the asset being acquired in accordance with ss. 1150 and 1153 and any non-cash consideration issued by the company (usually shares credited as fully paid).

s.600

▷ Valuation must be within the six-month period prior to the date of transfer of the assets and must be circulated to members and the other party to the transfer.

s.599(1)

▷ The transfer agreement is to be approved by members by ordinary resolution and a copy of the resolution must be forwarded to the other party involved in the transfer. **s.601**

▷ A copy of the ordinary resolution and the valuation report must be filed at Companies House within 15 days of the passing of the resolution. **s.602**

Procedure

▷ Convene a directors' meeting to appoint an independent valuer, usually the company's external accountant or auditor where appointed; recommend appropriate resolution(s) to members and to convene a general meeting. Ensure valid quorum present.

▷ A copy of the valuation report drawn up to a date not more than six months prior to the date of transfer must be received by the company. The valuation report must state those matters set out in s. 600(2). **s.599(1)(b)**

▷ Issue notice, signed by director or company secretary, together with a copy of the valuation report convening the general meeting on 14 clear days' notice for members to consider resolution to approve transfer agreement and valuation report. **ss.599(1)(c), 601(1)(a)**

▷ Enclose with the notice a form of proxy if desired. Listed companies must enclose a three-way form of proxy (see page 200). **LR9.3.6**

▷ Consider whether class meeting(s) also required.

▷ If the meeting is to be convened on short notice, the company secretary should arrange for agreement to short notice to be signed by each of the shareholders.

▷ Copy of valuation report and notice to be sent to the transferor of the assets if no longer a member. **ss.599(1)(c), 601(1)(c)**

▷ Hold general meeting. Ensure valid quorum is present. Resolution put to vote either by show of hands or by poll and to be passed by appropriate majority (ordinary resolution by 50% majority).

Filing requirement

▷ Signed copy of ordinary resolution and copy of the valuation report within 15 days of approval. **s.602(1)**

Notes

▷ The independent valuer's report must confirm that, in his or her opinion, the consideration to be received by the company is not less than the value of the consideration being paid (i.e. cash or shares).

▷ These provisions will apply even where the acquisition is only in part the acquisition of non-cash assets, provided that they exceed 10% in nominal value of the company's issued share capital.

▷ Transactions involving assets with an aggregate value representing less than 10% in nominal value of the company's issued share capital are exempt from these requirements.

s.598(1)(c)

▷ If these provisions have not been followed, the company is entitled to reclaim any consideration paid to its subscribers or members, in which case the agreement shall be void.

s.604

▷ If the consideration paid by the company is the allotment of shares credited as fully paid, the company shall be entitled to request from the allottee an amount equal to the nominal value of the shares together with any share premium.

s.604(3)

More information

▷ *Company Secretary's Handbook*, Chapter 13

Agreement to short notice

In most instances, members of private companies and small unquoted public companies can agree to accept shorter notice of a meeting than that prescribed by the Companies Act.

For any general meeting, other than an annual general meeting of a public company, a majority of the members holding between them at least 90% of the voting shares must agree to the meeting being held at short notice. This can be increased to not more than 95% by a provision contained in the company's articles of association.

s.307(6)

For an annual general meeting of a public company, all members must agree.

s.337(2)

It is not necessary for the members agreeing to the short notice to attend the meeting.

It is recommended that the agreement(s) to short notice are given in writing and that these are placed in the company's minute book, together with the minutes of the meeting.

If the meeting is being convened by a public company to consider the company accounts, the agreement to short notice must include agreement to accept receipt of the accounts less than 21 days prior to the meeting being held, if these are being sent with the notice convening the meeting.

s.424(4)

Although certain resolutions require that special notice be given, calling the meeting on short notice will not in itself invalidate the resolution.

However, caution must be taken when calling meetings on short notice of which special notice has been given.

Certain resolutions (e.g. purchase of own shares) require that documents be made available for inspection for a set period prior to the meeting. As a result, the option to convene the appropriate meeting on short notice is limited and for private companies, using the written resolution procedure may be an appropriate alternative (see page 255).

Checklist

▶ In addition to the requisite percentage of the issued share capital, is a majority of the members represented?

▶ Do any documents need to be made available for inspection for a minimum period prior to the meeting?

▶ Confirm consent to short notice verbally prior to issuing notice of meeting.

Procedure

▶ The company secretary circulates an agreement to short notice with the notice, and requests its signature and return.

Filing requirement

None.

More information

▶ *Company Secretary's Handbook*, Chapter 8

Annual general meeting

Private companies do not need to hold an annual general meeting unless their articles of association require this. Where a company is required to hold an annual general meeting by their articles of association, the notice period, in the absence of any provisions of the articles of association, is the same as for any general meeting.

A public company must hold an annual general meeting within six months of its accounting reference date. Where a company's accounting reference period is shortened, the annual general meeting must be held within three months of the giving of the notice to shorten the accounting period.

s.336(1)

s.336(2)

As a consequence, a public company may not need to hold an annual general meeting in any particular calendar year if it has a financial year in excess of 12 months.

The normal or 'ordinary' business of the AGM is to receive the most recent accounts, consider the remuneration report (quoted companies only), confirm the declaration of a final dividend (where appropriate), approve the remuneration of the auditors and re-elect the auditors and retiring directors, if necessary. Any other business is deemed to be 'special' business.

Checklist

▶ The meeting must be held within six months of the company's accounting reference date.

s.336(1)

▶ If the directors propose payment of a final dividend, this must be approved at a general meeting.

art.70 sch.3, SI 2008/3229

▶ If the company is quoted, a resolution to approve the directors' remuneration report will be required.

s.439

▶ Check the articles of association to see if the directors are required to retire by rotation. Directors of FTSE 350 companies are recommended to retire and offer themselves for re-election every year. All other directors of listed companies should offer themselves for re-election at least once every three years.

▶ Check the articles of association to see if any new directors appointed by the directors during the year are required to retire at the next

annual general meeting. If the company is a public company, each
director offering themselves for re-election will require a separate
resolution.   **s.160**

▷ Check the articles to see if there are any special requirements for the
election or re-election of directors.

▷ Check to see if any members have validly proposed any resolutions
required to be included in the notice.   **s.338**

▷ Are the auditors to be reappointed, or are new auditors being
appointed requiring special notice (see page 176)?   **ss.489,515**

▷ The remuneration of the auditors must be fixed by the members or in
such manner as they shall approve.   **s.492**

▷ If appropriate, a resolution to extend or renew any authority (see
page 271) to issue shares can be put as 'special business'.   **ss.549,551**

▷ If appropriate, a resolution to extend or renew any waiver of pre-
emption rights on allotment can be put as 'special business'.   **ss.561,570, 571,573**

▷ Consider whether there is any other business to be put before the
members.

Procedure

▷ Convene a directors' meeting to recommend appropriate resolution(s)
to members and to convene annual general meeting. Ensure valid
quorum present.

▷ Only the directors may convene an AGM as members' right to
requisition a meeting only applies to general meetings. The directors
should formally convene the meeting and approve the contents of the
notice and accompanying documents.   **s.302**

▷ Company secretary or director to give special notice to the company, if
required (such as appointment of auditor other than retiring auditor).   **s.312**

▷ Issue notice, signed by director or company secretary, convening
annual general meeting of a public company on 21 clear days' notice   **s.337**
(20 clear working days, for a quoted company) for members to
consider resolutions. Private companies holding an annual general
meeting need only give 14 clear days' notice, subject to the articles of   **s.307**
association.

▷ Notice must be given in hard copy, in electronic form (provided the   **s.308**
person has agreed to accept documents and notice in this way) or by
means of a website. Notice may be given partly by one such means
and partly by another.

▷ If notice is given by placing it on a website, members must be notified   **s.309**
where it may be viewed.

▷ Enclose with the notice a copy of any accounts and a form of proxy
if desired. Where issued forms of proxy must be sent to all members
entitled to vote at the meeting, listed companies must enclose a three-   **s.326**
way form of proxy (see page 200).   **LR 9.3.6**

▶ Consider whether class meeting(s) also required.

▶ If the meeting is to be convened on short notice, the company secretary should arrange for agreement to short notice to be signed by each of the members (see page 26).

▶ Copy of notice to be sent to non-member directors and auditors.   **s.502(2)**

▶ Hold annual general meeting. Ensure valid quorum is present.

▶ Resolutions put to vote either by show of hands or by poll and to be passed by appropriate majority (ordinary resolutions by 50% majority, special resolutions by 75% majority).

Filing requirement

▶ Copies of any special resolutions and those ordinary resolutions where notification required.   **ss. 29, 30**

▶ Any appropriate forms relating to non-reappointment of directors or auditors.   **ss. 167, 521**

Notes

▶ The company secretary should arrange a suitable venue for the meeting.

▶ Before the meeting the company secretary or, if appointed, the company's share registrars should check and count all the proxies received.

▶ At the meeting the company secretary should ensure that an attendance sheet is circulated.

▶ Arrangements should be made to ensure that members alone have access to the meeting; however, this is not always possible or desirable in practice.

▶ Unless waived by the meeting, the notice and the directors' report should be read to the meeting.

▶ There is no longer a statutory requirement for the audit report to be read to the meeting. However, if the auditor is present, it is common practice for him or her to read the audit opinion.

▶ For companies with a large number of shareholders, or at meetings where there may be questions from the floor, it is useful to prepare a chair's script prior to the meeting. Additionally, the directors should meet before the meeting to discuss any matters that might be raised at the meeting and decide who will deal with certain queries.

▶ If a poll is likely, the company secretary should arrange for poll cards to be available. Companies that use registrars will normally use their services when conducting a poll. The directors should ensure that as many proxy forms as possible are received prior to the meeting. It is important that proxy forms are received at the registered office, or the office of the registrars, before the deadline for receipt of proxies. Most companies adopt the standard, and maximum, period prior to the meeting of 48 hours, but the articles of association must be checked as companies can adopt a shorter period up to the start of the meeting itself. Proxy forms arriving later than this cannot be accepted, and any proxy forms brought to the meeting are invalid.

▶ Additional copies of the latest audited accounts and directors' service contracts must be available at the meeting, together with a copy of the register of members and minutes of previous shareholder meetings.

More information

▶ *Company Secretary's Handbook*, Chapter 8

Annual general meeting – best practice

This checklist sets out the main issues to be considered before, during and after an AGM.

In addition to the Companies Act requirements for general meetings, quoted companies must also comply with the provisions of the Listing Rules, Disclosure and Transparency Rules and the UK Corporate Governance Code. Finally, for most companies there will be provisions in the articles of association to be considered too.

Although this guidance is for AGMs, many of the requirements will apply equally to general meetings.

Checklist

Before the meeting

The venue

▷ Book a suitable venue with sufficient capacity for the expected number of attendees, suitable facilities for the disabled and presentation equipment.

▷ Confirm the date of the meeting with the board, registrars, advisers and others required to attend as early as possible.

▷ Companies with a large number of members and where the business is contentious should consider contingency plans in the event that attendees exceed the capacity of the room. Security arrangements should be considered.

▷ Arrangements may also need to be made to ensure that members alone have access to the meeting; however, this is not always possible or desirable in practice.

AGM notice – explanatory notes

While the core content of the notice is set out in the Act, it is good practice to provide additional information to clarify procedure or anticipate questions. This should include:

▶ the date and time not exceeding 48 hours by which members must be registered on the register of members to be entitled to attend and vote;

ss.311(3)(b) & 360B and regs 41(1) & (6) USR2001

▶ a statement of a corporate members' right to appoint one or more corporate representatives;

s.323

▶ a statement of the members' right to appoint one or more proxies and any more extensive rights conferred by the articles;

ss.324 and 325

▶ instructions as to how and when the proxy appointment should be returned, and a statement that the return of a completed form of proxy does not prevent a member from attending the meeting in person;

▶ a statement of the order of priority for signing a form of proxy in the case of joint holdings;

▶ if relevant, that the chair intends to call a poll on any or all resolutions; and

▶ an explanation of how the voting will take place at the meeting.

Proxies

▶ A proxy appointment should provide information on how to appoint a person or persons, other than the chair, as proxy.

s.324 and DTR 6.1.5

▶ If the company offers that a particular person, such as the chair, will act as proxy, that offer must be made to all shareholders.

s.326

▶ Include a note on how to change a proxy appointment and what happens if more than one proxy appointment is submitted.

▶ Provide details of how the proxy appointment should be completed and where it should be sent or delivered to and by when, which must not be more than 48 hours (excluding non-working days) before the meeting.

s.327

▶ Proxy forms for quoted and traded companies should be worded to provide for three-way voting by including a 'vote withheld' option and a note explaining that a 'vote withheld' is not a vote in law and will not be counted.

LR 9.3.6(2)

▶ Arrange regular updates on proxy voting totals. Where the chair has been appointed proxy, ensure that he or she is aware of the number of votes cast for and against the resolutions so that on a show of hands or a poll, he or she will know how to cast his or her vote(s).

Preparing the chair

▶ Brief the chair on the main provisions in the articles governing the organisation and procedure of the meeting, voting procedure and his or her role and powers as chair of the meeting.

▶ Prepare a script for the chair to use.

▶ Familiarise the chair with the process of taking questions from the floor. Prepare a questions and answers pack to anticipate questions, including any difficult issues which might be raised.

▶ Ensure that the chair of the board committees and the finance director will be present at the meeting and that they are fully briefed on possible questions that may be asked.

At the meeting

It may be useful to take the following items to the meeting:

▶ AGM notice and form of proxy;

▶ annual reports and accounts;

▶ the chair's script;

▶ copies of presentations;

▶ questions and answers pack;

▶ the documents that need to go on display at the meeting;

▶ articles of association;

▶ contingency plan; and

▶ spare paper poll cards and pens.

Documents available for inspection

Listed companies must have the following documents on display for at least 15 minutes prior to the start of the AGM until it closes:

▶ non-executive directors' terms and conditions of appointment; and

▶ directors' service contracts.

Any documents to be approved or amended that were not circulated to the members with the notice must be on display for at least 15 minutes prior to the start of the AGM until it closes. They must also be available for inspection in the City of London (or another place agreed with the FCA) from the date the notice is sent until the close of the meeting.

All directors should attend the AGM and all the company's directors should be seated with the chair, facing the shareholders.

The chair

▶ Check the articles to confirm who will be the chair of the meeting.

▶ Subject to the articles, a member, including a proxy, may be elected by resolution of the members present to be chair of the meeting. **ss.319 & 328**

▶ If the chair or chief executive is to give a presentation on the business, check that no inside information is being disclosed and that a copy is released to an RIS no later than the time the presentation is given to the meeting. **s.319A**

▷ The chair should not propose their own election or re-election or propose any resolution in which they have an interest.

Dealing with the business of the meeting

▷ The resolution to receive or adopt the accounts should be separate from any resolution to approve the payment of the final dividend recommended by directors. It is also good practice generally to deal with different items of business by way of separate resolutions.

▷ Ensure that adequate time is allowed for shareholder questions.

Voting

▷ If a poll is likely, the company secretary should arrange for poll cards to be available.

▷ Before each resolution is put to the vote, the chair should explain again its effect and purpose and, if necessary, elaborate on the information previously provided in the explanatory details circulated with the notice of the meeting. Shareholders may also be invited to speak.

▷ The chair should indicate the number of proxy votes held.

▷ When announcing the decision on a poll, the total number of votes cast for and against and withheld for the resolutions should be disclosed. The information should then be made available as soon as possible on the company's website.

▷ If a significant proportion of votes have been cast against a resolution at a general meeting, the company should explain when announcing the results of voting what actions it intends to take to understand the reasons behind the result.

After the meeting

Following the AGM, the company secretary is responsible for ensuring that all minutes, forms and resolutions are prepared, signed and filed at Companies House and/or the FCA, and made available on the company's website.

Minutes and registers

▷ Prepare the minutes of the meeting.   **s.355(1)**

▷ Once agreed, the minutes should be signed by the chair.   **s.356(4)**

▷ If appropriate, update the registers of directors, secretaries, members, charges or debenture holders.   **ss.113,876 & 743**

Statutory filings

▷ Any relevant Companies House forms.   **s.30(1)**

▶ For listed companies, arrange for two copies of all resolutions passed, other than resolutions concerning ordinary business passed at an AGM, to be forwarded to the FCA. In practice this requirement is met by forwarding a copy to the National Storage Mechanism. **LR 9.6.2**

▶ Listed companies should ensure that the appropriate announcements are made to an RIS as soon as possible.

Website

A summary of the poll results must be published on the company's website as quickly as practical and not later than 16 days after the meeting. **ss.341 (1A), (1B) & 353(4)(a)**

Dividends

If a dividend has been approved at the meeting, the necessary arrangements for it to be paid should be made.

Articles of association (adoption or change)

The articles of association are the rules governing the company's internal affairs. SI 2008/3229 contains model sets of articles, appropriate for private companies limited by shares, private companies limited by guarantee and public companies.

s.20

Under all previous Companies Acts, default articles of association were contained in Table A to the particular Companies Act in force when the company was incorporated.

Companies incorporated prior to 1 October 2009 will have as their default articles the version of Table A in force when the company was incorporated, and later versions do not apply unless specifically adopted by a company.

The model articles apply to any particular company, incorporated on or after 1 October 2009, to the extent that they are not excluded or varied by the company's articles.

s.20(1)(b)

Alteration of any particular regulation or adoption of new articles requires a special resolution of the members in a general meeting.

s.21

Articles may contain entrenched provisions. Amendment of entrenched provisions requires 100% consent from members entitled to vote or a court order.

s.22

Checklist

▷ If the company has more than one class of shares, a separate class meeting may also be required.

▷ Check whether rights to be amended are entrenched.

▷ Consider whether amendment can be undertaken by amending existing clauses, by the adoption of new clauses in addition to or in substitution for existing clauses or by the adoption of a complete new set of articles.

Procedure

▷ Convene a directors' meeting to recommend resolutions to members and to convene a general meeting or, in the case of a private company, circulate a written resolution if appropriate (see page 255).

▷ Issue notice, signed by director or company secretary, convening general meeting on 14 clear days' notice, or circulate written resolution for members to consider special resolution to amend the articles.   **s.21**

▷ As a special resolution, the resolution must contain the full text of the proposed changes.

▷ Consider whether a class meeting is also required.

▷ If the meeting is to be convened on short notice (see page 26), the company secretary should arrange for agreement to short notice to be signed by each of the members.

▷ Hold a general meeting. Ensure valid quorum is present. Resolutions put to vote either by show of hands or by poll and to be passed by appropriate majority (special resolution by 75% majority).   **s.283**

▷ If the resolution is circulated by means of a written resolution, the resolution must receive approval of the holders of at least 75% of the members entitled to vote within 28 days of the circulation date of the resolution (see page 254).

Filing requirement

▷ Signed copy of special resolution within 15 days.   **ss.29(1)(a),30(1)**

▷ Amended copy of the articles of association with copy of resolution.   **s.26**

Notes

▷ Although it is not necessary to issue new copies of the articles of association to the members, the company should ensure that it has a supply for issue to those members who request a copy. In addition, a copy will normally be sent to the company's bankers and to their auditors.

▷ If a company files a copy of a resolution amending its articles but does not file a copy of the amended articles, Companies House may issue a notice requiring an amended copy of the articles be filed within a specified time. Failure to file the amended copy within the specified time will mean the company is liable to a £200 fine.   **s.27, s.27(4)**

More information

▷ *Company Secretary's Handbook*, Chapter 3

▷ Companies House Guidance booklet GP3

Auditors – appointment to private company

With the exception of private companies that are exempt from audit, exempt subsidiaries, dormant companies and non-profit-making companies subject to public sector audit, all companies must appoint auditors and prepare audited accounts.

s.475

The members of a company which is exempt from audit may require it to appoint auditors, provided this request is made by members holding at least 10% in nominal value of its issued shares or 10% of the members for a company without shares.

s.476

Directors will usually appoint auditors where they are being appointed for the first time or following a period where an audit was not required.

Directors may appoint auditors at any time before the company's first or next period for appointing auditors (see below) or to fill a casual vacancy.

s.485(3)

If a company has no auditors, members may appoint auditors during a period for appointing auditors.

s.485(4)

The period for appointing auditors is the period of 28 days beginning on the end of the period for sending out the accounts to members for the previous financial year or, if earlier, the day the accounts for the previous financial year were sent out.

s.485(2)

If a company that is required to have its accounts audited fails to appoint auditors, notification of that must be sent to the Secretary of State and the Secretary of State may appoint auditors to fill the vacancy.

s.486

An auditor is required to be registered as an auditor, and must not be an officer or a servant of the company, or a partner or employee of such officers or servants. An auditor may be an individual, a partnership or a limited company.

ss.1211–1215

Checklist

▶ Does the company qualify for exemption from audit?

s.475

▶ Has an audit been requested by members?

s.476

▶ Does the person to be appointed meet the following eligibility criteria?

s.1211

▷ Member of a recognised supervisory body.

s.1212

▷ Not an officer or employee of the company or partner or
  employee of an officer or employee of the company.   **s.1214**

▷ Not connected with the company or an associated undertaking.   **s.1215**

Procedure

▶ Convene a directors' meeting to consider the appointment of an
  auditor. Ensure valid quorum present.

▶ Where the appointment is to be by the members, this is by an ordinary
  resolution either at a general meeting convened by the directors or by
  written resolution of the members.

▶ A company that has no auditors may have auditors appointed by the
  Secretary of State.

Filing requirement

▶ The appointment of auditors does not need to be notified to
  Companies House.

Notes

▶ The company may wish to notify its bankers, solicitors, subsidiaries,
  etc of the auditors' appointment.

More information

▶ *Company Secretary's Handbook*, Chapter 11

Auditors – appointment to public company

With the exception of dormant public companies that are exempt from audit, all public companies must appoint auditors and prepare audited accounts.

s.489(1)

Directors may appoint auditors at any time before the company's first general meeting to receive audited accounts or to fill a casual vacancy.

s.489(3)

Members may appoint auditors, by ordinary resolution, at a general meeting at which audited accounts have been laid or in circumstances when the company should have had auditors appointed but does not have auditors.

s.489(4)

If a public company that is required to have its accounts audited fails to appoint auditors, notification of that must be sent to the Secretary of State and the Secretary of State may appoint auditors to fill the vacancy.

s.490

An auditor is required to be registered as an auditor, and must not be an officer or a servant of the company, or a partner or employee of such officers or servants. An auditor may be an individual, a partnership or a limited company.

ss.1211–1215

Checklist

▶ Does the company qualify for exemption from audit?   **s.475**

▶ Does the person to be appointed meet the following eligibility criteria?   **s.1211**

  ▷ Member of a recognised supervisory body.   **s.1212**

  ▷ Not an officer or employee of the company or partner or employee of an officer or employee of the company.   **s.1214**

  ▷ Not connected with the company or an associated undertaking.   **s.1215**

Procedure

▶ Convene a directors' meeting to consider the appointment of an auditor. Ensure valid quorum present.

▶ Where the appointment is to be by the members, this is by an ordinary resolution either at a general meeting convened by the directors or by written resolution of the members.

▶ A public company that has no auditors may have auditors appointed by the Secretary of State.

▶ Auditors of a public company are appointed to hold office only until the conclusion of the next general meeting at which accounts are laid before the members, when they may be reappointed.

s.491

Filing requirement

▶ The appointment of auditors does not need to be notified to Companies House.

Notes

▶ The company may wish to notify its bankers, solicitors, subsidiaries, etc of the auditors' appointment.

More information

▶ *Company Secretary's Handbook*, Chapter 11

Auditor – appointment to a public interest entity

A public interest entity ('PIE') is defined as a company, which meets at least one of the following criteria:

s.519A

▶ an issuer with and transferable securities admitted to trading on a regulated market;

▶ a credit institution; or

▶ an insurance undertaking.

In order to promote transparency and competition in the audit market for listed companies the EU adopted the Statutory Audit Directive, an amending directive and the audit regulation adopted in the UK by SATCAR2016.

Under this legislation PIEs cannot appoint an auditor without first undertaking a formal tender process and where the existing audit firm has held office for ten years cannot be appointed without a formal tender being undertaken and may not be reappointed if they have served in office for 20 years.

Checklist

The maximum term of office for the auditor of a PIE is the longer of:

▶ 10 years from the first day of the first financial year in respect of which the auditor was appointed;

s.494ZA(1)

▶ 20 years from the first day of the first financial year in respect of which the auditor was appointed, provided that a tender process has been held for at least one financial year which begins every ten years in that period; or

s.494ZA(1)

▶ such other period not exceeding 20 years beginning with the first day of the first financial year in respect of which the auditor was appointed and ending on the last day of the relevant 10-year period.

s.494ZA(1)

Where the company has an audit committee there is a detailed procedure to follow – see below;

▶ Where there no audit committee the directors must carry out the tender process and it is for the directors to decide how to carry out that process.

Audit Regulation Art 16(3)

Procedure

Companies with an audit committee

▷ The opportunity to tender must be extended to at least two audit firms either of which has a reasonable chance of being appointed.

▷ At the conclusion of the tender process, the audit committee must make its recommendation to the full board of the preferred top two choices for auditor appointment.

▷ The committee must formally confirm that the recommendation is free from third party influence or contractual restriction.

▷ It is for the board as a whole to decide which of the two auditors to appoint.

▷ If the directors disagree with the preferred candidate of the audit committee, the directors must provide reasons.

Company without an audit committee

▷ The opportunity to tender must be extended to at least two audit firms either of which has a reasonable chance of being appointed.

▷ It is for the board as a whole to decide which auditor to appoint.

Small or medium-sized or in the case of a public company, a company with a reduced market capitalisation are exempt for these provisions.

Filing requirement

▷ None.

Notes

AIM and NEX Growth Market are not regulated markets and accordingly companies whose shares are traded on those markets will not be PIEs unless they are also a credit institution or insurance undertaking.

More information

▷ *Company Secretary's Handbook,* Chapter 11

Auditor – notification on ceasing to hold office

If the auditor to a company leaves office depending on the type of company and the circumstances of the auditor ceasing to hold that office the company, in addition to any obligations the auditor has, may be required to notify the relevant audit authority of that fact and may also be required to circulate a statement of reasons to their members.

s.519,523

A company must notify the relevant audit authority within 28 days that the auditor has ceased to hold office unless being a private company the cessation is at the end of the period for appointing auditors or in the case of a public company at the end of an accounts meeting.

s.523

Notification need not be made if the reason(s) for the cessation are exempt reasons.

The notification must contain a statement of the reasons the company believes to be the reasons for the auditor's resignation. Where the auditor has issued a statement of reasons with which the company agrees the notification may include a copy of the statement of auditor's reasons.

The auditor of a Public Interest Entity ('PIE') must, on ceasing to hold office at any time and for any reason, deliver a statement to the company of the reasons for doing so.

The auditor of a company that is not a PIE must send a statement of reasons unless either of the following two conditions is met:

- First condition

  - In the case of a private company at the end of the period for appointing auditors; or

    s.519

  - In the case of a public company at the end of the accounts meeting.

- Second condition

  - If the reason(s) for ceasing to hold office are all exempt reasons; and

  - There are no matters connected with the ceasing to hold office that the auditor considers need to be brought to the attention of members or creditors.

The exempt reasons are:

s.519A

▶ The auditor is no longer to carry out statutory audit work.

▶ The company is, or is to become, exempt from audit under section 477, 479A or 480.

▶ The company is a subsidiary undertaking of a parent undertaking that is incorporated in the United Kingdom and—

▷ the parent undertaking prepares group accounts;

▷ the auditor is being replaced as auditor of the company by the auditor who is conducting, or is to conduct, an audit of the group accounts;

▷ the company is being wound up under Part 4 of the Insolvency Act 1986 or Part 5 of the Insolvency (Northern Ireland) Order 1989.

Where a company receives a statement of reasons from their auditor on ceasing to hold office unless the company is both not a PIE and the statement notes that there are no matters connected with their ceasing to hold office that need notifying to the members or creditors the company must within 14 days either send a copy to every person entitled to receive a copy of the accounts or apply to court for an order not to circulate the statement.

S.520

Checklist

▶ Has a statement been received from the auditor concerning their ceasing to hold office?

▶ Does the statement contain details of any matters to be brought to the attention of the members or creditors?

▶ Within 14 days send statement to those entitled to receive copies of the accounts under s. 423 or apply to court for an order not to comply.

▶ If application is made to court notify the auditor.

▶ If the court refuse the application the statement must be circulated within 14 days of the court's decision.

▶ Is notification to the relevant audit authority required?

Procedure

▶ Where applicable circulate auditor's statement of reasons with 14 days or make application to court.

s.519

▶ Where applicable notify relevant audit authority with 28 days of the date the auditor ceases to hold office.

s.520

Filing requirement

▷ Notification to relevant audit authority within 28 days, as required.   **s.523**

Notes

For a company that is a PIE the relevant audit authority is the FRC; in all other cases it is the auditor's own recognised supervisory body and will be one of the ACCA, ICAEW, ICAS or CAI.

More information

▷ *Company Secretary's Handbook*, Chapter 11

Auditors – removal

The members of a company may remove the auditors from office by ordinary resolution. In practice the directors will normally invite the auditors to resign or will propose that the auditors are not reappointed at a general meeting at which accounts are to be laid.

s.510

Checklist

▶ Special notice must be given to the company of a proposed resolution to remove an auditor. **s.511**

▶ A copy of the special notice must be sent to the auditor whose removal is proposed. **s.511(2)**

▶ The auditor may make a written representation concerning their removal and request its notification to the members either by post or, if there is insufficient time, by reading it to the meeting. **s.511(3)**

▶ The auditor's representation need not be notified to members if an application to the court is upheld. **s.511(6)**

▶ On removal, notice of that removal must be filed at Companies House within 14 days. **s.512**

Procedure

▶ Special notice given by a director to the company.

▶ Convene a directors' meeting to recommend resolution to members and to convene a general meeting. Ensure valid quorum is present.

▶ Copy of the special notice sent to the auditor.

▶ Issue notice, signed by director or company secretary, convening general meeting with 14 clear days' notice for members to consider.

▶ Ordinary resolution to remove auditor.

▶ Consider whether a class meeting is also required.

▶ If the meeting is to be convened on short notice, the company secretary should arrange for agreement to short notice to be signed by each of the members.

▷ Representation of auditors circulated with notice, or separately.

▷ If appropriate, seek court order that representation need not be circulated or read out at meeting.

▷ If not circulated and no court order obtained, read auditor's representation to meeting.

▷ Hold general meeting. Ensure valid quorum is present. Resolutions put to vote either by show of hands or by poll and to be passed by appropriate majority (ordinary resolution by 50% majority).

▷ If removal approved, notify Companies House. Notification may be required to the relevant audit authority (see page 45)

Filing requirement

▷ Form AA03 within 14 days.

Notes

▷ If a member gives notice of their intention to propose the removal of the auditor, unless they also requisition a general meeting, there is no requirement for the directors to convene a meeting. The resolution would, however, be required to be put at the next general meeting.

▷ The written resolution procedure cannot be used and the resolution must be put to a general meeting of the members. Depending on whether the company is a public interest entity and the circumstances for the removal of the auditor the auditor may be required to send to the company a statement of circumstances connected with their cessation of office that they consider should be brought to the attention of the members or a statement that there are no such circumstances [s. 519]. See also 'Auditors – Notification on ceasing to hold office'.

More information

▷ *Company Secretary's Handbook*, Chapter 11

Auditors – resignation

Auditors may resign from office by giving notice in writing to the registered office of the company. If the company is a public interest company, the notice of resignation must be accompanied by a statement of any matters that they consider should be brought to the attention of members or, if there are no such circumstances, a statement to that effect.

s.516

s.516(2)

A resigning auditor of a non-public interest company may need to send a statement unless their resignation meets one of the conditions set out in s. 519(2A) or 2(B).

s.519

Checklist

▶ Auditor's resignation and statement, if any, received at the registered office.

▶ If there are circumstances to be notified to the members or creditors, the statement must be circulated to members within 14 days or an application be made to the court for an order that it need not do so.

s.520

▶ If court order sought, notify auditor.

s.520(3)

▶ Unless notice of application for court order received within 21 days, the auditors must file a copy of their statement with Companies House within 28 days of original notice of resignation.

s.521

▶ If court order not obtained, the company must circulate the statement to members within 14 days of the court's decision and notify the auditors, who shall file a copy of their statement at Companies House within the next seven days.

ss.520(5), 521(2)

▶ Notification to the relevant audit authority may be required (see page 45).

s.523

Procedure

▶ Circulate statement of circumstances, if any, to members or apply to court for order not to circulate. If court order sought, notify auditor within 21 days of original notice being received.

Filing requirement

▶ Copy of auditors' resignation letter within 14 days.

▶ Auditors to file statement of circumstances after 21 days but before 28 days, unless application to court made.

▶ If court upholds application, copy of that decision to be circulated to members.

▶ If application not upheld, statement to be circulated to members within 14 days and notify auditors, who must file their statement at Companies House within the next seven days.

More information

▶ *Company Secretary's Handbook*, Chapter 11

Bank account

The company's bank account and banking matters generally are controlled by the board of directors.

All banks have a standard Form of Mandate and this is usually presented as a draft minute. Once the text of the authority and the instructions have been approved by the directors, a copy of the signed mandate should be inserted in the company's minute book as evidence of the appropriate decisions having been reached.

The majority of banks require security or collateral for overdraft facilities and care must be taken to ensure that the directors have authority to charge the company's assets.

Checklist

- Completed bank mandate form.

- Approved by the directors.

- Originals or certified copies of memorandum and articles of association, certificate of incorporation and any changes of name certificate to commence trading (public companies only).

- Money laundering verification of identity documents as advised by the bank. Often original or certified copies of passport or driving licence and a utility bill showing residential address will suffice.

Procedure

- Convene a directors' meeting to consider the terms of the bank mandate and approve the opening of the account. Ensure valid quorum present.

Filing requirement

None.

Notes

▶ The bank will note and return the original Certificates of Incorporation and any change-of-name certificates.

▶ Care must be taken to ensure that the signatories required for cheques are reasonable in the circumstances. Many companies empower an authorised signatory to sign cheques up to a certain limit, with directors (often two) required to sign cheques of larger amounts.

▶ The frequency with which the company is to receive bank statements should also be agreed.

▶ The banks prefer the mandate to be expressed in terms of the position held by the signatories rather than their names. If a named person is shown, when that person leaves the company it is necessary to complete a new mandate rather than merely change the signatory.

▶ It is normal practice to inform the bank whenever there are changes to the company's directors, company secretary, registered office, the company's accounting reference date or the company's auditors.

▶ The bank will often require a copy of the company's latest audited accounts for their records.

More information

None.

Boardroom – best practice

Reliance on unwritten boardroom procedures and practices is no longer acceptable in the modern business environment. While it is acknowledged that company law should not attempt to prescribe any particular style of boardroom management, certain basic principles of good boardroom practice can be considered to be universally applicable.

The following is intended to be a guide to the matters that should be addressed and, wherever applicable, accepted formally by boards of directors in recognition of a commitment to adhere to an overall concept of best practice. Although particularly relevant to public companies with external shareholders, all companies will benefit from striving to carry out generally accepted best practice. It of course recognised that all company boards are different and that exceptions and adaptions of best practice will be appropriate.

Boardroom procedures should be periodically reviewed to ensure their scope remains relevant and allow for the identification of additional matters that individual companies could advantageously bring within their scope.

Checklist

▶ Establish written procedures and policies:

  ▷ Provide each director with a copy.

  ▷ Monitor and review compliance (including risk) and report breaches to the board.

▶ All new directors to be given appropriate induction to enable them to perform their duties.

▶ Guidance for non-executive directors should include procedures for:

  ▷ obtaining information; and

  ▷ requisitioning a board meeting.

▶ In the conduct of board business, all directors should:

  ▷ receive the same information at the same time; and

  ▷ be given sufficient time to consider the information.

- Identify matters reserved to the board and lay down procedures when a decision is required before its next meeting.

- All material contracts, and especially those not in the ordinary course of business, should be referred to the board.

- The board should approve definitions of 'material' and 'not in the ordinary course of business'.

- Agenda for individual meetings of the board to be settled by the chair in consultation with the company secretary.

- The company secretary should be responsible to the chair for the proper administration of meetings of the company, the board and any committees thereof.

- The minutes of meetings should record the decisions taken and provide sufficient background to those decisions.

- All papers presented at meetings should be identified and retained for reference.

- Minutes of committees' meetings should be circulated to the board.

- Where the articles of association allow the board to delegate any of its powers to a committee, the board should approve:

  ▷ the membership and quorum of any such committee;

  ▷ its terms of reference; and

  ▷ the extent of any powers delegated to it.

- Any director or the company secretary must be able to raise at any board meeting any matter, whether or not it is on the agenda for the meeting.

Bonus issue (capitalisation issue)

A bonus or capitalisation issue is the means by which the company allots shares that are partly or fully paid, by capitalising reserves. No further payment from the shareholder is normally required. However, if the bonus shares are partly paid, the unpaid portion may be called from the shareholder at some future date.

The company's capacity to issue partly or fully paid shares is included in the model articles for private and public companies, but also requires approval of the shareholders by ordinary resolution. Although a bonus issue is an issue of new shares, no new capital is raised; it is effected by capitalising some or all of the company's distributable reserves.

sch. I reg. 36, sch. 3
reg. 78, SI 2008/3229

Companies may wish to issue shares in this manner for a number of reasons. These include:

▷ to increase the company's issued share capital in order to meet the minimum capital requirement when re-registering as a public company without requiring the shareholders to inject further funds (see page 246);

▷ to declare a bonus issue in conjunction with a rights issue to reduce the potential dilution of the holdings of those shareholders who do not take up any shares under the offer; and

▷ to create a more substantial balance sheet by capitalising reserves into issued share capital.

Checklist

▷ Check the articles of association to ensure the issue of bonus shares is permitted and if any procedures have been stipulated.

▷ Check the articles to ensure that if the company has an authorised share capital, there are sufficient unissued shares available for issue.

▷ Check the articles of association to ensure the directors have authority in terms of s. 551 to issue shares. If not, a resolution to extend or renew the authority will be required (see page 271).

Procedure

▷ Convene a directors' meeting to recommend appropriate resolution(s) to members and to seek member approval either by circulating written resolution(s) or by convening a general meeting. Ensure valid quorum is present.

▷ Issue notice, signed by director or company secretary, together convening the general meeting on 14 clear days' notice for members to consider resolution. Alternatively, a private company may circulate the resolutions by written resolution.   **ss. 281, 307**

▷ Enclose with the notice a form of proxy if desired. Listed companies must enclose a three-way form of proxy (see page 200).

▷ Consider whether class meeting(s) also required.

▷ If the meeting is to be convened on short notice, the company secretary should arrange for agreement to short notice to be signed by the appropriate number of the members (see page 26).   **s. 307(5)**

▷ Copy of notice to be sent to non-member directors and auditor, if any.   **ss. 310, 502**

▷ Hold general meeting. Ensure valid quorum is present. Resolution put to vote either by show of hands or by poll and to be passed by appropriate majority (ordinary resolution by 50% majority).

▷ Following meeting, issue new share certificates and update register of members. If there is to be a delay before share certificates are issued, it may be appropriate to issue allotment letters giving details of each member's entitlement to new shares. In any event, new share certificates must be issued within two months.   **s. 554**

                    s. 769

Filing requirement

▷ Copies of approved member resolutions.   **s. 30**

▷ Form SH01 within one month.   **s. 555**

▷ Statement of capital.   **s. 555**

Notes

▷ As bonus shares are issued *pro rata*, it should not be necessary to waive any rights of pre-emption, unless the members have the option to renounce their entitlement.

▷ On completion of the bonus issue, the company's accountants, both internal and external, must be informed, so that the appropriate entries to the company's accounts can be made.

▷ If it is necessary to increase or renew s. 551 authority to issue shares (see page 271), it will be necessary to file a copy of the ordinary resolution within 15 days.

More information

▷ *Company Secretary's Handbook*, Chapter 13

Borrowing powers

All companies are deemed to have full capacity unless the articles place specific restrictions on the company.

The articles of listed companies will often restrict the directors' ability to exercise the full borrowing powers of the company. The limitation is often expressed as a multiple of the company's net assets and so will vary over time.

Directors of companies incorporated under previous Companies Acts require specific authority under their articles of association.

If the directors' capacity to exercise the company's borrowing power is not sufficient for their purposes, the articles of association will need to be amended by special resolution.

Checklist

▷ Check the articles of association for any restriction of either the company's capacity to borrow or the directors' authority to exercise that borrowing capacity.

Filing requirement

None.

More information

▷ *Company Secretary's Handbook*, Chapters 3 and 6

Business names

A business name is a name or title by which a company may trade other than its corporate or registered name.

There is no longer a register of business names.

The business stationery of a company using a business name must show the company's registered name in full as well as the business name, in addition to the other statutory requirements (see page 137).

reg. 24, SI 2015/17

Companies using business names must ensure they do not infringe registered names or trademarks, or pass themselves off as other registered companies, partnerships or sole traders. The use of sensitive words applies equally to business names and registered names (see page 173).

Checklist

reg. 24, SI 2015/17

▶ Is the company's registered name shown on all headed paper, email, website, invoices, cheques, etc?

regs 21 and 22, SI 2015/17

▶ Is the company's registered name displayed at all business premises?

Filing requirement

None.

Notes

reg. 21(2), SI 2015/17

A company that has always been dormant from the date of its incorporation need not have its name on display at its registered office.

More information

▶ *Company Secretary's Handbook*, Chapter 4

▶ Companies House Guidance – Incorporation and names

Calls

Where, for any reason, shares have been issued as partly or nil paid, the amounts unpaid can be called by the directors at any time, either in full or in part.

The liability for the unpaid amounts rests with the registered holder.

The company should not accept registration of a transfer of shares on which there remains an unpaid call unless the transferee is willing to pay the unpaid call.

The model articles for private companies do not permit partly or nil paid shares to be issued and accordingly if such shares are to be issued, the articles will require amendment. The model articles for public companies do contain provisions for the making of calls on partly paid shares.

art. 21 sch. 1, SI 2008/3229

arts 54–61 sch. 3, SI 2008/3229

Checklist

▷ Check the articles of association for the procedure to follow where a call is proposed. The procedure below follows the model wording for public companies.

Procedure

▷ Convene a directors' meeting to approve the making of a call.

▷ The company secretary should arrange the preparation and issue of call notices to members. Each call notice should be addressed to the registered holder or joint holders, as the case may be, and should contain details of the registered member(s), the amounts currently outstanding and the amount now being called, together with details of where and when the payment is due, which must be at least 14 days after the date of the call notice.

▷ Each call notice should carry a distinguishing number and this number should be noted on the register of members, together with a note of the amount being called. The company should compile lists of the payments as they are received and cleared by the bank. Once the date on which the call is due has passed, the list of payments should be reconciled with the register of members and a list of unpaid calls should be prepared.

▶ A reminder letter should be sent to all members that have not paid the call, requesting immediate payment and warning of the potential penalties for non-payment, including forfeiture of shares or suspension of voting rights.

▶ Members should return their share certificates together with a copy of the call notice so that the company can endorse the share certificates, giving details of the paid call. The endorsed share certificate should be returned to the shareholder. Alternatively, the share certificates can be cancelled and new, fully paid share certificates issued.

▶ The register of members should be amended to include details of the additional amounts now paid on the shares.

▶ If a call remains unpaid, interest is due at a rate to be set by the directors but not to exceed 5% above the base lending rate in force from time to time. Directors may waive the obligation to pay interest either in part or in full.

Filing requirement

None.

Notes

▶ Where calls remain unpaid, a number of actions can be taken, although the articles of association should be checked to ensure that the directors have the requisite authority.

▶ The directors may institute proceedings for the forfeiture of the shares, under which circumstance the shares are forfeited by the holder and cancelled or reissued. In the instance of reissue, the company should return to the shareholders the amounts paid by them on the shares.

▶ The articles of association may authorise the directors to withhold any dividends from the shareholder and credit these amounts to the share capital account until such time as the call has been paid.

▶ Alternatively, the shareholder may lose the right to vote until such time as the call has been paid.

▶ It will be necessary to inform the company's auditors of the call and the split between the calls that were paid and any unpaid calls. Occasionally, shares will be issued as partly paid with the balance payable on fixed instalment dates. The procedure to be followed in such circumstances is the same as that for making a call.

More information

▶ *Company Secretary's Handbook*, Chapter 13

Certification of shares

When members are transferring only part of their holding, they may be unwilling to forward their share certificate to the purchaser. In such circumstances, the transferor should forward the certificate and stock transfer form to the company or its share registrar for certifying. The company or its share registrar will then stamp the transfer form stating that the certificate representing the shares on the transfer form has been lodged with the company/share registrar and will return a balance certificate to the transferor if appropriate.

s.775

Certifications are most commonly used by stockbrokers and market-makers in respect of partial sales for quoted shares. These, however, are becoming less used following the introduction of the paperless settlement system, CREST.

Checklist

▷ Check the register of members to confirm that the share certificate has not previously been cancelled and is valid.

▷ Check that the transferor's details on the transfer form match the holder shown on the share certificate, and that the transfer form is signed by the transferor.

Procedure

▷ Cancel the share certificate and insert on the transfer form reference details for the certification.

▷ Update the register of members to record the certification details and the cancellation of the original share certificate.

▷ Return the now-certified transfer form to the person lodging it.

Filing requirement

None.

More information

▷ *Company Secretary's Handbook*, Chapter 18

Companies House – addresses of offices

England and Wales
Companies House
Crown Way
Maindy
Cardiff CF14 3UZ
DX 33050 Cardiff 1

Contact Centre: +44 (0)303 1234 500
Lines open: Monday to Friday, 8.30am–6.00pm

Website: www.companieshouse.gov.uk
Email: enquiries@companieshouse.gov.uk

London Information Centre
Companies House
Ground Floor
80 Petty France
Westminster
London
SW1H 9EX

Contact Centre: +44 (0)303 1234 500
Office hours: Monday to Friday, 9.00am–5.00pm

Scotland
Companies House
4th Floor, Edinburgh Quay 2
139 Fountainbridge
Edinburgh
EH3 9FF

Contact Centre: +44 (0)303 1234 500

Office hours: Monday to Friday, 9.00am–5.00pm

Northern Ireland

Companies House

2nd Floor, The Linenhall

32–38 Linenhall Street

Belfast

BT2 8BG

Contact Centre: +44 (0)303 1234 500

Office hours: Monday to Friday, 9.00am–5.00pm

More information

▷ Companies House website for directions and maps:
www.gov.uk/government/organisations/companies-house/about/
access-and-opening

Companies House – charges

The fees charged by Companies House in force as at 1 May 2019 for incorporation and registration services are as follows.

Service	Web filed	Software	Paper
Incorporation fee		£10	£40
Incorporation fee via Companies House	£12		
Same-day incorporation fee		£30	£100
Change-of-name fee	£8	£8	£10
Same-day change-of-name fee	£30	£30	£50
Re-registration fee			£20
Same-day re-registration fee			£50
Same-day simultaneous re-registration and change-of-name fee			£100
Confirmation fee	£13	£13	£40
Overseas company registration fee			£20
Overseas company change-of-name fee			£10
Overseas company filing accounts fee			£20
Registration of a charge	£15	£15	£23
Voluntary dissolution fee			£10
Reduction of capital supported by solvency statement			£10
Same-day reduction of capital supported by solvency statement			£50
Administrative restoration			£100
Application to suppress address information from public search			£55
Application to suppress address information from credit reference			£100

More information

▷ Full price list available from Companies House website: www.gov.uk/government/organisations/companies-house/about-our-services

Companies House – software filing

Software filing is only available using an approved software package. At present there are about 40 suppliers of software offering some or all of the ability to incorporate companies, file accounts, file forms and register mortgages. A full list and contact information for these suppliers can be found on the Companies House website (www.gov.uk/company-filing-software/filing-other).

Checklist

▶ Proprietary software.

▶ Registration with Companies House.

Procedure

▶ Presenters must first register with Companies House. As part of this process, an account will be opened for the payment of any filing fees.

▶ The company must notify Companies House of a password to authenticate documents and of the presenter transmitting the documents. This password will replace the signature of the company secretary or a director currently required to authenticate all forms.

▶ Groups of companies can choose to have the same password. In order to comply with the Companies Act, the password must be delivered to Companies House in writing by the company, and signed by a serving officer of the company.

▶ When a form detailing the appointment of a director or company secretary is delivered, the appointee is required to indicate his or her consent to act as a director or company secretary by providing three pieces of information that other people would not normally be expected to know. This information will not be displayed on the public file, but will be stored so that it can be retrieved should any question arise as to the validity of the appointment. Such personal information includes: place of birth, mother's maiden name, NI number, passport number, etc. Alternatively, a director or company secretary may agree with Companies House a six-digit personal identification code.

More information

▶ www.gov.uk/government/organisations/companies-house

Companies House – web filing

Companies House has introduced an electronic web filing service, currently limited to the more popular forms, with further ones becoming available according to demand. Currently the following forms may be filed using the web filing service:

Company forms

AA01	change of accounting reference date
AA02	dormant company accounts
AD01	change of situation or address of registered office
AD02	notification of single alternative inspection location (SAIL)
AD03	change of location of the company records to the single alternative inspection location (SAIL)
AD04	change of location of the company records to the registered office
annual accounts	audit exempt small full accounts (with abbreviated option)
annual accounts	audit exempt abbreviated accounts
annual accounts	micro-entity accounts
AP01	appointment of director
AP02	appointment of corporate director
AP03	appointment of secretary
AP04	appointment of corporate secretary
CH01	change of particulars for director
CH02	change of particulars for corporate director
CH03	change of particulars for secretary
CH04	change of particulars for corporate secretary
CS01	confirmation statement (£13 charge)
DS02	withdrawal of application to strike off
incorporation (IN01)	private company limited by shares adopting their model articles in their entirety
MR01	particulars of a charge

MR02	particulars of a charge subject to which property or undertaking has been acquired
MR04	statement of satisfaction in full or in part of a charge
MR05	statement that part or the whole of the property charged (a) has been released from the charge (b) no longer forms part of the company's property
NM01	notice of change of name by resolution and special resolution (RES15) (£8 charge)
SH01	return of allotment of shares
TM01	terminating appointment as director
TM02	terminating appointment as secretary
PSC01	notice of individual person with significant control
PSC02	notice of relevant legal entity with significant control
PSC03	notice of other registrable person with significant control
PSC04	notice of change of details for PSC
PSC05	notice of change of details for relevant legal entity with significant control
PSC06	notice of change of details of other registrable person with significant control
PSC07	notice of ceasing to be a PSC
PSC08	notice of PSC statements
PSC09	notice of update to PSC statements
EH01	elect to keep register of directors information on the public register
EH02	elect to keep directors' residential addresses on the central register
EH03	elect to keep register of secretaries information on the central register
EW01	withdraw register of directors information from the central register
EW02	withdraw usual residential addresses information from the central register
EW03	withdraw register of secretaries' information from the central register

It is not possible to web file full audited accounts.

Limited liability partnership forms

LL AA01	change of accounting reference date of an LLP
LL AD01	change of registered office address of an LLP
LL AD02	notification of the single alternative inspection location (SAIL) of an LLP
LL AD03	change of location of the records to the single alternative inspection location (SAIL) of an LLP

LL AD04	change of location of the records to the registered office of an LLP
LL AP01	appointment of member of an LLP
LL AP02	appointment of corporate member of an LLP
LL AR01	annual return of an LLP (£13 charge)
LL CH01	change of details of a member of an LLP
LL CH02	change of details of a corporate member of an LLP
LL CS01	confirmation statement (£13 charge)
LL DS02	withdrawal of application to strike off
LL MR01	particulars of a charge created by an LLP
LL MR02	particulars of a charge subject to which property or undertaking has been acquired by an LLP
LL MR04	statement of satisfaction in full or in part of a charge by an LLP
LL MR05	statement that part or the whole of the property charged (a) has been released from the charge (b) no longer forms part of the LLP's property
LL TM01	termination of appointment of member of an LLP
LL PSC01	notice of individual person with significant control
LL PSC02	notice of relevant legal entity with significant control
LL PSC03	notice of other registrable person with significant control
LL PSC04	notice of change of details for PSC
LL PSC05	notice of change of details for relevant legal entity with significant control
LL PSC06	notice of change of details of other registrable person with significant control
LL PSC07	notice of ceasing to be a PSC
LL PSC08	notice of PSC statements
LL PSC09	notice of update to PSC statements
LL EH01	elect to keep register of members information on the central register
LL EH02	elect to keep register of LLP members' residential addresses information on the central register
LL EH04	elect to keep register of PSC information on the central register
LL EW01	withdraw register of LLP members' information from the central register for an LLP
LL EW02	withdraw register of LLP members' usual residential addresses information from the central register
LL EW04	withdraw register of PSC information from the central register for an LLP

Checklist

▷ Registration with Companies House.

Procedure

▷ Presenters must first register with Companies House. As part of this process, an account will be opened for the payment of any filing fees.

▷ The company must notify Companies House of a password to authenticate documents and of the presenter transmitting the documents. This password will replace the signature of the secretary or a director currently required to authenticate all forms.

▷ Groups of companies can choose to have the same password. In order to comply with the Companies Act, the password must be delivered to Companies House in writing by each company, and signed by a serving officer of the relevant company.

More information

▷ www.gov.uk/government/organisations/companies-house/about-our-services#webfiling

Company secretary – appointment and reporting lines

A public limited company must appoint a suitably qualified individual to the role of company secretary. Private companies need not appoint or retain a company secretary, but may do so if they wish. Nevertheless, all companies must ensure their statutory obligations are met, so it is good practice for all but the simplest organisations to have an appropriately qualified and experienced company secretary.

ss. 271, 273
s. 270

Regardless of the size of the organisation, the company secretary is a key member of the executive team who is appointed by the board as an officer of the company. They have specific responsibility for advising the board through the chair on all governance matters. The company secretary is also responsible for ensuring good information flows within the board and its committees and between senior management and non-executive directors, as well as facilitating induction and assisting with professional development. The UK Corporate Governance Code states that the UK Governance Code – provision 16 appointment and removal of the company secretary is a matter for the board as a whole. The company secretary is responsible to the board of directors collectively rather than to any individual director.

The company secretary will need to have knowledge of the legal, regulatory and administrative framework in which the organisation operates. This will vary from a premium listed public limited company with thousands of shareholders, to a private limited company, a charity or a service provider in the public sector. The individual appointed should have the experience and/or ability to understand the additional demands of the role.

Reporting lines

The company secretary should be in a position to give independent, impartial advice and support to all the directors individually and to the board as a whole. The company secretary should not be subject to undue influence from one or more of the directors and appropriate reporting lines should be established. If the board fails to protect the integrity of the company secretary's position, one of the important in-built internal controls available to the company is likely to be undermined. Appropriate reporting lines for the company secretary will also help to ensure the delivery of the best company secretarial service and the most positive impact on the performance of the board and the organisation.

The Chartered Governance Institute recommends that the company secretary should report to the chair on all matters relating to corporate governance and other duties and responsibilities that concern the whole board. If the company secretary has other executive or administrative duties, they should report to the chief executive or other director who has delegated responsibility. The Chartered Governance Institute also recommends (particularly where the company secretary reports to the chair on all matters) that decisions on remuneration and benefits should be taken (or at least noted) by the board as a whole or the relevant board committee to avoid undue influence.

Checklist

▷ The person named as company secretary, if any, on form IN01 delivered on incorporation of a company is deemed to have been appointed as company secretary upon incorporation.

▷ Subsequent appointments of company secretaries are made by the board of directors in accordance with the provisions of the Act or any provisions contained in their articles of association. **s.276**

▷ If a public company fails to appoint a company secretary, the Secretary of State may issue a direction requiring the appointment of a company secretary and specifying the period in which the appointment must be made, being between one and three months of the date of the direction. **s.272**

▷ The company's auditor cannot be appointed as company secretary. **s.1214**

▷ Company secretaries of public companies must be qualified by profession or experience: **s.273**

  ▷ They have held the position of secretary in a public company for at least three of the five years preceding their appointment.

  ▷ They are a member of any of the specified bodies. **s.273(3)**

  ▷ They are a barrister, advocate or solicitor called or admitted in the UK.

  ▷ They are a person who, through holding or having held another position, or being a member of another body, appears to the directors to be capable of fulfilling the functions of the role.

Procedure

▷ Convene a directors' meeting to approve the appointment of the company secretary. Ensure valid quorum is present.

▷ File form AP03 or AP04 as appropriate. **s.276**

▷ The necessary entry must be made in the Register of Secretaries. **s.275**

▷ The company secretary is frequently a signatory on the company's bank account, and accordingly it may be necessary to amend the company's bank mandate in addition to notifying the bank of the new appointment and supplying specimen signatures to the bank.

▶ The board will normally consider it necessary for the company secretary to have a service contract.

▶ If the company secretary is to carry out executive duties, it may be considered necessary to include the company secretary on any policy of directors' and officers' indemnity insurance.

Filing requirement

▶ Form AP03 or AP04 within 14 days.

Notes

▶ The appointment of a company secretary may be terminated by the directors. There is no need for shareholder approval. The company secretary may be able to bring an action for breach of contract in such circumstances, and accordingly a compromise agreement may be appropriate.

▶ The company secretary must provide a service address; this need not be their residential address. Unlike with directors, there is no need to notify the company of the secretary's usual residential address.

s.277

More information

▶ *Company Secretary's Handbook*, Chapter 1

▶ Companies House Guidance booklet GP3

Company secretary – role and responsibilities

The role of the company secretary can cover all areas of a company's activities, depending on the size and nature of the company. The duties of the company secretary are not specified in detail in the Companies Act, although as an officer of the company, the company secretary is liable, along with the directors, for any breaches of the regulations imposed by the Act.

The company secretary plays a central role in the legal operation of the organisation and, by ensuring high standards of corporate governance, shareholder relations and board effectiveness, the company secretary can contribute to the company's performance. The UK Corporate Governance Code recognises explicitly the secretary's responsibility for corporate governance, particularly as an independent, impartial adviser.

Research published in July 2014 by The Chartered Governance Institute and Henley Business School identified that the independence and discretion of the company secretary, bridging the executive team and main board NEDs, played an increasingly important role in promoting a well-functioning board, which in turn helped to build stakeholder trust. The Chartered Governance Institute guidance on the duties and reporting lines of the company secretary divides the role and responsibilities into three broad areas – the board, the company and the shareholders – and then sets out the core duties, which are summarised below.

Checklist

The board
▶ Board/ committee meetings

▷ Organising board and board committees.

▷ Formulating meeting agendas in consultation with the chairman and/or the chief executive and advising management on content and organisation of memoranda or presentations for the meeting.

▷ Collecting, organising and distributing high-quality information, documents or other papers required for the meeting.

▷ Ensuring that all meetings are conducted in accordance with the Articles of Association minuted and that the minute books are maintained with certified copies of the minutes.

▷ Ensuring that the board and its committees are properly constituted and advised, that the latter are provided with clear terms of reference and that there is clear co-ordination between the board and the various committees.

▶ Directors' duties and transactions

▷ Ensuring that the directors are aware of their statutory duties under the Act and advising the directors on those duties.

▷ Ensuring that the directors are properly advised on their duties and responsibilities to creditors in the event that the company may become, or has become, insolvent.

▷ Ensuring compliance with the restrictions in the Act in relation to transactions with directors, including directors' service contracts, the sale or purchase of non-cash assets from directors and (in the case of public companies) loans and credit transactions with directors.

▷ Devising, implementing and administering directors' and employees' share ownership schemes and directors' long term incentive plans.

▶ Corporate governance

▷ Review developments in corporate governance and fulfilling all requirements of the Code and assisting the chairman and directors in complying with the Code.

▶ Acquisitions, disposals and mergers

▷ Participating as a key member of the company team established to implement corporate acquisitions, disposals and mergers.

▷ Protecting the company's interests by ensuring the effectiveness of all documentation.

▷ Ensuring that due diligence disclosures enable proper commercial evaluation prior to completion of a transaction.

▷ Ensuring that the correct authority is in place to allow timely execution of documentation.

▶ Powers of the company secretary and the company seal

▷ Ensuring the safe custody and proper use of any company seals.

The company

▶ Articles of Association

▷ Ensuring that the company complies with its Articles of Association and be responsible for drafting and incorporating amendments to the Articles in accordance with the Act, the LPDT Rules and any other relevant regulations.

▶ UKLA

▷ Monitoring and ensuring compliance with the LPDT Rules, the Takeover Code when relevant and supervising the implementation of the company's code for dealing in the company's securities by Persons Discharging Managerial Responsibilities and their connected persons, as appropriate.

▷ Releasing 'regulated information to the market through a Regulatory Information Service (RIS) including 'inside information'

▷ Ensuring the security of inside information prior to disclosure.

▷ Updating corporate websites with inside information issued via an RIS and filing certain documents with the National Storage Mechanism such as circulars and prospectuses.

▷ Making applications for listing of additional issues of securities.

▶ Statutory registers

▷ Maintaining the statutory registers.

▶ Statutory returns

▷ Filing information with the Registrar of Companies, as required.

▶ Report and accounts

▷ Co-ordinating the preparation, publication and distribution of the company's annual report and accounts and interim statements, in consultation with the company's internal and external advisers.

▷ Assisting the directors to draft the narrative reporting sections of the report, as required, covering corporate governance, the work of the board and the board committees, the directors' report and environmental/corporate social responsibility areas.

▷ Publication of electronic versions of the documents on the company website.

▶ Registered office

▷ Establishing and administering the registered office.

▷ Ensuring the provision of facilities and procedures for the public inspection of company documents.

▶ Company identity

▷ Ensuring that all business letters, order forms and websites of the company show the name of the company and the other information required by the Act.

▷ Ensuring that the company's name is displayed in a conspicuous place at the company's registered office and any other place it conducts business or has records available for inspection.

▶ Subsidiary companies

▷ Ensuring that procedures are in place for the correct administration of subsidiary companies including all aspects of their corporate procedures, company books, records and filings.

▷ Maintaining a record of the group's corporate structure.

▶ General compliance

▷ Monitoring and laying in place procedures which allow for compliance with relevant regulatory and legal requirements.

▷ Ensuring that procedures are in place for the retention of documents, retaining the minimum set of records required for commercial reasons and ensuring that procedures are in place to allow adequate historical archive to be maintained.

The members

▶ General meetings

▷ Ensuring that annual and other general meetings are held in accordance with the requirements of the Act, the LPDT Rules, and the company's Articles of Association, obtaining internal and external agreement to all documentation for circulation to members.

▷ Preparing and issuing notices of meetings, and distributing proxy forms.

▷ Assisting directors to prepare for any member questions including the creation of briefing materials.

▷ Overseeing the preparations for security arrangements.

▷ Ensuring that proxy forms are correctly processed and that the voting is carried out accurately.

▷ Co-ordinating the administration and minuting of meetings, for larger companies often carried out in association with the company's share registrar.

▶ Share registration

▷ Maintaining the company's register of members.

▷ Dealing with transfers, share certificates and other matters affecting share holdings including co-ordination of all requirements relating to dividend and interest payments to shareholders dealing with queries and requests from shareholders.

▶ Shareholder communications

▷ Communicating with the shareholders about corporate actions (e.g. through circulars), in connection with payments and general meetings.

▷ Issuing documentation regarding rights issues and capitalisation issues.

▷ Maintaining good general shareholder relations.

▷ Assisting in the maintenance of good relations between the company and institutional shareholders and their investment committees.

▶ Shareholder monitoring

▷ Monitoring movements on the register of members to identify any apparent 'stake building' in the company's shares by potential take-over bidders.

▷ Making appropriate inquiries of members as to beneficial ownership of holdings.

▶ Share and capital issues and restructuring

▷ Implementing properly authorised changes in the structure of the company's share and loan capital, in accordance with the Articles of Association, the Act and the LPDT Rules.

▷ Ensuring that the restrictions and prohibitions in the Act in relation to maintenance of share capital are complied with.

Notes

There are many other areas in which company secretaries can and often do become involved relating to the management of companies. These might include other aspects of company law, regulation and compliance such as risk management, pensions administration, information security and data protection, and health and safety.

More information

▶ *Company Secretary's Handbook*, Chapter 1

Confirmation statement

Introduced under SBEE2015 as a deregulating measure, the confirmation statement is intended to offer an easier and more efficient way for companies to check and confirm information held by the Registrar of Companies rather than having to provide information in the form of the annual return, which for many companies remains unchanged from year to year.

All companies must make a confirmation statement up to a date not more than 12 months after the previous confirmation (or 12 months after incorporation), although a company may choose to make it up to an earlier date. The confirmation statement must be filed with the Registrar of Companies within 14 days of the confirmation date, together with a fee (currently £13 if filed online or £40 if filed in hard copy).

s.853A(1)

The statement confirms that all information that the company is required to have delivered to the Registrar of Companies under s. 853B (Relevant Events) has been delivered or is being delivered at the same time as the confirmation statement. In addition to the statement concerning relevant events, companies must provide updated information primarily relating to their share capital, share ownership and beneficial ownership.

s.853A(2)(a)

s 853A(2)(b)
ss.853C-I

Checklist

▶ Check if the records at Companies House are up to date and either confirm or complete the confirmation statement information together with any additional forms required to update the public record as set out below.

▶ Provide details of any changes in relevant events during the confirmation period.

▶ Provide details of any changes in:

  ▷ the company's business activities or SIC code;

  ▷ information about people with significant control or any changes;

  ▷ statement of capital;

  ▷ trading status of shares; and

  ▷ member information.

▶ File the confirmation statement within 14 days of end of the review period to which it relates, together with the appropriate filing fee, if any: £40 if being filed in hard copy, and £13 if being filed electronically or online.

s.853A(5)

ss.853A(4),(6)

Procedure

▶ A company's first review period begins on the date of incorporation and ends 12 months later. Subsequent review periods are the period of 12 months beginning on the day after the previous confirmation statement. Companies may choose to file a confirmation statement covering a shorter period than 12 months, but the period cannot exceed 12 months.

s.853(A)(1)

▶ A confirmation statement is required even where there have been no changes.

▶ For all companies, details of any relevant events must have already been notified or be being notified at the same time as the confirmation statement is submitted using the usual statutory forms. The relevant events are:

▷ company's registered office;

s.853B

▷ company's directors and any changes to their registered or registrable information (see page 65);

▷ company's secretary and any changes to their registered or registrable information (see page 65); and

▷ changes to the location of any of the company's registers.

▶ In addition, if there has been a change to any of the details set out below, updated information must be provided with the confirmation statement:

▷ If the company's business activities have changed, the relevant SIC code(s).

s.853C

▷ If the company has shares, any change to the statement of capital. The statement of capital was simplified at the same time as the introduction of the confirmation statement and comprises details of the total number of shares of the company, of all classes, aggregate nominal value and aggregate amount unpaid on those shares, whether of nominal value or share premium. In addition, for each share class there must be provided details of the prescribed particulars of the rights attached to the shares, total number of shares of that class and the aggregate nominal value of the shares of that class.

s.853D

▷ Any changes in trading status of the shares. The requirement is to notify if any of the shares were at any time during the period admitted to trading on a regulated market and if so whether the shares were admitted to that market throughout the period and whether the company was a DTR5 issuer.

s.853E

▷ Any changes in members' information. A non-traded company that has not elected to keep its register of members on the public register must provide information about any changes to the names of any members, number of shares of each class held by members, and number and date of registration of any shares transferred during the confirmation period.

▷ If the company is a traded company, for every member who held 5% or more of the issued shares at any time during the period covered by the return, their name, address and holding of shares.

s.853G

Filing requirement

▶ Form CS01.

▶ Filing fee: £40 or £13 as appropriate.

Notes

If a company files more than one confirmation statement in any 12-month period, there is no fee payable for filing the second or subsequent statements.

More information

▶ *Company Secretary's Handbook*, Chapter 7

▶ Companies House Guidance – Confirmation statement

Corporate governance – principles and key issues for listed companies

The overarching corporate governance principles under the 2018 UK Corporate Governance Code are as follows.

1   Board Leadership and Company Purpose

A. A successful company is led by an effective and entrepreneurial board, whose role is to promote the long-term sustainable success of the company, generating value for shareholders and contributing to wider society.

B. The board should establish the company's purpose, values and strategy, and satisfy itself that these and its culture are aligned. All directors must act with integrity, lead by example and promote the desired culture.

C. The board should ensure that the necessary resources are in place for the company to meet its objectives and measure performance against them. The board should also establish a framework of prudent and effective controls, which enable risk to be assessed and managed.

D. In order for the company to meet its responsibilities to shareholders and stakeholders, the board should ensure effective engagement with, and encourage participation from, these parties.

E. The board should ensure that workforce policies and practices are consistent with the company's values and support its long-term sustainable success. The workforce should be able to raise any matters of concern.

2   Division of Responsibilities

F. The chair leads the board and is responsible for its overall effectiveness in directing the company. They should demonstrate objective judgement throughout their tenure and promote a culture of openness and debate. In addition, the chair facilitates constructive board relations and the effective contribution of all non-executive directors, and ensures that directors receive accurate, timely and clear information.

G. The board should include an appropriate combination of executive and non-executive (and, in particular, independent non-executive) directors, such that no one individual or small group of individuals dominates the board's decision-making. There should be a clear division of responsibilities between the leadership of the board and the executive leadership of the company's business.

H. Non-executive directors should have sufficient time to meet their board responsibilities. They should provide constructive challenge, strategic guidance, offer specialist advice and hold management to account.

I. The board, supported by the company secretary, should ensure that it has the policies, processes, information, time and resources it needs in order to function effectively and efficiently.

3   Composition, Succession and Evaluation

J. Appointments to the board should be subject to a formal, rigorous and transparent procedure, and an effective succession plan should be maintained for board and senior management. Both appointments and succession plans should be based on merit and objective criteria and, within this context, should promote diversity of gender, social and ethnic backgrounds, cognitive and personal strengths.

K. The board and its committees should have a combination of skills, experience and knowledge. Consideration should be given to the length of service of the board as a whole and membership regularly refreshed.

L. Annual evaluation of the board should consider its composition, diversity and how effectively members work together to achieve objectives. Individual evaluation should demonstrate whether each director continues to contribute effectively.

4   Audit, Risk and Internal Control

M. The board should establish formal and transparent policies and procedures to ensure the independence and effectiveness of internal and external audit functions and satisfy itself on the integrity of financial and narrative statements.

N. The board should present a fair, balanced and understandable assessment of the company's position and prospects.

O. The board should establish procedures to manage risk, oversee the internal control framework, and determine the nature and extent of the principal risks the company is willing to take in order to achieve its long-term strategic objectives.

5   Remuneration

P. Remuneration policies and practices should be designed to support strategy and promote long-term sustainable success. Executive remuneration should be aligned to company purpose and values and be clearly linked to the successful delivery of the company's long-term strategy.

Q. A formal and transparent procedure for developing policy on executive remuneration and determining director and senior management remuneration should be established. No director should be involved in deciding their own remuneration outcome.

R. Directors should exercise independent judgement and discretion when authorising remuneration outcomes, taking account of company and individual performance, and wider circumstances.

Good corporate governance should promote the best long-term interests of the company. Composition of the board, its functions and responsibilities and its effectiveness are therefore key issues of corporate governance.

More information

▷ *Company Secretary's Handbook*, Chapter 17

Corporate governance – Wates principles

The original corporate governance code was focused on providing additional safeguards for investors and holding directors to be more accountable. As a consequence, the guidance only applied to Listed companies. Over the years corporate governance has evolved and the scope of the protection has widened to include additional stakeholders relevant to both public and privately-owned groups. During recent years there have been a number of high-profile collapses among large privately held companies which has led to the call for better corporate governance among those companies too.

Under the chairmanship of James Wates, the Coalition Group published six guiding principles for large private companies (the Wates principles).

Checklist

▶ **Purpose:** An effective board promotes the purpose of a company, and ensures that its values, strategy and culture align with that purpose.

▶ **Composition:** Effective board composition requires an effective chair and a balance of skills, backgrounds, experience and knowledge, with individual directors having sufficient capacity to make a valuable contribution. The size of a board should be guided by the scale and complexity of the company.

▶ **Responsibilities:** A board should have a clear understanding of its accountability and terms of reference. Its policies and procedures should support effective decision-making and independent challenge.

▶ **Opportunity and risk:** A board should promote the long-term success of the company by identifying opportunities to create and preserve value and establishing oversight for the identification and mitigation of risks.

▶ **Remuneration:** A board should promote executive remuneration structures aligned to the sustainable long-term success of a company, taking into account pay and conditions elsewhere in the company.

▶ **Stakeholders:** A board has a responsibility to oversee meaningful engagement with material stakeholders, including the workforce, and have regard to that discussion when taking decisions. The board has a responsibility to foster good stakeholder relationships based on the company's purpose.

Procedure

Following the lead of the UK Corporate governance Code the application of the Wates principles adopts the comply or explain approach.

The principles will apply to private companies meeting either of the following criteria:

▶ Turnover of more than £200m and balance sheet of more than £2bn; or

▶ More than 2,000 employees

Filing requirement

None.

More information

https://www.frc.org.uk/getattachment/31dfb844-6d4b-4093-9bfe-19cee2c29cda/Wates-Corporate-Governance-Principles-for-LPC-Dec-2018.pdf

▶ *Company Secretary's Handbook*, Chapter 17

CREST settlement

'CREST-compliant articles' is the term used to describe companies whose articles permit settlement in CREST, the dematerialised settlement system for shares of listed, AIM and NEX companies operated by Euroclear UK and Ireland Limited.

New applicants to either of the markets will be required to ensure that their articles are CREST-compliant as a condition of entry. For existing companies this could be by way of either a directors' or a shareholders' resolution. For newly incorporated companies, this power would be incorporated in the articles of association adopted for the purposes of admission.

Enabling the shares to be settled in CREST requires the register of members to be split into two parts: a wholly electronic sub-register maintained by CREST and the certificated part of the register maintained by or on behalf of the company.

The company will need to ensure it has the necessary systems to allow for real-time updating and synchronisation between the electronic sub-register and the certificated register; this task is usually outsourced to a specialist share registration company.

Checklist

▷ Do the articles permit dematerialised holdings?

▷ Has appropriate software been acquired or the share register been outsourced to ensure the register of members is capable of interacting with CREST?

Procedure

▷ Convene a directors' meeting to approve appropriate resolution to amend the articles of association. Ensure valid quorum is present.   reg. 16, SI 2001/3755

▷ Alternatively, the amendments may be made by special resolution of the shareholders (see page 254).

▷ Where changes are made by directors' resolution, notice must be given to shareholders within 60 days of the date of the resolution.

Filing requirement

▶ Copy of directors' resolution or special resolution within 15 days.

Notes

▶ Enabling CREST settlement is one of the few occasions where the directors can resolve to change the company's articles of association.

▶ Prior to commencement of CREST settlement, an application form must be submitted to Euroclear UK and Ireland Ltd, the system operator, to enable CREST settlement. This process will usually be arranged by the company's share registrars.

More information

▶ *Company Secretary's Handbook*, Chapter 18

▶ www.euroclear.com

Data Protection registration

2018 saw a significant change to data protection legislation across Europe with the implementation of the pan European General Data Protection Regulation ('GDPR'), supported in the UK by the Data Protection Act 2018 (DPA2018), and the Privacy and Electronic Communications Regulations (PECR). In formulating their data protection policies, practices and procedures public bodies must also be aware of the requirements of the Freedom of Information Act 2000.

Although data controllers are no longer required to register with the Information Commissioner's Office ('ICO') they are instead required to provide limited information and pay an annual fee. This fee is primarily to ensure the continuing funding for the ICO.

'Data controller' means the natural or legal person, public authority, agency or other body which, alone or jointly with others, determines the purposes and means of the processing of personal data.

GDPR Art. 4 (1), (2) & (7)

'Data processor' means a natural or legal person, public authority, agency or other body which processes personal data on behalf of the controller, and 'personal data' means any information relating to an identified or identifiable natural person.

Data controllers must pay an annual Data Protection fee unless all the processing of personal data they undertake qualifies as exempt processing.

Checklist

▶ Is the company a data processor?

▶ Is all processing exempt processing (for the purposes of registration)?

Procedure

Data controllers other than those only undertaking exempt processing must provide the following information to the ICO:

▶ the name and address of the controller;

▶ the number of members of staff;

▶ the turnover for the latest financial year; and

▶ any other trading names.

Names and contact details of the following people:

▶ the person completing the registration process; and if different

▶ a relevant person in the organisation to contact on ICO matters.

The data protection fee depends on the size of the company measured in terms of turnover or numbers of staff. There are three different tiers of fees as set out below. An organisation meets the Tier test if it meets either of the criteria for that Tier.

Tier	ICO Fee*	Turnover not exceeding	Average number of employees not exceeding
Tier 1	£40	£632,000	10
Tier 2	£60	£36m	250
Tier 3	£2,900	No limit	No limit

*Where paid by direct debit the fee is reduced by £5

Filing requirement

None.

Notes

Any organisation which is processing personal data only for at least one of the following activities will be exempt from the requirement to pay a fee:

▶ staff administration;

▶ advertising, marketing and public relations;

▶ accounts and records;

▶ not-for-profit organisation purposes;

▶ personal, family or household affairs;

▶ maintaining a public register;

▶ judicial functions; or

▶ processing personal information without an automated system such as a computer.

These exemptions are only in relation to payment of ICO fees.

More information

▶ *Company Secretary's Handbook*, Chapter 7

▶ www.ico.gov.uk

Debenture stock

The procedures for issuing, transferring, payment of interest on and redemption of debentures are, broadly speaking, the same as for the issuing of ordinary shares.

Debentures, unlike shares, are loans to the company and are secured against the assets of the company.

Unless restricted by the articles of association, companies have an implied power to issue debentures.

Checklist

▶ Do articles restrict the directors' power to create and issue debentures?

▶ Create trust deed containing:

▷ details of the stock, terms of issue, payment of interest, conversion into shares and/or redemption;

▷ provisions constituting charges over the assets of the company in favour of the trust deed and giving details of the events by which the charge would be enforceable;

▷ details of the Trustees' powers to concur with the company in dealings with the charged assets;

▷ where the security is by way of floating charge, a prohibition on the company issuing any further security ranking in priority to the debenture stock without previous consent; and

▷ details setting out the form of stock certificate, conditions of redemption, conversion rights and regulations in respect of the Register of Holders, transfer and transmission, and regulations for the conducting and holding of meetings of the debenture holders.

▶ Register allotment of debentures as soon as practical in register of debenture holders and in any event within two months of issue.

s.741

▶ Ensure register is available for inspection at the registered office or at its SAIL address (see page 285).

s.743

▶ If register is not kept at registered office, file form AD02.

Procedure

▶ Convene a directors' meeting to approve the terms of the trust deed and the issue of debentures.

▶ The company secretary should arrange the preparation and issue of debenture stock certificates to each debenture holder.   **s. 741**

▶ The company secretary should record the details of the debentures issued in the register of debenture holders.   **ss. 859A, 859B**

▶ As debentures are secured on the assets of the company, the trust deed and form MG07 or MG08 as appropriate must be submitted to Companies House within 21 days of the creation of the trust deed.

Filing requirement

▶ Trust deed.

▶ Form MG07 or MG08 within 21 days.

▶ Form AD02, if required.

▶ Filing fee £23 (paper), £15 (electronic).

More information

▶ *Company Secretary's Handbook*, Chapter 12

▶ Companies House Guidance booklet GP3

Directors – appointment of corporate director

The Small Business, Enterprise and Employment Act 2015 (SBEE2015) contains additional restrictions on the appointment of corporate directors; however, at the time of writing these provisions have not been implemented and there is no guidance on when they are to be brought into effect.

s. 12 reg. 17 sch. 1 or reg. 20 sch. 3, SI 2008/3229

Although the Act introduced a general ban on the appointment of corporate directors, there are to be a number of exemptions to this ban.

Accordingly, once brought into force, the detail of the legislation must be checked to ensure any proposed appointment of a corporate director is permitted.

Checklist

▶ If there is to be a corporate director, there must also be appointed at least one other director that is a natural person.

s. 155

▶ Is the director disqualified from acting by statute or the articles of association?

▶ Obtain written consent from the entity consenting to be appointed as a director. This can be included in the service contract rather than a stand-alone document if preferred. Ensure that any cap on the maximum number of directors set out in the Articles has not been reached or amend if required.

Procedure

▶ The following details will be required in order to complete form AP02.

- Corporate name and registered or principal office.
- For an EAA company details of the registry it is registered in and its registered number.
- For a non EAA company its legal form and if applicable details of the registry it is registered in and its registered number.

▶ Although not explicitly prohibited, the duties and responsibilities of the UK corporate governance code make it very unlikely that a corporate director can be appointed to a listed company.

▷ If directors' names are shown on the headed paper, this will need to be updated.

▷ Amend bank mandate if necessary.

▷ Convene a directors' meeting to approve the appointment of a new director. Ensure valid quorum is present.

▷ File completed form AP02 at Companies House.

▷ Notify employees, customers and/or bank, if appropriate.

▷ Update the registers of directors and directors' residential addresses as necessary.

Filing requirement

▷ Form AP02 within 14 days.

Notes

▷ Those persons representing the corporate director should notify the board of any interest in contracts or other companies with which the company has dealings.

▷ The company secretary should inform those persons representing the new director of the dates on which forthcoming board meetings are to be held, if these are known.

▷ If the articles of association require that the directors hold a share qualification, it is essential that the director acquires the appropriate shares within two months, or the time limit set down by the articles if shorter.

▷ Appointees are no longer required to sign a statement on the form AP02 consenting to act as a director; instead a statement confirming the entity has consented is confirmed on behalf of the company. Accordingly confirmation of consent should be obtained and retained in the event of any disputed appointments (see page 111).

▷ It may be necessary to add the director to the company's directors' indemnity insurance policy, or indeed it may be necessary to effect such a policy.

More information

▷ *Company Secretary's Handbook*, Chapter 6

▷ Companies House Guidance booklet GP3

Directors – appointment of individual

When a company is incorporated, the people named in the incorporation papers (form IN01) as directors and who have consented to act are deemed to be appointed on the date of incorporation. Following the appointment of these first directors, any further directors to be selected should be appointed in accordance with the regulations laid down by the company's articles of association.

In general, the articles will allow the existing directors to fill any casual vacancy in their number by themselves or by the members by ordinary resolution.

Occasionally, the articles of association will stipulate qualifications to be held for eligibility for appointment as a director. This often used to be a share qualification, although this is no longer a popular practice.

Additional qualifications would more normally be the holding of a particular professional or technical qualification (e.g. chartered surveyor, architect, etc).

s. 12
reg. 17 sch. 1 or
reg. 20 sch. 3,
SI 2008/3229

Checklist

▷ Check the articles of association to establish whether directors or only shareholders may appoint the new director(s).

▷ Check the articles to ensure any maximum number of directors stipulated in the articles has not already been reached.

▷ Is the proposed director at least 16 years old?   *s. 157*

▷ If there is to be a sole director, is the proposed director a natural person?   *s. 155*

▷ Is the director disqualified from acting by statute or the articles of association?

▷ Obtain the director's details required to complete form AP01, including their residential address in addition to a service address.

▷ If appointment is as a non-executive to a listed company, ensure appropriate independence tests can be met if appropriate.

▷ Obtain written consent from the individual consenting to be appointed as a director. This can be included in their employment contract rather than a stand-alone document if preferred.

▷ If directors' names are shown on the headed paper, this will need to be updated.

▷ Amend bank mandate if necessary.

Procedure

▷ Convene a directors' meeting to approve the appointment of a new director. Ensure valid quorum is present.

▷ File completed form AP01 at Companies House.   **s.167**

▷ Notify employees, customers and/or bank, if appropriate.

▷ Notify Stock Exchange if company's shares are listed or traded on AIM.   **LR 9.6.11, AR 17**

▷ Notify NEX if company's shares are traded on the NEX market.   **NE RFI 66**

▷ Update the registers of directors and directors' residential addresses as necessary.   **ss.163–165**

Filing requirement

▷ Form AP01 within 14 days.

Notes

▷ The new director should notify the board of any interest in contracts or other companies with which the company has dealings.   **ss.177,182**

▷ The company secretary should inform the new director of the dates on which forthcoming board meetings are to be held, if these are known.

▷ If the articles of association require that the directors hold a share qualification, it is essential that the director acquires the appropriate shares within two months, or the time limit set down by the articles if shorter.

▷ If the new director is to be an executive director, it may be considered necessary for the director to have a formal service contract with the company.

▷ It may be necessary to add the director to the company's directors' indemnity insurance policy or indeed it may be necessary to effect such a policy.

▷ Appointees are no longer required to sign a statement on form AP01 consenting to act as a director; instead a statement confirming the individual has consented is confirmed on behalf of the company. Accordingly, confirmation of consent should be obtained and retained in the event of any disputed appointments (see page 111).

▶ If this is the director's first appointment as director, he or she should
   be given guidance as to his or her duties and responsibilities in terms
   of the Companies Act and his or her duties and responsibilities to
   members.

▶ HM Revenue & Customs should be informed of the director's
   appointment.

More information

▶ *Company Secretary's Handbook*, Chapter 6

▶ Companies House Guidance booklet GP3

Directors – ceasing to hold office

A director may cease to hold office as a result of his or her death, by statute or under the provisions of the articles of association.

A director may be barred from holding or continuing to hold office as director for the following reasons:

▶ If the articles require that the director hold a share qualification and the director does not acquire the necessary shares within the time limit specified by the articles if shorter.

▶ If the director becomes bankrupt (unless permitted to continue by the court).

▶ If the director is disqualified from holding a directorship by a court order.

Additionally, the articles may stipulate certain events that will require the director to vacate office, including:

▶ If a director resigns: resignation will not normally require consent of the remaining directors, although this may be required by the articles.

▶ If a director is absent from board meetings for a specific period without the authority of the board.

▶ If a director has a Receiving Order made against him or her, or if he or she enters into arrangements with his or her creditors.

▶ If the director is, or may be, suffering from a mental disorder and either the director has been admitted to hospital pursuant to the Mental Health Act or a court order has been made requiring his or her detention under the Act.

▶ If a director is removed from office by the remaining directors or by the members in some specified manner. This may include by written resolution of the remaining directors, by notice in writing of the company's holding company or in certain circumstances by their appointer. (For example, the holders of a particular class of shares may have the right to appoint a director and this person may be removed by them.)

In addition to the powers contained in the articles of association or by statute, the shareholders of the company have the right at all times to remove a director by ordinary resolution. Care must be taken when using these provisions.

s. 168

Checklist

▶ The company's bankers should be informed and any necessary amendments made to the bank mandate.

▶ The company secretary should amend the company's register of directors and the register of directors' residential addresses.

ss. 162, 165

▶ If the director's name is shown on the company's letter heading, this should be amended.

▶ If the company maintains a directors' indemnity insurance policy, the insurers should be informed.

▶ The auditors should be informed.

▶ HM Revenue & Customs should be notified.

▶ Any outstanding fees should be paid to the director and arrangements made for the return of any company property (car, computer equipment, etc).

▶ If appropriate, the director should be reminded of any restrictions on his or her future employment contained in his or her contract of employment with the company.

Procedure

▶ Convene a directors' meeting to consider the circumstances of the director whose appointment has ceased. Ensure valid quorum is present.

▶ File completed form TM01 at Companies House.

▶ Update register of directors and register of directors' residential addresses as necessary.

ss. 162, 165

▶ Amend headed paper if directors' names are shown.

▶ Notify Stock Exchange if company's shares are listed or traded on AIM.

LR 9.6.11, AR 17

▶ Notify NEX if company's shares are traded on the NEX market.

NE RFI 66

Filing requirement

▶ Form TM01 within 14 days.

Notes

None.

More information

▶ *Company Secretary's Handbook*, Chapter 6

▶ Companies House Guidance booklet GP3

▶ Enterprise Act 2002

▶ Company Directors' Disqualification Act 1986

▶ Insolvency Act 1986

▶ Small Business, Enterprise and Employment Act 2015

Directors – disqualification

▷ The Company Directors' Disqualification Act 1986 (CDDA1986) consolidated a number of enactments relating to the disqualification of persons from being directors of companies and from being otherwise concerned with company management.

▷ CDDA1986 sets out circumstances where a court may or will (depending on the section) make a disqualification order that prohibits that person from being a director, liquidator or administrator of a company, a receiver or manager of a company's property, or being in any way involved in the promotion, formation or management of a company for the specified period.

CDDA1986 ss. 1–6, 10

▷ Under provisions introduced by the Insolvency Act 2000, a director facing prosecution may voluntarily apply to be disqualified as a director. This voluntary procedure speeds up the disqualification process and significantly reduces the costs for all parties.

▷ SBEE2015 introduced new provisions allowing the courts to take into account overseas convictions for the purposes of determining whether or not to disqualify a person from acting as a director in the UK.

form DQ01

Checklist

▷ Ensure the court order or copy bears the seal of the court.

▷ The company's bankers should be informed and any necessary amendments made to the bank mandate.

▷ The secretary should amend the company's register of directors.

▷ If the director's name is shown on the company's letter heading, this should be amended.

▷ If the company maintains a directors' indemnity insurance policy, the insurers should be informed.

▷ The auditors, if any, should be informed.

▷ HM Revenue & Customs should be notified.

▷ Any outstanding fees should be paid to the director and arrangements made for the return of any company property (car, computer equipment, etc).

▷ If appropriate, the director should be reminded of any restrictions on his or her future employment contained in his or her contract of employment with the company.

Procedure

▷ File completed form TM01 at Companies House.   **s. 167**

▷ Update register of directors as necessary.

▷ Amend headed paper if directors' names are shown.

▷ Notify Stock Exchange if company's shares are listed or traded on AIM.   **LR 9.6.11, AR 17**

▷ Notify NEX if company's shares are traded on the NEX.   **NE RFI 66**

Filing requirement

▷ Form TM01 within 14 days.   **s. 167**

▷ Copy of disqualification order.

More information

▷ *Company Secretary's Handbook*, Chapter 6

▷ Companies House Guidance booklet GP3

Directors – duties

A director's prime duty, which he or she holds together with his or her fellow directors, is to manage the company for the benefit of its members. The directors may delegate some or all of their powers to particular directors (perhaps constituting a committee of the board) and/or other senior officers in the company, but they cannot delegate their duties.

The Companies Act 2006 introduced seven duties of directors. These duties codified, with some amendments, existing case law.

The directors must ensure that suitable arrangements are in place to enable the company to meet its statutory duties and are liable to penalties if the company is in default. Directors of many companies will delegate these duties to the company secretary, and as it is the directors who are liable in the event of default, care must be taken to ensure that the company secretary is suitably qualified.

Companies other than those that qualify as medium sized must include in their strategic report a statement describing how the directors have had regard to their duties set out in CA2006 s. 172(1)(a) to (f). This obligation applies for financial periods beginning on or after 1 January 2019.

s.414CZA

In many small private companies the directors will often rely on their professional advisers to undertake some of their responsibilities, such as filing accounts and preparing annual returns. Directors must act on the advice of their advisers to ensure that the statutory obligations are met. It is the directors and not the professional advisers who are liable, and in the event of default and prosecution it is the directors who will be called to account.

Checklist

The seven statutory duties are:

1. **To act within their powers:** Directors must act in accordance with the company's constitution and only exercise powers for the purposes for which they are conferred. The company's articles of association should be consulted to ascertain the extent of a director's powers and any limitations placed upon them.

s.171

2. **To promote the success of the company:** A director must act in the   s.172
way he or she considers, in good faith, would be most likely to promote
the success of the company for the benefit of its members as a whole, and
in doing so have regard (among other matters) to:

▶ the likely consequences of any decision in the long term;

▶ the interests of the company's employees;

▶ the need to foster the company's business relationships with suppliers,
customers and others;

▶ the impact of the company's operations on the community and the
environment;

▶ the desirability of the company maintaining a reputation for high
standards of business conduct; and

▶ the need to act fairly as between members of the company.

3. **To exercise independent judgement.**   s.173

4. **To exercise reasonable care, skill and diligence:** The duties   s.174
imposed by ss. 173 and 174 require that a director owes a duty to exercise
the same standard of care, skill and diligence that would be exercised by a
reasonably diligent person with:

▶ the general knowledge, skill and experience that may reasonably be
expected of the person carrying out the same functions as a director in
relation to that company (an objective test); and

▶ the general knowledge, skill and experience that the director actually
has (a subjective test).

(For example, a finance director would be expected to have a greater
knowledge of finance issues than, say, the HR director (the objective
test); but if the HR director is also a qualified accountant, then he or she
would be expected to have a greater knowledge than would normally be
expected of a HR director, although not necessarily the same knowledge
as the finance director (the subjective test).)

5. **To avoid conflicts of interest:** Directors must avoid situations in   s.175
which they have or might have a direct or indirect interest that conflicts or
might conflict with the interests of the company. Of particular importance
are conflicts relating to property, information or opportunity regardless of
whether the company could take advantage of such opportunities.

▶ The duty does not apply to conflicts arising out of transactions or
arrangement between the company and the director.

▶ Where the company is a private company, authorisation may be   s.175(5)
given by resolution of the directors, provided there is nothing in the
company's articles of association that invalidated the authorisation.

▶ Where the company is a public company, authorisation may be given
by resolution of the directors, provided there is specific authority in
the company's articles of association that permits directors to authorise
such transactions.

▷ Such authorisation, whether for a private or public company, is only valid if the necessary quorum for a meeting of the directors is present, excluding the director with the conflict of interest and without that director voting.

s. 175(6)

6. **Not to accept benefits from third parties:** Directors must not accept a benefit from a third party being given by virtue of their being a director or due to any action or inaction by the director.

s. 176

Benefits received by a director from a person by whom his or her services are provided are not to be regarded as paid by a third party.

The duty is not infringed if the acceptance of the benefit cannot reasonably be regarded as likely to give rise to a conflict of interest.

7. **To declare interests in any proposed transaction or arrangement:** A director must declare the full nature and extent of any direct or indirect interest in any proposed transaction or arrangement before that transaction or arrangement is entered into. The declaration may be given at a meeting of the directors or by general notification on appointment.

s. 177

ss. 184, 185

Where a previous notification or interest becomes inaccurate or incomplete, additional notification(s) must be made.

Notification is not required where the director is not aware of the interest or is not aware of the transaction or arrangement.

Notification is not required where the nature of the interest is such that it cannot reasonably be regarded as likely to give rise to a conflict of interest, to the extent that the other directors are already aware of the interest without requiring specific notification or where the transaction relates to the director's service contract.

More information

▷ *Company Secretary's Handbook*, Chapter 6

▷ Companies House Guidance booklet GP3

Directors – meetings – private companies

There are no fixed rules regarding operation of the board of directors. The articles of association will govern the powers of directors. The maximum or minimum number of directors and the quorum necessary for meetings of the directors will be stipulated.

regs 7–16 sch. 1, SI 2008/3229

Meetings of the directors should be held upon 'reasonable' notice, according to the circumstances of the company or the meeting concerned. Where the board of directors all work in the same office, reasonable notice may well be two to three hours. Where the directors normally meet on a quarterly basis only and do not work at the same location, then reasonable notice may be two weeks, or more.

Meetings are usually called by the company secretary on instructions of the chair, although any director may request that a meeting be convened or convene it themselves.

reg. 9 sch. 1, SI 2008/3229

Votes at a directors' meeting are taken on the basis of one vote per director. All resolutions are passed by a simple majority. The articles of association of the company may give the chair a casting vote in circumstances where there are an equal number of votes both for and against a particular resolution.

regs 7, 8, 13, SI 2008/3229

In certain circumstances, usually where one director has invested the majority of the company's funding, the articles may provide for enhanced voting rights for certain specified directors.

Directors may be empowered by the articles of association to appoint someone to attend and vote in their place (an alternate director), when circumstances dictate that they are unable to attend the meeting themselves. Such authority is not contained in the CA2006 model articles for private companies.

In addition to allowing the reaching of decisions at meetings, the model articles permit private company directors to reach decisions by indicating to each other by any means that they share a common view on any particular matter. Although many formal matters may be decided upon by circulating written resolutions, where a contentious matter requires consideration and an exchange of views, it is important to ensure that all directors are able to participate fully in that debate.

reg. 8(2) sch. 1, SI 2008/3229

Although the day-to-day running of the company will be left to the managing director and the other executive directors, the board should meet to decide upon matters of policy and matters requiring signature on behalf of the board.

Checklist

▷ Pre-CA2006 articles may provide for directors not in the UK not to be entitled to receive notice of meetings.

▷ Has notice been given to all directors entitled to notice?

▷ Have all relevant board papers been circulated sufficiently in advance of the meeting?

▷ At the meeting, is a quorum present at the start and throughout the meeting?

reg. 11 sch. 1, SI 2008/3229

▷ Have participating directors declared any conflicts of interest and considered their statutory duties in reaching their decision?

reg. 16 sch. 3, SI 2008/3229

ss. 171–177

▷ Have minutes been taken and, once approved, kept in the minute book?

reg. 15 sch. 1, SI 2006/3229

Notes

s 248

▷ Members have no right to view the minutes of the directors.

More information

▷ *Company Secretary's Handbook*, Chapter 9

Directors – meetings – public companies

There are no fixed rules regarding operation of the board of directors. The articles of association will govern the powers of directors. The maximum or minimum number of directors and the quorum necessary for meetings of the directors will be stipulated.

regs 7–19 sch. 3, SI 2008/3229

Meetings of the directors should be held upon 'reasonable' notice, according to the circumstances of the company or the meeting concerned. Where the board of directors all work in the same office, reasonable notice may well be two to three hours. Where the directors normally meet on a quarterly basis only and do not work at the same location, then reasonable notice may be two weeks, or more.

Meetings are usually called by the company secretary on instructions of the chair, although any director may request that a meeting be convened or convene it themselves.

reg. 8 sch. 3, SI 2008/3229

Votes at a directors' meeting are taken on the basis of one vote per director. All resolutions are passed by a simple majority. The articles of association of the company may give the chair a casting vote in circumstances where there are an equal number of votes both for and against a particular resolution.

regs 13, 14, SI 2008/3229

In certain circumstances, usually where one director has invested the majority of the company's funding, the articles may provide for enhanced voting rights for certain specified directors.

Directors may be empowered by the articles of association to appoint someone to attend and vote in their place (an alternate director), when circumstances dictate that they are unable to attend the meeting themselves. If a director is appointed as an alternate for another director, that director will have two votes and may cast each vote differently.

reg. 15 sch. 3, SI 2008/3229

In addition to allowing the reaching of decisions at meetings, the model articles permit public company directors to reach decisions by any other means, provided they can communicate with each other. Accordingly decisions may be reached by conference video or telephone facilities. Written resolutions of directors are permitted by the model articles. As decisions may require an exchange of views, it is important to ensure that all directors are able to participate fully in that debate.

reg. 9(1)(b) sch. 3, SI 2008/3229

regs 17, 18 sch. 3, SI 2008/3229

Although the day-to-day running of the company will be left to the managing director and the other executive directors, the board should meet to decide upon matters of policy and matters requiring signature.

Checklist

▶ Pre-CA2006 articles may provide for directors not in the UK not to be entitled to receive notice of meetings.

▶ Has notice been given to all directors entitled to notice?

▶ Have participating directors declared any conflicts of interest and considered their statutory duties in reaching their decision?

        reg. 16 sch. 3, SI 2008/3229 ss. 171–177

▶ Have all relevant board papers been circulated sufficiently in advance of the meeting?

▶ At the meeting, is a quorum present at the start and throughout the meeting?

        reg. 10 sch. 3, SI 2008/3229

▶ Have minutes been taken and, once approved, kept in the minute book?

        s. 248

Notes

▶ Members have no right to view the minutes of the directors.

More information

▶ *Company Secretary's Handbook*, Chapter 9

Directors – objection to appointment

The Small Business, Enterprise and Employment Act 2015 introduced a new procedure under which a person can object to their appointment as a director on the grounds that they did not consent to be appointed.

ss. 1095(4A–4D)

If the objection is upheld, the Registrar has power to rectify the company record and remove form AP01 or AP02 from the company's file.

s. 1095(1)

Checklist

▷ Application can only be made by or on behalf of the person claiming to have been appointed without their consent.

Procedure

▷ The applicant or someone on their behalf must complete and file form RP02a setting out details of the incorrect form lodged and confirming that the application complies with the requirements of s. 1095.

s. 1095(4A)(b)

▷ On receipt of the application the Registrar will send a notice to all directors and company secretary, if any, the registered office and the presenter giving notice of the intention to remove the relevant form from the company's file unless an objection is received within 28 days.

▷ Provided no objection is received, the relevant form will be removed and the register will be annotated accordingly.

▷ If there are any objections these are indicated by filing form RP03, which must be filed within 28 days of the date of notice by the Registrar.

s. 1095(4B)

▷ To object, the company need only provide evidence that the person consented to act.

Filing requirement

▷ Form RP02.

▷ Form RP03, if applicable.

Notes

▶ In the case of any objections, the Registrar is not permitted to remove the form and has no authority to decide the merits of any claim. Where the applicant maintains they have been appointed in error, it will be necessary to make an application to the court.

▶ Application for rectification and removal of forms should only be used in cases of fraud or genuine dispute. Where a form contains a factual inaccuracy, rectification is not normally appropriate and a replacement document should be filed.

More information

▶ *Company Secretary's Handbook*, Chapter 6

▶ Companies House Guidance booklet GP6

Directors – removal

Irrespective of any provisions contained in the company's articles of association or a director's service contract, the shareholders can, at any time, remove a director by ordinary resolution.

s.168

Checklist

▶ Will the director resign?

▶ Check the articles to see if the director can be removed by a vote of the remaining directors or by notice from, say, the holding company.

▶ Is the director due to retire by rotation at the next annual general meeting (public companies only)?

▶ Special notice (see page 176) of the proposed removal needs to be given to the company by an officer.

s.168(2)

▶ The director whose removal is proposed must be sent a copy of the special notice.

s.169(1)

Procedure

▶ Company secretary, director or a shareholder to give special notice to the company of proposal to remove a director. The special notice must be received at least 28 clear days before the meeting.

s.169(1)

▶ If the removal is proposed by shareholders, it may be appropriate for them to requisition a general meeting as well (see page 132).

s.303

▶ A copy of the special notice must be sent to the director whose removal has been proposed.

s.169(1)

▶ Convene a board meeting to consider the special notice and convene a general meeting if appropriate.

▶ Company secretary or a director to issue a notice convening a general meeting on 14 clear days' notice to consider the resolution as an ordinary resolution. The notice should state on it that special notice has been given. The director whose removal is proposed is entitled to have a written representation circulated with the notice.

s.168

s.169(3)

▶ If the resolution is approved, file form TM01 with Companies House.

▶ The company secretary should ensure that the register of directors is amended.

▶ Listed, AIM or NEX companies must make an appropriate announcement no later than the day following the removal.

LR 9.6.11, AR 17, NE RFI 66

Filing requirement

▶ Form TM01 within 14 days.

Notes

▶ The director to be removed has the right to be heard at the general meeting even if he or she is not a shareholder.

▶ Although the meeting can be held at short notice without contravening the provisions relating to the giving of special notice, this may be seen as prejudicial to the director's case and care must be taken when convening the meeting on short notice.

▶ Although the shareholders can remove the director from office, this would not prejudice the director's rights under any service contract, nor would it affect his or her right to take action against the company for any breach.

▶ The removal of a director must be put to a meeting of the members and cannot be dealt with by means of a written resolution by a private company.

s. 168(1)

More information

▶ *Company Secretary's Handbook*, Chapter 6

Directors – residential address

Directors, other than corporate directors (and in the case of an overseas company registered in Great Britain, a representative), must give details of a service address on form AP01 and any change in that address on form CH01.

s. 167

If the service address of a director is not their usual residential address, the director must notify the company of their usual residential address and the company must maintain a register of directors' residential addresses. Where the service address is a director's usual residential address, the register of directors' residential addresses need only contain an entry to that effect.

s. 165

Although details of the residential address are contained in form AP01, those details are not disclosed on the public file unless required by a court order or where the Registrar has cause to believe that the service address is not effective at bringing documents to the notice of the director.

ss. 240–246

More information

▷ *Company Secretary's Handbook*, Chapter 6

▷ Companies House Guidance booklet GP3

Directors – residential address suppression

Directors' private address information is no longer disclosed on the public record, for new filings, after 1 October 2009 when directors and company secretaries were permitted to provide a service address.

However, previous forms still show the residential address information.

Due to the nature of the business activities of certain companies, overseas companies and LLPs, their directors, company secretaries and members might be at risk of violence or intimidation.

Such individuals can apply for their residential address information to be suppressed.

ss. 243, 790(ZF) & (ZG), 1088

Checklist

Application may only be made by an individual who is or proposes to be:

▶ a director of a company;

▶ a member of an LLP; or

▶ a director or permanent representative of an overseas company.

Procedure

▶ Applications are available on request from Companies House contact centre, 0303 1234 500.

▶ Complete and file appropriate application form. There are a number of different forms depending on which section the application is being made under and whether it relates to an individual, company, charge holder or a subscriber. All the forms have the prefix 'SR'.

Whichever SR form is used the following information is required:

– statement of the grounds for making the application;

– identifying the company whose activities may place the applicant at risk;

– the applicants details; and

– application fee of £100.

Filing requirement

▶ SR form as appropriate.

▶ Statement of grounds and evidence.

▶ Application fee.

▶ Details of company whose activities give rise to the risk of violence or intimidation.

ss. 243, 790(ZF), (ZG), 1088

More information

▶ Companies House Guidance booklet GP3

Dissolution

The Registrar is authorised by the Companies Act 2006 to remove from the register those companies that are believed to be defunct. This procedure will frequently be used where a company has failed to file accounts or annual returns, and no response is received to letters sent to the company's registered office. **s.1000**

In addition, the directors of a company may voluntarily request that a company be struck off. **s.1003**

This procedure may not be used if, within three months of the proposed application, the company has changed its name, traded, disposed of property or rights for value, or engaged in any activity other than that required to effect the dissolution, or where application for a scheme of **s.1004(1)** arrangement or petition or order under the Insolvency Act has been made. **s.1005**

Checklist

▶ Has the company any assets or liabilities, or does it hold title to any property or assets?

▶ During the three months preceding the application, has the company:

▷ changed its name;

▷ traded;

▷ disposed of any property or rights for value; or

▷ engaged in any activity other than that required to effect the dissolution?

▶ Check that insolvency or administration procedures have not commenced.

Procedure

▶ Convene a directors' meeting to consider the dissolution of the company.

▶ If part of a group, enter into a transfer of assets agreement with another group company to 'sweep' up any assets not previously disposed of.

- File completed form DS01 at Companies House signed by all directors, where there are no more than two, or a majority of directors, if there are three or more.

- A copy of the application must be sent within seven days to any person who at any time on or after the date of application but prior to dissolution or withdrawal was: **ss. 1006, 1007**

  ▷ an employee;

  ▷ a member;

  ▷ a creditor;

  ▷ a director; or

  ▷ a manager or trustee of any pension fund established for the employees.

- VAT-registered companies must notify their VAT office.

- On receipt of the application, the Registrar will publish a notice in the *Gazette* inviting any objections as to why the company should not be struck off.

- If no objections are made within two months of publication in the *Gazette*, the Registrar will strike off the company and publish a further notice in the *Gazette* notifying that the company has been dissolved.   **s. 1003(3)**

Filing requirement

- Form DS01.

- £10 filing fee.

Notes

- The directors may halt the dissolution process by submitting form DS02.   **ss. 1009, 1010**

- Care must be taken to ensure that there are no assets remaining in the company as these will pass to the Crown on dissolution under the *bona vacantia* (ownerless property) regime. Within groups of companies, leases are frequently left in the name of dormant subsidiaries.

- Where the company has only recently ceased to trade, it will be necessary to contact the company's corporation tax office to settle any liability to tax or confirm that no tax is due, otherwise HM Revenue & Customs are likely to object to the dissolution as a matter of course.

More information

- *Company Secretary's Handbook*, Chapter 22

- Companies House Guidance – Strike off, dissolution and restoration

Dividends

Unless shares of any particular class carry a fixed dividend, the declaration and payment of a dividend are at the directors' discretion as set out in its articles. ·

reg.30(2) sch. I,
SI 2008/3229 (Ltd Co)
reg.70(2) sch.3,
SI 2008/3229 (PLC Co)

Dividends can be paid only if the company has sufficient distributable profits.

s.830

The directors may declare a dividend as they see fit in the case of an interim dividend, or subject to the approval of the members by ordinary resolution in the case of the final dividend.

reg.30 sch. I, reg.70
sch.3, SI 2008/3229

The declaration of any dividend should be made by reference to the relevant accounts. These would normally be the most recent annual accounts except where those accounts show that there is insufficient profit available or the dividend is proposed to be paid in the first accounting period. In such cases, interim or initial accounts, as appropriate, will be required. If the annual accounts have a qualified auditors' report, the auditor must issue a statement about whether the qualification is material for determining if a distribution can be made in terms of s. 836.

s.836(2)

s.837(4)

For a private company, the interim or initial accounts must enable a reasonable judgement to be made as to the availability of distributable reserves. For a public company, those accounts must be properly prepared in accordance with ss. 395, 396 and 397 of the Companies Act 2006.

ss.838(1),839(1)

Where interim accounts are prepared, these must be signed and a copy filed with the Registrar of Companies.

In the case of initial accounts, these must contain a report from the company's auditor and, if the audit report is qualified, a statement from the auditor about whether the qualification is material for determining if a distribution can be made in terms of s. 836. A copy of the signed accounts, audit report and any auditors' statement, if required, must be laid before the members in a general meeting and delivered to the Registrar of Companies.

s.838(2)–(6)

s.839(2)–(7)

Checklist

▶ Dividends are usually declared stating both a record date and a later payment date. The record date establishes the date on which the entitlements are to be calculated, and any changes in ownership after that date are ignored.

- On the payment date, dividend cheques and tax vouchers should be completed and issued to members.

- With effect from 31 March 2016, dividend payments no longer have an associated tax credit. Companies are however still required to provide members with a dividend confirmation confirming the amount of tax deducted (currently £nil).

Procedure

- Interim dividend.
  - ▷ Convene a directors' meeting to consider the payment of an interim dividend. Ensure sufficient distributable profit is available by reference to relevant accounts.
  - ▷ The company secretary arranges the printing of dividend warrants and tax vouchers.
  - ▷ Dividend warrants and tax vouchers are despatched to the shareholders.
- Final dividend.
  - ▷ Accounts and notice of general meeting are issued to members. If accounts have a qualified audit report, the auditors' statement on their qualification is circulated with the accounts.
  - ▷ The general meeting is held.
  - ▷ If approval is given to the final dividend, the company secretary arranges payment in the same way as for an interim dividend. Although members can reduce the amount of dividend payable, they cannot approve a payment at a higher rate than that recommended by the directors.

Filing requirement

- Interim or initial accounts if prepared by a public company.

Notes

- The secretary should liaise with their bank or, if relevant, their share registrars concerning the format of the dividend warrant.

- Schedule of payments and non-cashed cheques must be maintained.

- Often companies maintain a separate dividend account, as once declared and dividend cheques issued, the uncashed funds are no longer a company asset.

More information

- *Company Secretary's Handbook*, Chapter 19

Documents – suggested retention periods

Type of document	Period of retention	
Statutory records		
Certificate of incorporation	Original to be kept permanently	
Certificate to commence business (public company)	Original to be kept permanently	
Articles of association	Original to be kept permanently	
Seal book/register	Original to be kept permanently	
Register of directors and secretaries	Original to be kept permanently	**s.162**
Register of directors' residential addresses	Original to be kept permanently	**s.165**
Register of interests in voting shares	Original to be kept permanently	**s.808**
Register of charges created prior to 6 April 2013	Original to be kept permanently	**s.59P & 859Q**
Register of members	Current members permanently Former members 10 years	**s.113** **s.121**
Register of debenture or loan stockholders	Original to be kept permanently	**s.743**
Meeting records		
Minutes of general and class meetings, written resolutions	Originals to be kept permanently for meetings held prior to 1 October 2007	**para.40 sch.1, SI 2007/2194**
	Ten years after meeting for meetings held after 1 October 2007	**s.355**
Directors' minutes	Originals to be kept permanently for meetings held prior to 1 October 2007	**para.19 sch.1, SI 2007/2194**
	Ten years after meeting for meetings held after 1 October 2007	**s.248(2)**
Circulars to shareholders including notices of meetings	Master copy to be kept permanently	

Proxy forms/polling cards	One month if no poll demanded One year if poll demanded	

Accounting and financial records

Annual report and accounts	Signed copy to be kept permanently (a stock of spare copies should be maintained for up to five years to meet casual requests)	
Accounting records required by the Companies Acts	Six years for a public company Three years for a private company	**s. 388(4)(b)** **s. 388(4)(a)**
Taxation returns and records	Six years	
Internal financial reports	Six years	
Statements and instructions to banks	Six years	
Tax returns	Permanently	
Expense accounts	Seven years	
Customs and Excise returns	Six years	

Share registration documents

	Refer to articles, but typical periods are:	
Forms for application of shares, debentures, etc, forms of acceptance and transfer, renounceable letters of acceptance and allotment, renounceable share certificates, request for designation or redesignation of accounts, letters of request, allotment sheets, letters of indemnity for lost share certificates, stop notices and other court orders	Ten years from date of registration	**reg. 82 sch. 3,** **SI 2008/3229**
Powers of Attorney	Ten years after cessation of membership to which power relates	**s. 121**
Dividend and interest bank mandate forms	Two years after registration	
Cancelled share or stock certificates	One year after cancellation	
Notification of change of address	Two years	
Any contract or memorandum to purchase the company's own shares	Ten years	
Report of an interest in voting shares for investigations requisitioned by members	Six years	
Register of interest in shares when company ceases to be a public company	Six years	

Property records

Deeds of title	Permanently
Leases	Twelve years after lease has terminated
Agreements with architects, builders, etc	Six years after contract completion
Patent and trademark records	Permanently

HR records

Staff personnel records	Seven years after employment ceases
Patent agreements with staff	Twenty years after employment ceases
Applications for jobs	Up to twelve months
Payroll records	Twelve years
Salary registers	Six years
Employment agreements	Permanently
Time cards and piecework records	Two years
Wages records	Six years
Medical records	Twelve years
Industrial training records	Six years
Accident books	Twelve years

Pension records

Trustees and rules (pension schemes)	Permanently
Trustees' minute book	Permanently
Pension fund annual accounts and Inland Revenue approvals	Permanently
Investment records	Permanently
Actuarial valuation records	Permanently
Contribution records	Permanently
Records of ex-pensioners	Six years after cessation of benefit
Pension scheme investment policies	Twelve years after cessation

Insurance records

Group health policies	Twelve years after final cessation of benefit
Group personal accident policies	Twelve years after cessation of benefit
Public liability policies	Permanently
Product liability policies	Permanently

Employers' liability policies	Permanently
Sundry insurance policies	Three years after lapse
Claims correspondence	Three years after settlement
Accident reports and relevant correspondence	Three years after settlement
Insurance schedules	Ten years

Other records

Vehicle registration records, MOT certificates and vehicle maintenance records	Two years after disposal of vehicle
Certificates and other documents of title	Permanently or until investment disposed of
Trust deeds	Originals to be kept permanently
Contracts with customers, suppliers or agents	Six years after expiry
Licensing agreements	Six years after expiry
Rental and hire purchase agreements	Six years after expiry
Indemnities and guarantees	Six years after expiry

Dormant companies

Where a company has not traded during any particular financial period, the company can dispense with the obligation to prepare audited accounts and need only file an abbreviated balance sheet and notes with Companies House. This is a separate dispensation from the audit exemptions considered on page 9.

s.480

Checklist

▶ There must have been no transactions required to be made in the company's accounting records.   **s.1169**

▶ The company must not: **s.481**

  ▷ be an authorised insurance company, a banking company or e-money issuer, a MiFID investment firm or a UCITS management company; or

  ▷ carry on insurance market activity.

▶ The company must not be required to prepare group accounts.   **s.480(2)(b)**

▶ The company must qualify as a small company (see page 21), or would have but for the fact that it is: **s.480(2)(a)**

  ▷ a public company; or

  ▷ a member of an ineligible group.

▶ The balance sheet must contain statements immediately above the director's/directors' signature(s) that:

  ▷ the company is entitled to the exemption;   **s.475(2)**

  ▷ the director(s) acknowledge their responsibilities;   **s.475(3)(b)**

  ▷ the accounts give a true and fair view;   **s.396(2),)**

  ▷ the members have not required the accounts to be audited (this only applies to the set of accounts filed at Companies House).   **s.475(3)(a)**

Procedure

▶ Non-trading non-audited accounts must be prepared.

▶ Convene a directors' meeting to approve the accounts.

▶ Signed copy to be filed with the Registrar within the same timescales for a trading company (see page 12).

Filing requirement

▶ Copy of the accounts within the appropriate timescale: six months for a public company and nine months for a private company.

Notes

▶ For a company to remain dormant, any costs must be paid by someone other than the company itself and any cash held in a bank must be in a non-interest-bearing account.
s. 1169(3)

▶ Receipt of payment by the company for the shares taken by the subscribers or any payment made in respect of any change of name, re-registration fees, annual returns or late filing penalties may be disregarded for the purposes of assessing whether a company is dormant.

▶ Although the copy that is filed with the Registrar may be abbreviated and not contain a directors' report, the copy circulated to shareholders must be full accounts, and accordingly a directors' report will be required.

More information

▶ *Company Secretary's Handbook*, Chapter 10

▶ Companies House Guidance – Filing accounts

Electronic communications

Subject to any provisions in their articles, and obtaining shareholder consent under schedule 5 to the Companies Act 2006, companies may send written resolutions, notices, annual accounts and related documents to their members in hard copy, in electronic form or by making the documents available for download from a website.

ss. 293(2), 308, 309

When making written resolutions available on a website, these are not valid unless the document(s) is/are available throughout the period commencing with the circulation date and ending on the date the resolution lapses.

s. 299

Notice of a meeting given by publication on a website is not valid unless the notification sent to members states that it concerns a notice of a general meeting, specifies the place, date and time of the meeting and, in the case of a public company, states that the meeting is to be an AGM. The documents must be available throughout the period commencing on the date of notification and ending at the conclusion of the meeting.

s. 309

Notification of the website address may be given in hard copy or by electronic communication, provided the member has provided an address for that purpose.

Quoted companies are required to make their annual report and accounts available on a website as soon as reasonably practical and ending no earlier than the date the following year's annual report and accounts are made available on the website.

s. 430

Any member receiving documents or information by electronic communication or by publication on a website can request that they receive copies of documents in hard copy and the company must supply those copies within 21 days.

s. 1145

Checklist

▷ To enable shareholders to communicate electronically with the company, ensure notices and forms of proxy contain details of an electronic address to be used by shareholders to send documents or proxies relating to the meeting to the company.

▷ For a company to communicate with its shareholders in electronic   **para. 4 sch. 5**
form, it must have obtained specific or general consent from
shareholders and to an address supplied for that purpose.

▷ For a company to make information and documents available on a   **para. 9 sch. 5**
website, it must have specific or general consent from shareholders or
where the shareholder is deemed to have consented.

▷ In addition, listed companies are required to obtain shareholder   **DTR 6.1.8**
consent in general meeting to the use of electronic communications.

Notes

None.

Forfeiture

When shares have been allotted as either nil or partly paid, the balance outstanding on the shares can be called at any time by the directors (see page 61). The amount of this call can be all or part of the balance outstanding.

Any shares on which a call has been made and which remains outstanding may be forfeited provided there is authority contained in the company articles. Public companies incorporated after 1 October 2009 and adopting the model articles for a public company will have such provisions in their articles. A private company incorporated after 1 October 2009 and adopting the model articles for a private company will not have such provisions in their articles, as reg. 21 of the model articles for private companies only permits shares to be issued fully paid.

regs 54–62 sch. 3, SI 2008/3229

The procedures for making a call and subsequent forfeiture must be strictly adhered to. If they are not, the court may overturn any forfeiture. The provisions under which shares may be forfeited are contained in the company's articles of association.

Checklist

▶ Do the articles of association contain forfeiture provisions?

Procedure (taken from the model articles for public companies)

▶ If a call notice has not been paid and forfeiture is to be implemented, the directors must give the member(s) concerned notice.

▶ The company secretary is to issue a notice to the member(s) giving not less than 14 days' notice requiring payment of all outstanding amounts and must state that if the notice is not complied with, the shares are liable to forfeiture.

▶ If the call remains unpaid, the directors must convene a board meeting to consider forfeiture of the shares. This is accomplished by the directors resolving that the shares be forfeited.

▷ Notice of forfeiture is usually sent to the member(s) by the company secretary, but it is not a requirement.

▷ Forfeited shares may be sold or cancelled as the directors see fit.

▷ Details of the forfeiture must be entered in the register of members.

Filing requirement

None.

Notes

▷ If the shareholder cannot or will not pay the call, he or she may wish to surrender the shares. Shares can only be surrendered if they are already liable to be forfeited.

▷ The member whose shares have been forfeited ceases to be a member in respect of such shares as soon as the forfeiture has been entered in the register of members. Such a person does, however, remain liable for any amounts unpaid on the shares.

▷ Forfeited shares may be sold or disposed of on such terms and in such manner as the directors think fit. Forfeited shares that are reissued must be issued at a price not less than the amounts remaining unpaid. When shares are reissued, the original member will no longer be liable for the uncalled amounts once the full amount has been received by the company, from whatever source.

s.662

▷ Where the shares are reissued at a price greater than the unpaid amount, then the company shall pay to the original member the additional monies received up to the amount paid by them.

▷ At the end of the financial year, it will be necessary to inform the auditors that certain shares have been forfeited and whether or not they have been reissued.

More information

▷ *Company Secretary's Handbook*, Chapter 13

General meetings

All meetings of members of a private company are general meetings unless there are express provisions in the company's articles that provide for it to hold an annual general meeting or an extraordinary general meeting.

s.301

Any meeting of a public company which is not an annual general meeting is a general meeting. If there is express provision in its articles, an extraordinary general meeting may be held. Where an extraordinary general meeting is held, there is no longer any distinction between that and a general meeting.

s.336

All matters that can be considered at a general meeting of a private company may be undertaken by written resolution, with the exception of considering resolutions for the removal of a director or an auditor.

Procedure

▶ Convene a board meeting to consider the business to be put to shareholders and convene a general meeting if appropriate.

s.302

▶ The company secretary or a director is to issue a notice convening the general meeting on 14 clear days' notice. If appropriate, the notice should state on it that special notice has been given.

s.307

Filing requirement

▶ Copies of relevant resolutions and appropriate forms within 15 days.

s.30

Notes

None.

More information

▶ *Company Secretary's Handbook*, Chapter 8

Gender pay gap reporting

Introduced in 2017 by the Equality Act 2010 (Gender Pay Gap Information) Regulations 2017 (172/2017) all companies with 250 or more employees must publish details of the relative pay rates for men and women in their business (the gender pay gap).

The gender pay gap is the difference between the average earnings of men and women, expressed relative to men's earnings. For example, 'women earn 15% less than men per hour'.

The legislation sets out details of how the rates of pay are to be calculated so as to ensure all companies report in the same way so as to facilitate accurate comparisons between companies and industry sectors.

Qualifying employers must publish their gender pay gap data and a written statement on their public facing website, if they have one, and submit those figures to an online government portal. If the employer does not have a public facing website the information can be made available on a group website or failing that on an internal intranet or otherwise circulated to employees.

Employers with fewer than 250 employees may voluntarily report their gender pay gap data but are not obliged to do so.

The requirement to report falls on the employing entity and for groups it may be that several subsidiaries have their own obligation to report their gender pay gap data. Groups may also publish aggregated group gender pay gap data but are not obliged to do so.

Checklist

▶ Does the employing entity employ 250 or more employees?

▶ The online portal includes a template publication page but organisations can create their own provided it meets the template criteria. The portal can be accessed at www.gov.uk/report-gender-pay-gap-data.

Procedure

▶ Publish gender pay gap data on the entities website, if it has one.

▶ Submit the gender pay gap data to the government online portal.

▶ Public sector employers must publish the data by the following 30 March and businesses and charities by the following 4 April.

▶ The data that must be published is:

▷ mean gender pay gap in hourly pay

▷ median gender pay gap in hourly pay

▷ mean bonus gender pay gap

▷ median bonus gender pay gap

▷ proportion of males and females receiving a bonus payment

▷ proportion of males and females in each pay quartile

Filing requirement

None.

Notes

The gender pay gap data must relate to the pay paid to employees in the pay period which includes the 'snapshot date' which is 31 March for public sector employers and 5 April for businesses and charities.

There are complex rules regarding how the pay data is complied and what to include but broadly the data includes full-time employees being paid their normal pay and their working hours, the employees gender, the gross amount of any bonus payments paid in the pay period incorporating the snap shot date and in the previous 12 months. Using this information the employer needs to calculate the normal hourly rate for each employee and from that data the statistics can be calculated.

More information

▶ www.gov.uk/guidance/gender-pay-gap-reporting-overview#data-you-must-publish-and-report

General meetings – requisition

Subject to the company's articles of association, a member or members holding not less than 5% of the paid-up issued share capital and carrying the right to vote may requisition a meeting of the members.

s.303(3)

If the directors do not convene a meeting within 21 days of receiving the requisition, those who have requisitioned it may convene the meeting themselves for a date not more than three months thereafter.

s.303(3)

The directors are deemed not to have duly convened the meeting if it is convened for a date more than 28 days after the date of the notice convening the meeting.

s.305
s.304

Checklist

▷ Does the requisitionist(s) hold the necessary number of shares?

▷ Has notice of the requisition been served on the company either in hard copy or electronic form, and has it been authenticated by the requisitionist(s)?

▷ The request must state the general nature of the business to be considered and may include the text of a resolution that may be properly moved at the meeting.

s.303(6)

▷ A resolution may be properly moved unless it would be ineffective due to inconsistency with any legislation or the company's constitution, or it is defamatory or is frivolous or vexatious.

s.303(4)

Procedure

▷ A letter or electronic communication of requisition and the text of the desired resolution(s) or general nature of the business must be delivered to the company.

s.303(5)

▷ Convene a board meeting to consider the request and convene a general meeting if appropriate. If a meeting has been requested, it is not sufficient for the directors of a private company to circulate the proposed resolution as a written resolution.

▶ The directors must convene the meeting within 21 days of receipt. **s. 304**
If approved, the company secretary or a director is to issue a notice
convening a general meeting to be held within 28 days on appropriate
notice to consider the resolution(s).

Filing requirement

▶ There are no requirements specific to the meeting having been
requested, but it will be necessary to file copies of any special
resolutions or relevant ordinary resolutions meeting the criteria
set out in s. 29 within 15 days.

More information

▶ *Company Secretary's Handbook*, Chapter 8

Headed paper

s. 82

regs 24, 25,
SI 2015/17

The full name of the company as registered must be shown on all letters, notices and other official publications, e-mails, its website, bills of exchange, promissory notes, cheques and orders for money or goods signed by or on behalf of the company, invoices, receipts and letters of credit. If this provision is not complied with, the signatory of the document in question may be personally liable in the event of default by the company.

Where the company operates under a trading name other than its registered name, the registered name will usually be shown at the foot of the page.

Checklist

▷ The company name as registered must be shown.

▷ The place of registration must be shown, e.g. registered in England and Wales, Cardiff, Wales, Scotland or Edinburgh.

▷ The company's registration number must be shown.

▷ The address of the company's registered office must be shown. Where the company's business address and registered office are the same, the fact that the address shown on the headed paper is the registered office must be stated unless the address of the registered office is shown separately.

▷ Where the company is an investment company, as defined in s. 833, this fact must be stated on the headed paper.

▷ In the case of a charity where the company's name does not include the word 'Charity' or 'Charitable', the fact that it is a charity must be stated on the headed paper. If this provision is not complied with, the signatory to any documents may be personally liable in the event of any default by the company.

▷ Where directors' names are shown on headed paper, all the directors' names must be shown and not just some of them. This is particularly important to remember where the directors have personalised stationery. It is not necessary to show the nationality of directors.

▶ If the company has been permitted not to include the word 'limited' in its registered name, the headed paper must disclose that the company is a limited company.

Filing requirement

None.

Notes

▶ When a company changes its registered office, the company's headed paper must be changed to show the new address within 14 days of the date of change. The date of change is the date of registration of form AD01 by the Registrar of Companies.

s. 87(3)

▶ Although not necessary, if there is a reference to the company's share capital on the headed paper, this must be to the paid-up share capital.

reg. 4,
SI 2015/17

More information

▶ *Company Secretary's Handbook*, Chapter 4

HM Revenue & Customs – Stamp Duty Office

Except in cases where the transactions is exempt from stamp duty, all stock transfer forms with a transfer value of £1,000 or more must be stamped by HM Revenue & Customs.

Companies must not register transfers that are liable to duty if not stamped, as registering such a transfer does not give good title to the underlying shares.

For all enquiries, please contact the HMRC dedicated Enquiry Line.

Enquiry Line Number: 0300 200 3510

Written enquiries should be addressed to the Customer Service office:

Customer Service Manager
HMRC Birmingham Stamp Office
9th Floor
City Centre House
30 Union Street
Birmingham
B2 4AR

More information

▷ *Company Secretary's Handbook*, Chapter 18

▷ HMRC www.gov.uk/topic/business-tax/stamp-taxes

Incorporation

The majority of companies are formed directly with Companies House, although many are still incorporated on behalf of the ultimate owners by registration agents. It is open to anyone, however, to incorporate a company using the procedure set out below.

Checklist

▶ Check the index of company names maintained by the Registrar of Companies to ensure that the proposed name is not the same as, or too similar to, the name of an existing company. The register can be checked either at Companies House or by accessing the Companies House website at www.gov.uk/government/organisations/companies-house **s.66**

▶ Additionally, certain words ('sensitive' words) may require justification or approval by some third party (see page 263). **s.66(4)**

▶ All companies must have at least one subscriber. **s.7**

▶ Private companies must have at least one director and may have a company secretary; public companies must have at least two directors and a company secretary (who can also be a director). **s.154**

Procedure

▶ The following documents must be submitted to the Registrar of Companies. **s.7**

  ▷ The memorandum of association. This must be signed by the subscriber(s) in the presence of at least one witness.

  ▷ Articles of association, which again must be signed by the subscriber(s) and the signature(s) witnessed. Alternatively if the model articles are to be adopted without amendment, there is no requirement to file a copy, as the model articles are adopted by default. **ss.9(5),20,55**

▷ An application to register a company (form IN01) containing details of the proposed company name, the country of the situation of its registered office, whether the members' liability is limited and if so whether by shares or guarantee and whether the company is to be a private or public company, the names and addresses of the first director(s), company secretary if there is to be one and the situation of the registered office. This form must be signed by the first director(s) and company secretary (if one is being appointed), agreeing to act in that capacity, and must also be signed by the subscriber(s) or their agent(s). **ss. 9–12**

▷ A statement of compliance made by a solicitor or by one of the first directors or company secretary confirming that the necessary documents have been properly prepared. **s. 13**

▷ Where appropriate, formal justification of a 'sensitive' name must be submitted with the incorporation papers. **s. 66**

▷ Where appropriate, a statement on form NE01 to exempt the company from using the word 'limited' as part of its name. **s. 60**

▷ The registration fee payable (£40 if filed in hard copy, £10 if using a software package and £12 if made directly with Companies House). Same day incorporation fees are £40 if web filed and £100 if made in hard copy.

Filing requirement

▶ Form IN01.

▶ Memorandum and articles of association.

▶ Filing fee.

▶ Form NE01 if required.

▶ Justification for name if required.

▶ Statement of compliance.

Notes

▶ By using an appropriate software package, companies can now be incorporated electronically.

▶ Upon incorporation, the Registrar of Companies issues a certificate of incorporation which shows the date of incorporation, the status of the company (i.e. private or public) and the company's registered number.

▶ A private company is entitled to commence business immediately and there is no requirement for the company to obtain a certificate to commence business.

▶ The incorporation process for a public company is essentially the same as that for a private company, with the exception that the form of memorandum and articles of association is different and that the company must have a minimum of two directors and a company secretary.

▷ Before a public company may commence business or exercise its borrowing powers, it must apply for a trading certificate using form SH50. This certificate will only be issued once the company has a nominal issued capital of at least £50,000 (or euro equivalent) with the nominal value of each share at least 25% paid up plus the whole of any premium, if any.

s.761

s.584

More information

▷ *Company Secretary's Handbook*, Chapter 2

▷ Companies House Guidance booklet GP1

Incorporation – completion formalities

Once a company has been incorporated, there are a number of matters that should be formally noted or approved by the directors.

The first director(s), company secretary, if any, and situation of the registered office will have been determined and shown on application for registration (form IN01), filed with the Registrar of Companies. Particularly where companies are incorporated by registration agents, the first director and any company secretary may well be the agent themselves and accordingly will resign and the registered office will be changed immediately following incorporation.

Some or all of the following matters will require attention.

Checklist

- Appoint director(s) and company secretary, if any, to replace incorporation agents.

- Appoint a managing director or chair of the board.

- Appoint bankers, including approval of the relevant bank mandate.

- Appoint solicitors to act on behalf of the company.

- Appoint accountants and auditors.

- Change the company's default accounting reference date.

- Approve the transfer of the subscriber share(s), if appropriate.

- Allot shares in the capital of the company and approve the issue of share certificates.

- Dispense with the need for distinguishing numbers on fully paid shares.

- Notify the Registrar, if appropriate, of the place where directors' service contracts and the statutory books are situated, if elsewhere than at the registered office.

- Some or all of the directors may require service contracts.

- The directors may decide to effect directors' indemnity insurance.

▷ Consider arrangements regarding PAYE, VAT, insurance and the possible need to register trademarks in the company's name.

▷ If the company is to have employees, then employers' liability insurance is compulsory.

▷ Appropriate company headed stationery should be obtained. See page 137.

Procedure

▷ Convene a directors' meeting for directors to consider and approve any changes required. Ensure valid quorum is present.

▷ Write up the statutory books to record changes in director(s) and company secretary, transfers or allotment of shares and directors interests. As an alternative to keeping their own statutory registers the directors can opt to keep the registers on the central register maintained by Companies House. See page 225.

Filing requirement

▷ As required, forms AP01, AP02, AP03, AP04, AD01, SH01 and AA01 within 15 days.

▷ Form SH50 prior to commencing to trade (public companies only).

Notes

▷ Form AA01, notifying the Registrar of the company's accounting reference date, should be submitted to the Registrar. If this form is not received by the Registrar, the company's first financial year will end on the last day of the month of the anniversary of its incorporation. **s. 390**

▷ If a company subsequently decides to have a different accounting reference date, it will be necessary to amend this default accounting reference date on form AA01.

▷ If the company is to adopt a company seal, this should be formally approved by the directors. It is no longer necessary for a company to have a seal, as the company may rely on s. 46 of the Companies Act 2006. If the company does rely on this section, documents executed by the directors must be expressed as having been executed on behalf of the company, i.e. 'Executed as a deed this . . . day of . . . 20 . . . on behalf of . . . Limited in the presence of . . . '. **s. 45**

More information

▷ *Company Secretary's Handbook*, Chapter 2

▷ Companies House Guidance booklet GPI

Insolvency – administration

Insolvency legislation is complex and outside the scope of this book. However, it is appropriate for company secretaries to be aware of the procedures applicable to the appointment of an administrator, and these are detailed below.

A company becomes insolvent when it is unable to pay its debts as they fall due. In circumstances where the directors realise the company will become insolvent, but has not reached that point, they might wish to appoint an administrator to manage the company until it is able to continue, be sold or, if these are not possible, to wind up the company.

Part II EA2002

s. 123 IA1986

Checklist

A company is deemed unable to pay its debts if:

▶ it is unable to pay a debt of £750 or more within 21 days of a formal demand in the prescribed form;

▶ execution issued on a judgement remains unsatisfied in whole or in part (England and Wales);

▶ the court is satisfied that the company is unable to meet its debts as they fall due;

▶ the court is satisfied that the value of the company's assets is less than the amount of its liabilities;

▶ a charge for payment on an extract decree, extract registered bond or extract registered process has expired without payment (Scotland); or

▶ a certificate of unenforceability has been granted in respect of judgement (Northern Ireland).

Procedure

▶ There are a number of methods for appointing an administrator, including:

▷ on application to the court by the company, a majority of its directors, a qualifying floating charge holder or one or more creditor;

▷ an out-of-court appointment by a qualifying floating charge holder;

▷ the company or a majority of its directors;

▷ the liquidator of the company; and

▷ the supervisor of a CVA.

▶ Once a company is in administration, all business documents issued by it must state the name of the administrator and that the business and affairs of the company are being managed by the administrator.

▶ As soon as practical after appointment, the administrator must publicise their appointment, file notice at Companies House and forward a copy to the company and all known creditors.

▶ While an administration order is in force, the company cannot be wound up and an administrative receiver cannot be appointed or, if previously appointed, they must vacate office. There are restrictions on enforcing any security over the company's property, selling any goods and starting any legal proceedings.

Filing requirement

▶ Form AM01.

Notes

None.

More information

▶ *Company Secretary's Handbook*, Chapter 22

▶ Companies House Guidance - Liquidation and insolvency, booklets GP08n and GP08s

▶ The Insolvency Service www.gov.uk/guidance/guidance-on-personal-debt-relief-options-company-liquidation-investigation-and-enforcement

Insolvency – receivership

Insolvency legislation is complex and outside the scope of this book. However, it is appropriate for company secretaries to be aware of the procedures applicable to the appointment of a receiver, and these are detailed below.

An administrative receiver is a receiver or manager of the whole or substantially the whole of a company's property and business, appointed by or on behalf of the holders of debentures of the company secured by a floating charge. An appointee under a fixed charge will normally have no power to manage the business and is, as such, known merely as 'a receiver'.

Receivers are appointed either by the courts or by debenture holders.

Checklist

▶ Check the deed of appointment and a copy of the debenture (or Trust Deed) in order to consider the validity of the debenture and the receiver's appointment.

Procedure

Appointment by the court

▶ A court may appoint a receiver on the application of a mortgagee or a debenture holder in the following circumstances:

▷ where repayment of principal and/or interest is in arrears;

▷ when the security has become crystallised into a specific charge by the making of a Winding-up Order or passing of a resolution to wind up;

▷ where the security of the mortgagee or the debenture holder is in jeopardy;

▷ a receiver may also be appointed by the court on the application either of a contributory (i.e. a person liable to contribute to the assets of the company in the event of its being wound up) or of the company. The court will sometimes appoint a receiver and a manager on a short-term basis if the directors are not fulfilling their functions of management – for instance, because of a dispute between them, and pending a general meeting where there has been no governing body. A court will not, however, appoint a receiver if winding up would be more appropriate.

Appointment by debenture holders

▶ The appointment is made under a deed executed by the debenture holder and is, together with the debenture, evidence of his or her capacity. The appointment of a receiver usually arises in the following circumstances:

▷ failure to pay the principal and/or interest in accordance with the terms of the debenture;

▷ where a borrowing limit has been exceeded and has not been reduced within a specified period; or

▷ a breach of some other provisions in the debenture or trust deed.

Filing requirement

▶ Form RM01.

Notes

▶ The appointment as receiver or manager must be accepted before the end of the next business day following receipt of the instrument of appointment, and shall be deemed to be effective from the time and date the instrument of appointment was received.

More information

▶ *Company Secretary's Handbook*, Chapter 22

▶ Companies House Guidance – Liquidation and insolvency, booklets GP08n and GP08s

▶ The Insolvency Service
www.gov.uk/guidance/guidance-on-personal-debt-relief-options-company-liquidation-investigation-and-enforcement

Insolvency – winding up (liquidation)

Insolvency legislation is complex and outside the scope of this book. However, it is appropriate for company secretaries to be aware of the procedures applicable to the appointment of a liquidator, and these are detailed below.

A company becomes insolvent when it is unable to pay its debts as they fall due. Once this stage has been reached, in order to protect the interests of creditors, employees and shareholders, the directors must take steps for the company's affairs to be wound up. Winding up involves the realisation of the company's assets. The process is administered by a licensed insolvency practitioner who is appointed as liquidator of the company. Winding up is frequently known as liquidation.

Checklist

There are several methods of winding up.

▷ Members' voluntary winding up, only available where the company is solvent, requiring the directors to give a declaration that the company can meet its debts in full, with interest, during the period of 12 months commencing on the date of commencement of winding up. **ss. 89, 90 IA 1986**

▷ Creditors' voluntary winding up, applicable where a declaration of solvency cannot be given. **s. 98 IA 1986**

▷ Winding up by the courts.

▷ Winding up by special resolution of the members.

▷ On petition of a judgement creditor where a debt of not less than £750 has not been paid within 21 days of a demand in the prescribed form. **s. 123 IA 1986**

▷ It is just and equitable that the company be wound up.

▷ The company fails to meet specific statutory requirements such as minimum number of shareholders. **ss. 122, 124 IA 1986**

Procedure

Members voluntary

▶ The company's board of directors resolves to make a declaration of solvency, which must embody a statement of assets and liabilities, and be made within five weeks immediately before the passing of the resolution to wind up. The declaration has to be filed with the Registrar of Companies within 15 days of the passing of the resolution to wind up.

▶ The board of directors will also authorise the calling of a general meeting at which a special resolution to wind up will be considered. An ordinary resolution will suffice if the period of life of the company has expired or the occurrence of an event on the happening of which the articles provide that the company should be wound up.

▶ If the resolution is passed, it will be necessary to appoint a liquidator. This may be done by an ordinary resolution of the company.

▶ The resolution to wind up, signed by the chair of the meeting, should be published in the *London Gazette* or the *Edinburgh Gazette*, as appropriate, within 14 days of being passed. The resolution and all documents for publication in each *Gazette* must be authenticated by a solicitor or a member of an established body of accountants or secretaries. The resolution to wind up must also be filed within 15 days with the Registrar of Companies.

▶ The liquidator must, within 14 days of his or her appointment, advertise his or her appointment in each *Gazette* and give notice to the Registrar of Companies.

Creditors voluntary

▶ A meeting of the board of directors will authorise the calling of a general meeting to consider an ordinary resolution that the company, by reason of its liabilities, cannot continue and that it is advisable to wind up.

▶ A meeting of the creditors should be called by the company to be held within 14 days of the members' meeting to consider the resolution to wind up. At least seven days' notice of the meeting must be given to the creditors. Notice of the creditors' meeting should be advertised in the appropriate *Gazette* and two local newspapers.

▶ The notice must state either:

▷ the name and address of the insolvency practitioner who will give such information to the creditors before the meeting takes place as they may reasonably require; or

▷ a place in the principal area of business of the company where a list of names and addresses of the company's creditors will be available for inspection without charge.

▶ The creditors' meeting will be presided over by one of the directors, who should prepare a statement of affairs in the prescribed form, verified by affidavit, to be laid before the creditors' meeting.

▶ At the general meeting an ordinary resolution is passed to wind up and an ordinary resolution is passed to nominate the liquidator.

▶ At the creditors' meeting, which must be attended by the proposed liquidator, the directors may answer questions put to them by the creditors concerning the administration of the company, although there is no legal requirement for them to do so.

▶ The liquidator shall be the person nominated by the creditors or, where no other person has been so nominated, the person (if any) nominated by the company. Where a different person is nominated by the creditors, any member or creditor of the company may apply to the court within seven days for an order that the members' nomination shall remain liquidator instead of, or jointly with, the creditors' nomination, or that some other person be appointed.

By the court

▶ When the court makes a Winding-up Order, the official receiver becomes the liquidator.

▶ The official receiver may require officers of the company or other persons as specified to prepare, swear and submit a statement of affairs within 21 days.

▶ Separate meetings of creditors and contributories may be summoned by the official receiver at his or her discretion for the appointment of some other person to be liquidator of the company. Contributions are defined by the IA s. 79, but are usually synonymous with the term 'members'. The official receiver remains liquidator if another person is not appointed. The official receiver must summon a meeting for the appointment of another liquidator if 25% of the creditors requisition him or her to do so.

▶ The court may make any appointment or order to give effect to the wishes of the meetings or make any other order that it may think fit.

▶ The creditors and contributories may nominate as liquidator any person who is qualified to act as an insolvency practitioner, and in the absence of a nomination by the creditors, the contributories' nominee (if any) will be the liquidator.

▶ At any time the official receiver may apply to the Secretary of State for the appointment of a liquidator in his or her place. Any such liquidator must send notice of his or her appointment as the court may direct.

Filing requirement

▶ There are a variety of forms that are required depending upon which of the three methods of winding up is used. The liquidator or proposed liquidator will normally arrange filing of the relevant forms and this will not fall to the company secretary.

Notes

▶ On the appointment of a liquidator, all the powers of the directors cease.

▶ The creditors have the power to appoint a liquidation committee, which may sanction the continuation of some of the directors' powers.

▶ The remuneration of the liquidator is fixed by the liquidation committee or, if there is no committee, by the creditors.

More information

▶ *Company Secretary's Handbook*, Chapter 22

▶ Companies House Guidance - Liquidation and insolvency, booklets GP08n and GP08s

▶ The Insolvency Service www.gov.uk/guidance/guidance-on-personal-debt-relief-options-company-liquidation-investigation-and-enforcement

Inspection of registers and other documents

The Act requires that every company keep various registers, and stipulates where they must be held and provisions regarding their inspection, other than the register of directors' residential addresses. Inspection of all the registers is free to members and, in the case of the historic register of charges, free to creditors. Anyone else may be required to pay a fee.

Requests to inspect the register of members must be accompanied by a statement identifying the person requesting the information and the purpose for which they require the information. If the company does not believe that the request is being made for a proper purpose, application may be made to the court for a direction either to supply the information or to order the company not to comply with the request. Any application to the court must be made within five days of the request being made.

s. 116

s. 117

Where a private company has elected to hold some or all of its registers on the central record, entries on those registers after the date of election are automatically available for public inspection, although application to the company will still be required for any earlier entries.

s. 128D

Checklist

▶ The general position is that all the registers must be kept at and be available for inspection either at the registered office, the single alternative inspection location (see page 285) or Companies House where an election to keep a register on the central record has been made.

s. 1136

▶ The following registers and documents must be available for inspection:

▷ s. 114 (register of members);

▷ s. 128D (historic register of members);

▷ s. 162 (register of directors);

▷ s. 228 (directors' service contracts);

▷ s. 237 (directors' indemnities);

▷ s. 275 (register of secretaries);

▷ s. 358 (records of resolutions, etc);

> s. 702 (contracts relating to purchase of own shares);

> s. 720 (documents relating to redemption or purchase of own shares out of capital by private company);

> s. 743 (register of debenture holders);

> s. 790N (register of people with significant control);

> s. 790Z (historic PSC register);

> s. 805 (report to members of outcome of investigation by public company into interests in its shares);

> s. 809 (register of interests in shares disclosed to public company); and

> s. 859Q (instruments creating charges).

Filing requirement

▶ Forms AD02, AD03 and AD04 as required.

Notes

▶ The registers and other documents of a public company must be available for inspection for at least two hours between 9.00am and 5.00pm on business days.   **reg. 5, SI 2008/3006**

▶ The registers and other documents of a private company must be available for inspection for at least two hours between 9.00am and 3.00pm on business days, and the company must be given two days' notice of inspection where such request is made during the notice period of a meeting or during the circulation period of a written resolution, and ten days' notice at all other times.   **reg. 4, SI 2008/3009**

            reg 2 SI 2008/3007

▶ Fees payable:

> The company is obliged to provide copies of certain registers and documents upon payment of a fee.   **reg 3 SI 2007/2612**

> Fees in respect of inspection of registers by non-members.   **reg 3 SI 2007/3535**

> The fee for the inspection of the register of members, register of interests in shares and register of debenture holders.

> £3.50 per hour or part thereof during which the register(s) is/are inspected.

> Fees for provision of copies of entries in registers and copies of reports.   **reg. 6 SI 2016/339**

> The fees for copies of the registers of debentures, register of interests in voting shares and registers of debenture holders or members are:

>> £1.00 for the first five entries;

▷ £30.00 for the next 95 entries or part thereof;

▷ £30.00 for the next 900 entries or part thereof;

▷ £30.00 for the next 99,000 entries or part thereof; and

▷ £30.00 for the remainder of the entries in the register.

▶ The fee for provision of copies of trust deeds, service contracts and minutes is 10 pence per 500 words or part thereof.

▶ The fee for providing a copy of all or part of a PSC register is £12 per request.

More information

▶ *Company Secretary's Handbook*, Chapter 7

Joint shareholders

Occasionally, shares will be issued or transferred jointly to two or more persons. The articles of association of the company may place a limit on the number of holders. Under Stock Exchange and NEX Market rules, listed, AIM and NEX public companies must allow for a minimum of four joint holders.

Suggested solutions are given below to particular problems or queries that can arise in relation to joint holdings.

Joint holders may request that the shares registered in their names be split into two or more accounts, with the holders' names being shown in a different order. Such requests are commonly dealt with without the need for a stock transfer form, provided the request is in writing and signed by all the joint holders. Additionally, it will be necessary for the share certificate to be returned for cancellation and new certificates issued. For ease of administration, however, companies may prefer to deal with such requests by designation of accounts rather than by rearranging the order of the names.

Occasionally, the joint holders will request that the order of the names on the joint account be changed and again most companies will process this without the need for a formal stock transfer form, provided the request is in writing, is signed by all the joint holders and includes confirmation that no sale or disposition has taken place. Again, the share certificate should be returned for cancellation. All communications for the shareholders will be sent to the first-named of the joint holders.

The joint holders may request that communications be sent to someone other than the first-named; however, for administrative reasons this may be impractical. Additionally, the articles of association may prohibit such a request.

Notes

None.

More information

▶ *Company Secretary's Handbook*, Chapters 2 and 18

Joint shareholders – death of one shareholder

When a joint shareholder dies, the surviving holder or holders in whose name or names the shares are registered become the beneficiaries of the share. There is no need for a stock transfer form to be completed.
The company will require sight of the death certificate or an authenticated copy of it. The register of members should be amended to note the death of one holder.

The company may require a new dividend mandate to be given.

The share certificate may be either endorsed or cancelled and a new certificate issued.

It is important to establish the correct address for the surviving joint shareholder(s), as if it is the first-named holder that has died, the address details for the next first-named holder may be several years old.

Checklist

▷ Amend register of members.

▷ Endorse or issue a replacement share certificate. (Replacement is often more appropriate as otherwise the surviving joint holders will be reminded of the deceased joint holder whenever the records are reviewed.)

Procedure

▷ Note death details on register of members.

▷ Confirm correspondence address for surviving joint holder(s).

Filing requirement

None.

Notes

None.

More information

▷ *Company Secretary's Handbook*, Chapter 18

Loan stock

The procedure for the issue of loan stock, and thereafter the payment of any interest and the holding of meetings, are, subject to a trust deed creating the loan stock, similar to the procedures for the issue, declaration of dividend and requirements for meetings of ordinary shares.

The most important difference is that the loan stock will be created by a trust deed setting out the rights attaching to the stock.

Checklist

▶ Check the articles to ensure directors have authority to create loan stock.

▶ The trust deed should cover:

▷ details of the stock, aggregate amount of stock, the units in which it may be issued or transferred and details of repayment and interest;

▷ provisions creating a charge over the company's assets and stipulating under what circumstances the security is enforceable;

▷ the powers of the trustee. In particular the trustee is usually instructed to concur with the company in all dealings relating to the charged assets;

▷ provisions stipulating that no additional charges can be created ranking ahead of the stock without written consent of the loan stockholders; and

▷ schedules detailing the repayment conditions, transfer conditions, regulations for meetings and the form of stock certificate.

Procedure

▶ Convene a directors' meeting to approve the creation of the loan stock deed and issue of loan stock. Ensure valid quorum is present.

▶ Enter details in register of loan stock (if kept).

▶ Issue appropriate loan stock certificates.

Filing requirement

▶ None unless secured, in which case the charge needs to be registered (see page 223).

Notes

▶ The company is not required by statute to keep a register of loan stockholders. However, for practical reasons this is usually done and, in such circumstances, the register of loan stockholders should be in the same form as the register of members.

▶ Stock is issued by resolution of the directors as with the share capital, although there is no requirement to file a return with the Registrar of Companies.

More information

▶ *Company Secretary's Handbook*, Chapter 12

Loan stock – convertible

It is common for the terms of issue of loan stock (more usually *unsecured* loan stock) to include provisions for the loan stock to be converted into share capital. Usually the loan stock will be convertible into equity shares, although the stock may be convertible into another class of shares.

Checklist

▶ Ensure there is no restriction on the number of shares that may be allotted without seeking the consent of members (see page 271).

▶ Ensure directors have authority to grant rights to convert securities into shares.

s.549(1)(b)

Procedure

▶ Convene a directors' meeting to consider the conversion of the stock, whether in full or in part. Ensure valid quorum is present. The precise procedures to be followed will be stipulated in the loan stock deed.

▶ The company secretary should prepare a circular letter to the holders giving details of the conversion procedure, including a form of nomination and acceptance for their use. A form of nomination is necessary in the event that any particular stockholder requires the shares to be registered in another person's name.

▶ As the completed notices of conversion and forms of nomination and acceptance are received, these should be checked against the register of stockholders to ensure that the details are correct. The loan stock certificates should be returned for cancellation. Once the period for conversion has elapsed, a list of shares to be issued should be compiled and the directors should formally allot the shares. A return of allotments should be submitted to the Registrar of Companies within 15 days.

▶ Share certificates evidencing the shares issued should be prepared and issued to the shareholders within two months of the date of allotment.

▶ The register of members should be amended to record the shares now issued, and the register of loan stock should be amended to show the loan stock that has been cancelled.

▷ Where the conversion of the loan stock is only for part of the stock, a balancing loan stock certificate should be issued.

Filing requirement

▷ Form SH01 within 15 days.

Notes

None.

More information

▷ *Company Secretary's Handbook*, Chapter 12

Loan stock – unsecured

Unsecured loan stock carries a greater risk for investors than secured loan stock and as a result will usually attract a higher rate of interest. Additionally, as an added incentive, the holders may be given options to acquire equity capital in the future, usually by conversion of the unsecured loan stock into equity shares rather than by repayment of the loan. As with secured loan stock, the issue of unsecured loan stock and the rights and privileges attaching to the stock are governed by a trust deed.

Checklist

▶ Check the articles to ensure directors have authority to create loan stock.

▶ The trust deed should cover:

▷ details of the terms of issue, amounts payable on the stock and, where these are payable by more than one instalment, dates and terms of the instalments, details of the repayment or redemption of the stock and interest payments, and any rights of conversion or options on shares in the capital of the company;

▷ restrictions on further issues of unsecured loan stock without the approval of the existing loan stockholders;

▷ restriction on the borrowing powers of the company without prior approval;

▷ restrictions on the disposal by the company of certain assets or other sale agreements without prior approval;

▷ guarantees by the company that it will maintain sufficient unissued share capital to satisfy any conversion or option rights given to the loan stockholders;

▷ the actions open to the stockholders in the event of non-payment of interest or non-redemption of the stock on the due date;

▷ details of the trustees to the issue and of any remuneration payable; and

▷ schedules containing the form of stock certificates, option certificates, notices of redemption and detailed conditions concerning the redemption, whether in whole or in part, and any conversion rights or options given to the holders.

Procedure

▶ Convene a directors' meeting to approve the creation of the loan stock deed and issue of loan stock. Ensure valid quorum is present.

▶ Enter details in register of loan stock (if kept).

▶ Issue appropriate loan stock certificates.

Filing requirement

None.

Notes

▶ The procedures to be followed for the issue or repayment of unsecured loan stock are the same as for loan stock (see page 162).

▶ The conversion procedure, where relevant, is the same as for convertible loan stock (see page 160).

More information

▶ *Company Secretary's Handbook*, Chapter 12

Loans to directors

Except under specified circumstances, companies are not permitted to make loans or quasi-loans, nor enter into credit arrangements with their directors, directors of their holding company or persons connected to them unless the transaction has been approved by ordinary resolution of the members. Where the director concerned is a director of the holding company, the transaction must be approved by members of the holding company.

ss. 197–203

Approval is not required where funds are being made available to meet expenditure made or to be made for the purposes of the company or to enable the director to perform his or her duties as a director of the company.

s. 204

Checklist

The following transactions do not require approval from members:

▶ quasi-loan of up to £10,000 where repayment required within two months;

s. 207

▶ loan to director of company or holding company not exceeding £10,000;

s. 207

▶ loan to director by relevant company in ordinary course of business on an arm's length, commercial basis. Where a loan is proposed for the purchase of a home, this must be for the director's only or main residence or for the improvement of such a residence; and

s. 209

▶ loan to cover out-of-pocket expenses to be incurred in performance of duties not exceeding £50,000.

s. 204

Procedure

▶ Check if proposed loan falls within one of the permitted exceptions.

▶ Convene a directors' meeting to consider the making of a loan or credit arrangement to a director. Ensure valid quorum is present.

▶ Ensure director notifies interest in proceedings (see page 105).

▶ Convene general meeting to approve ordinary resolution or, if a private company, circulate a written resolution.

Filing requirement

None.

Notes

None.

More information

▶ *Company Secretary's Handbook*, Chapter 6

Memorandum of association

Unlike previous Acts, the Companies Act 2006 gave all companies general authority to undertake all acts unless there are specific restrictions in the articles of association. As a consequence, the content of the memorandum of association changed and now only contains details of the subscribers.

s.8

To form a company, one or more persons must subscribe to a memorandum of association.

For an existing company, any other provisions set out in their memorandum are deemed to form part of their articles of association.

Filing requirement

▶ On incorporation, a copy of the memorandum of association is required to be filed with the other incorporation documents.

s.9

Notes

None.

More information

▶ *Company Secretary's Handbook*, Chapter 3

Memorandum of association – deletion

For companies incorporated prior to 1 October 2009, the provisions of their memorandum will be treated as provisions in the articles of association. The only exception to this is the details of the subscribers.

s. 28
s. 8

Accordingly the clauses stating the company name, the liability of the company, the objects of the company, the country of registered office and details of the share capital can now be altered, updated or deleted by amending the articles.

Procedure

- Convene a directors' meeting to recommend resolutions to members and to convene a general meeting or, in the case of a private company, circulate a written resolution if appropriate.

- Issue notice, signed by director or company secretary, convening general meeting on 14 clear days' notice, or circulate written resolution for members to consider special resolution to amend the articles.

- As a special resolution, the resolution must contain the full text of the proposed changes.

  s. 21

- Consider whether a class meeting is also required.

- If the meeting is to be convened on short notice, the company secretary should arrange for agreement to short notice to be signed by each of the shareholders.

- Hold general meeting. Ensure valid quorum is present. Resolutions put to vote either by show of hands or by poll and to be passed by appropriate majority (special resolution by 75% majority).

  s. 283

- If the resolution is circulated by means of a written resolution, the resolution must receive approval of the holders of at least 75% of the members entitled to vote within 28 days of the circulation date of the resolution.

Filing requirement

▶ Signed copy of special resolution within 15 days.   ss. 29(1)(a), 30(1)

▶ Amended copy of the articles of association with copy of the   s. 26
resolution.

▶ If the resolution adds, removes or alters the statement of the   s. 31
company's objects, form CC04 must be filed within 15 days.

Notes

▶ Although it is not necessary to issue new copies of the articles of
association to the shareholders, the company should ensure that it
has a supply for issue to those shareholders who request a copy. In
addition, a copy will normally be sent to the company's bankers and
to their auditors.

▶ If a company files a copy of a resolution amending its articles but does
not file a copy of the amended articles, Companies House may issue   s. 27
a notice requiring an amended copy of the articles be filed within a
specified time. Failure to file the amended copy within the specified s. 27(4)
time will mean the company is liable to a £200 fine.

More information

▶ *Company Secretary's Handbook*, Chapter 3

▶ Companies House Guidance booklet GP3

Minutes

Directors are required to ensure that minutes are kept of all directors',
shareholders' and class meetings, and members' resolutions approved
otherwise than at a general or class meeting, and that these are kept in
appropriate minute books.

ss. 248, 355

Checklist

▷ Minutes should state the name of the company, the place, date and
time of the meeting.

▷ If a list of attendees is not included or attached to the minutes, the
minutes should state that a quorum was present.

▷ The minutes should record decisions reached by the meeting together
with sufficient detail of the discussions to enable the sense of the
meeting to be established.

▷ Any specific disagreement by a director with a particular resolution or
course of action should be recorded.

▷ Companies that have external regulators will often have particular
requirements for their directors' minutes to include more detail of
discussions leading up to decisions. For instance, the impact of a
business decision or declaration of dividends on the regulated capital
of an FCA-regulated company.

Procedure

▷ It is normally the company secretary who takes the minutes of
proceedings and who prepares the first draft.

▷ The draft minutes are circulated to those attending for comments.

▷ Although not a requirement, it is useful for the chair to sign the agreed
minutes.

▷ Signed minutes are evidence of the discussions and agreement
reached.

s. 249

Filing requirement

None.

Notes

▶ When draft minutes are circulated for comments, care must be taken to ensure that any suggested amendments do not reflect what a speaker meant to say rather than what was actually said.

▶ Directors are entitled to have access to directors' minutes.

▶ Shareholders may inspect the minutes of shareholder meetings or, on payment of a prescribed fee, request that copies of shareholder minutes be sent to them, within 14 days. Shareholders have no right to inspect minutes of directors' meetings.   **s.358**

▶ Minutes of directors' and shareholders' meetings must be kept for at least 10 years from the date of the meeting.   **ss.248(2), 355(2)**

More information

▶ *Company Secretary's Handbook*, Chapters 8 and 9

Modern Slavery Act statement

All organisations meeting four criteria are required to publish an annual statement setting out the steps taken to prevent modern slavery in their business and their supply chain. Each organisation is responsible for assessing for itself whether or not it meets the four criteria.

Modern Slavery Act 2015 (MSA2015) s.54

Checklist

The four criteria are:

▶ it is a body corporate or partnership, wherever incorporated or formed;

▶ it carries on a business or part of a business in the UK;

▶ it supplies goods and services; and

▶ its annual turnover is at least £36 million.

MSA2015 s.54(2) & (12)

Procedure

▶ Annually assess whether the organisation meets the criteria and review the organisation's policies and procedures for ensuring there is no modern slavery within the business or supply chain.

▶ Although not stated in the legislation the Home Office guidance notes that the statement should be made within six months of the financial year to which it relates.

▶ Statement must be published on the organisation's UK website, if it has one.

▶ If an organisation does not have a website, it must provide a copy of the statement within 30 days of a written request for a copy being received.

▶ The statement should be formally approved by the board of directors.

▶ Where a group statement is published covering two or more entities the statement should identify all entities meeting the criteria.

Filing requirement

None

Notes

▶ Total turnover means the amount received by itself and any subsidiaries for the provision of goods and services within the ordinary activities of the organisation after deducting trade discounts, VAT and other taxes.

▶ Groups may comprise subsidiaries which meet the criteria on their own in additional to the parent company. In these circumstances the group can publish one statement covering all qualifying entities or each entity can publish its own statement.

More information

▶ Home Office guidance: Transparency in Supply Chains etc. A practical guide

▶ https://assets.publishing.services.gov.uk/government/uploads/ systems/uploads/attachment_data/file/649906/transparency_in_ supply_chains_a_practical_guide_2017.pdf

Name change

A company may change its name by special resolution of the members or by other means provided for in its articles of association.

ss. 77(1), 79

Certain words are deemed to be 'sensitive' and require justification or due authority before the Registrar of Companies will allow their use (see page 263).

ss. 55–57, 1193–1198

Checklist

▷ If the change is to be authorised other than by the members ensure that the articles contain the necessary authority and procedure. Check that the proposed name is available by checking the register of company names (www.gov.uk/government/organisations/companies-house).

s. 66
ss. 1080, 1085

▷ The name of a private company must end with either 'limited' or 'ltd', or the Welsh equivalents 'cyfyngedig' or 'cyf'. Certain guarantee or non-profit-making companies and charitable companies are exempt from this provision if they meet qualifying criteria or are a community interest company.

ss. 60–62

s. 33 C(AICE)A 2004

▷ The name of a public company must end with either 'public limited company' or 'PLC', or the Welsh equivalents 'cwmni cyfngedig cyhoeddus' or 'ccc'. Community interest companies are not subject to this provision.

s. 58
s. 33 C(AICE)A2004

▷ Does the name contain only permitted characters?

s. 57
reg. 4 and sch. 2,
SI 2008

▷ Is the name misleading or does it contain sensitive words or expressions?

ss. 54–56, 65
SI 2015/17

▷ Although not a legal requirement, it is advisable to check the proposed names against the trademark registry and registered internet domain names so as to limit the possibility of objections being raised with the company names adjudicator by third parties with goodwill in the name.

s. 69

Procedure – by directors

▷ Convene a directors' meeting to use any relevant procedure contained in the company's articles of association. Ensure valid quorum is present.

▷ Amend articles of association if these contain a company name clause. If any changes to the articles are required other than references to the company name a special resolution of the members will be required.

▷ Alternatively the directors may be directed by the Secretary of State to change the name of the company, in which case a resolution of shareholders is not required.   **ss. 64, 1033**

Procedure – by members

▷ Convene a directors' meeting to recommend a special resolution to the members and circulating a written resolution or convening a general meeting as appropriate.   **s. 79**

▷ Where a general meeting is to be held, issue meeting notice, signed by a director or company secretary, on at least 14 clear days' notice.

▷ If the meeting is to be convened on short notice, the company secretary should arrange for consent to short notice to be signed by each member.

▷ Enclose with the notice a form of proxy if desired. Listed companies must enclose a three-way form of proxy (see page 200).

▷ If the meeting is to be convened on short notice, the company secretary should arrange for agreement to short notice to be signed by each of the members.

▷ Hold general meeting. Ensure valid quorum is present. Resolution put to vote either by show of hands or by poll and to be passed by appropriate majority (special resolution by 75% majority).

▷ Amend articles of association if these contain a company name clause.

Filing requirement

▷ Copy of change of resolution within 15 days.   **ss. 78(1), 79(1)**

▷ Form RES15.

▷ Notice of change of name on form NM01, NM02, NM04 or NM05 as appropriate.

▷ Filing fee £10 (same-day fee £50). Filing fee £8 if filed online (£30 for same-day change filed online).

▷ Justification for sensitive word(s) if required.   **s. 26**

▷ Amended copy of articles of association, if required.

Notes

▷ The change of name only takes effect when the Registrar issues a revised certificate of incorporation.   **ss. 80(3), 81**

▷ Once the Registrar has issued the revised certificate of incorporation, **s.82**
it will be necessary to obtain new headed stationery, amend email
and website disclosures, and obtain a new company seal where the
company has a seal.

▷ Arrange for the name of the company's bank accounts to be changed
and arrange for the company's articles of association to be amended
and reprinted.

▷ Notify the company's suppliers and customers of the change of name,
the VAT authorities, HM Revenue & Customs for both corporation
tax and PAYE, pension scheme, title deeds, trademark registrations,
data protection registration, insurers, etc. Signs at the company's
premises or on the company's cars, vans and lorries will also require
amendment.

▷ Listed, AIM and NEX companies must make appropriate market
disclosures.

More information

▷ Companies House Guidance booklet GP3

Notice – special

Certain resolutions require that 28 days' special notice of the intention to put that resolution be given to the company. Other than where resolutions are proposed by shareholders, this special notice would be given by a director or the company secretary.

s.312

Checklist

The following resolutions require special notice to be given to the company:

▶ removal of a director (see page 113);

s.168

▶ removal of auditors or appointment as auditors of persons other than the retiring auditors (see page 48); and

s.511

▶ appointment of auditors to fill casual vacancies or reappointment of auditors following appointment by directors to fill casual vacancies (see pages 39 and 47).

s.515

Procedure

▶ Letter to the company stating the intention to propose appropriate resolution and stating that special notice is being given must be lodged at the company's registered office at least 28 days prior to the meeting.

s.312

▶ The company must, where practical, give its members notice of any such resolution in the same manner and at the same time as it gives notice of the meeting. If that is not possible, it must give at least 14 days' notice by newspaper advertisement or such other method provided in its articles.

s.312(2)

s.312(3)

▶ If the resolution relates to the proposed removal of a director, a copy of the special notice must be sent as soon as possible to the director concerned.

Filing requirement

None.

Notes

▷ If after special notice has been given the meeting is convened for a date sooner than in 28 days, notice is deemed properly given, although not within the time required.

s.312(4)

More information

▷ *Company Secretary's Handbook*, Chapter 8

Notices – content

Checklist

▷ Notices should contain:

  ▷ company name;

  ▷ date and time of meeting;   **s.311(1)(a)**

  ▷ place of meeting; and   **s.311(1)(b)**

  ▷ general nature of business to be transacted.   **s.311(2)**

▷ Notice of a public company or traded private company AGM must state that the meeting is to be an AGM.   **s.337(1)**

▷ Where a special resolution is to be proposed, the notice must state that the resolution is to be proposed as a special resolution and contain the text of the resolution.   **s.283(6)**

▷ For listed, AIM and NEX companies, resolutions on substantially different matters should be separate resolutions and not bundled.

▷ Public companies must consider the appointment or reappointment of directors as separate resolutions unless a resolution permitting multiple appointments by single resolution has previously been approved.   **s.160**

▷ A statement that members may appoint proxies who need not themselves be members.   **s.325**

▷ Companies whose shares are settled in CREST will usually state a date not more than 48 hours before the meeting as the cut-off for registrations to determine entitlement to attend and vote. In practice, due to the difficulty in establishing the entitlement to attend part-way through a trading day, the cut-off is usually stated as being the holdings at the close of business on the pre-penultimate day before the day of the meeting.   **s.41 USR1985**

Procedure

▷ Convene a directors' meeting to recommend appropriate resolution(s) to members and to convene a general meeting. Ensure valid quorum is present.

▶ Issue notice either in hard copy, in electronic form or by means of a website. **s.308**

▶ Issue with the notice a form of proxy if desired. Listed companies must enclose a three-way form of proxy (see page 200).

▶ Consider whether class meeting(s) also required.

▶ If the meeting is to be convened on short notice, the company secretary should arrange for agreement to short notice to be signed by each of the shareholders.

Filing requirement

None.

Notes

None.

More information

▶ *Company Secretary's Handbook*, Chapter 8

Notices – periods

Although directors' meetings may be held on 'reasonable' notice, there are strict rules governing the minimum notice periods for shareholders' meetings.

Checklist

▶ Annual general meeting of a public company	21 days	s.307(2)(a)
▶ General meeting of a public company	14 days	s.307(2)(b)
▶ General meeting of a private company	14 days	s.307(1)
▶ Notice to company of intention to put resolution	28 days	s.312
▶ General meeting of a traded company that is not an AGM, where electronic proxy voting is available and a resolution permitting notice of not less than 14 days has been passed at either the previous AGM or a subsequent general meeting	14 days	s.307A

Procedure

▶ Convene a directors' meeting to recommend appropriate resolution(s) to members and to convene a general meeting. Ensure valid quorum is present. — s.308

▶ Issue notice either in hard copy, in electronic form or by means of a website.

▶ Issue with the notice a form of proxy if desired. Listed companies must enclose a three-way form of proxy (see page 200).

▶ Consider whether class meeting(s) also required.

▶ If the meeting is to be convened on short notice, the company secretary should arrange for agreement to short notice to be signed by each of the shareholders.

Filing requirement

None.

Notes

▶ Period of notice is stated in 'clear' days. The articles should be consulted to ascertain what constitutes 'clear' days for the particular company. For example, the company's articles may state that the day of receipt must be classed as 48 hours and not 24 hours after posting.

▶ Under the UK Corporate Governance Code, listed companies should give at least 20 working days' notice of their AGM and 14 for a GM.

▶ Companies formed prior to 1 October 2009 must take great care to check their articles, as these are very likely to contain the notice periods under the former Companies Act which are longer in certain circumstances. Other than a quoted company, a general meeting may be held upon shorter notice if 90% of the members entitled to attend and vote agree in the case of a private company and 95% for a public company general meeting. Members can agree to shorter notice of a **s.307(5)** general meeting excluding a meeting that is an AGM. Agreement must be given by a majority in number of the members who between them hold at least 90% of the voting rights in the case of a private company or 95% in the case of a public company. **s.307(5)&(6)**

More information

▶ *Company Secretary's Handbook*, Chapter 8

Overseas company

The provisions relating to overseas companies are contained in ss. 1044–1059 and the Overseas Companies Regulations 2009 SI 2009/1801 ('OCR').

Any overseas company that opens a UK establishment must register certain particulars with the Registrar of Companies. A UK establishment is either a branch within the meaning of the eleventh Company Law Directive or a place of business that is not a branch.

OCR reg. 3

If an overseas company has already registered details for another UK establishment, details applicable to both registrations need not be repeated but may be referred to.

OCR reg. 5(2)

Checklist

▶ If the parent company's incorporation documents are not in English, a certified translation will be required.

▶ If another UK establishment has been registered, details of that registration will be required.

OCR regs. 5 and 6

Procedure

▶ Complete form OS IN01, containing:

  ▷ the company's registered name;

  ▷ its legal form (public, private, etc);

  ▷ if registered in its country of incorporation, its registered number and the identity of the register;

  ▷ details of directors and secretary, or their equivalents;

  ▷ the authority of the directors to represent the company and their capacity to bind the company in dealings with third parties together with a statement of whether this authority may be exercised solely or jointly with other directors; and

  ▷ whether the company is a credit or financial institution.

▶ If the overseas company is not incorporated in a member state of
   the European Union, the following additional information must be   **OCR reg. 5(2)**
   provided:

   ▷ the legislation under which the company was incorporated;

   ▷ the address of the principal place of business, the country of
   incorporation, the objects of the company and the amount of its
   issued share capital; and

   ▷ the accounting reference date and time allowed for filing of
   accounts available for public inspection (required if the company
   wishes to take advantage of the right to file in the UK accounts
   prepared and disclosed in its country of incorporation).

▶ In respect of the UK establishment, the following information should
   be registered: **OCR reg. 6(2)**

   ▷ the address of the establishment;

   ▷ the date on which it was opened;

   ▷ the business carried on;

   ▷ the establishment's trading name if different from the company's
   registered name;

   ▷ the name and service address of all persons resident in the UK
   authorised to accept service on behalf of the company in respect
   of that establishment;

   ▷ the name and address of all persons authorised to represent the
   company as permanent representatives for the business of that
   establishment; and

   ▷ the authority of the permanent representatives to contract on
   behalf of the establishment and whether they may exercise such
   authority solely or, if jointly, the name of the person(s).

▶ A statement of how the company intends to meet its obligations
   relating to accounts and whether those will be met by the   **OCR reg. 7**
   establishment being registered or by another UK establishment.

Filing requirement

▶ Form OS IN01.

▶ A certified copy of the company's constitutional documents.

▶ A copy of the latest set of audited accounts required to be published
   by parent law.

▶ If these documents have been previously filed by another UK
   establishment, they may be referred to rather than filed again.

▶ Registration fee of £20, same-day registration £100.

Notes

▷ The constitutional document need only be submitted once and must be referred to for other branch registrations.

▷ Any alterations to the constitutional documents must be notified on the appropriate form.

OCR reg. 14

▷ Each overseas company with a UK establishment that is required by its parent law to prepare, have audited and disclose accounts or is incorporated in an EAA state and is required by its parent law to prepare and disclose accounts but is not required to have those accounts audited to deliver them must register its annual report and accounts.

OCR regs. 68–74

OCR regs. 31 and 32

OCR regs. 36 and 37

▷ Each overseas company to which the above criteria do not apply must prepare accounts and deliver a copy to companies as if it were a company incorporated in the UK.

OCR regs 58–65

▷ A UK establishment owning property over which charges have been given is required to register details of the charge with the Registrar.

▷ Every UK establishment of an overseas company shall state the registered branch number and the place of registration of the branch on its headed paper, invoices, etc. If the overseas company is not from an EU member state, the following additional information must be stated:

  ▷ the identity of the register and its country of incorporation;

  ▷ its registered number, if any;

  ▷ the legal form of the company;

  ▷ if the liability of its members is limited, that fact;

  ▷ the location of its registered office or principal place of business; and

  ▷ whether it is in liquidation or other form of insolvency.

▷ Where an overseas company that has UK establishment(s) is being wound up it must, within 14 days of the commencement of the winding up, give details of its name, particulars of the winding up and the date upon which the winding up is or will be effective. Within 14 days of appointment, the liquidator must notify his or her name and address, the date of his or her appointment and a description of his or her powers. Following the termination of the winding up for whatever reason, the liquidator must file details of the termination within 14 days. Details must be given for each UK establishment, although one return may be made, provided the registered numbers of each UK establishment are stated on the return.

More information

▷ *Company Secretary's Handbook*, Chapter 24

▷ Companies House Guidance booklet GP01

Payment practices disclosures

Implemented to encourage companies to pay their suppliers more quickly qualifying businesses are required to submit details of their payment terms and performance to a government online portal every six months. The data collected is available to the public.

The obligation is individual to all Companies and accordingly groups may comprise one or more Companies that are required to report their own payment practices. Group practices and performance are not required to be disclosed.

SBEE2015 s.3 and The Reporting on Payment Practices and Performance Regulations 2017 (SI 395/2017)

Checklist

▷ Is the business incorporated under the Companies Act 2006, or earlier legislation, or as an LLP under the Limited Liabilities Partnerships Act 2000.

▷ Did the business meet any two of the criteria at each of its previous two balance sheet dates:

　▷ Turnover of at least £36m (£43.2m gross)

　▷ Balance sheet total of at least £18m (£21.6m gross) (meaning the aggregate of amounts shown as assets

　▷ At least 250 employees

Turnover means the amounts received for the sale of goods and services, excluding financial services.

The gross amounts are applicable only to parent companies.

Procedure

▷ Businesses are required to report in respect of each 6 month period commuting on the first day of its financial year and within 30 days of the end of each reporting period

▷ If the financial year is shorter than 9 months only one report is required, and three reports are required if the financial year is longer than 15 months.

▶ The following information must be submitted to the online government portal:

▷ Narrative description of: standard payment terms including normal length of time for payment, maximum payment period and any changes to standard payment period and how suppliers have been notified or consulted in respect of any changes.

▷ Description of the process to resolve disputes.

▷ Statistics showing: average number of days to pay invoices from date of receipt of invoice, percentage of payments made in less than 30 days, between 31 & 60 days and in 61 days or more and the percentage of payments made within the agreed payment terms.

▷ Confirmation on whether suppliers are offered e-invoicing, availability of supply chain financing, whether a charge is made for the supplier to remain on a supplier's list and if so if a charge has been made in the reporting period and whether the company is a member of a payment code and if so the name of the code.

Filing requirement

None.

More information

▶ assets.publishing.service.gov.uk/government/uploads/system/ uploads/attachment_data/file/649941/payment-practices- performance-reporting-requirements-oct-2017.pdf

Polls

The rules governing the demanding of a poll will be laid down in the company's articles or in the appropriate model articles if the company has not adopted its own articles. The provisions of ss. 321 and 322 must be considered, however, when drafting a company's articles covering voting on a poll, since by those sections certain provisions are rendered void.

The checklists and procedure set out below are based upon the relevant model articles set out in SI 2009/3229.

Private companies – *sch. 1, SI 2009/3229*

Checklist

▶ Check articles to see if model articles provisions adopted.

▶ Has the demand for a poll been validly made: reg. 44(1)

  ▷ in advance of the general meeting; or

  ▷ at the meeting on or before the declaration of the result on a show of hands?

▶ Where model article provisions have been adopted, a poll may be demanded by: reg. 44(2)

  ▷ the chair;

  ▷ the directors;

  ▷ at least two persons having the right to vote at the meeting; or

  ▷ one or more persons representing not less than one-tenth of the total voting rights of all the members having the right to vote at the meeting.

▶ Demand for a poll may only be withdrawn if the poll has not taken place and the chair agrees.   reg. 44(3)

▶ The poll must be taken immediately in such manner as the chair directs.   reg. 44(4)

Public companies – *sch. 3, SI 2009/3229*

Checklist

▶ Check articles to see if model articles provisions adopted.

▶ Has the demand for a poll been validly made: reg.36(1)

  ▷ in advance of the general meeting; or

  ▷ at the meeting on or before the declaration of the result on a show of hands?

▶ Where model article provisions have been adopted, a poll may be   reg.36(2)
demanded by:

  ▷ the chair;

  ▷ the directors;

  ▷ at least two persons having the right to vote at the meeting; or

  ▷ one or more persons representing not less than one-tenth of the total voting rights of all the members having the right to vote at the meeting.

▶ Demand for a poll may only be withdrawn if the poll has not taken   reg.36(3)
place and the chair agrees.

▶ The poll may be taken in such manner as the chair directs, but must be reg.37(5)
taken within 30 days.

▶ The chair may appoint scrutineers, who need not be members, and   reg.37(2)
may decide how, where and when the results will be declared.

▶ Polls on the election of a chair or adjournment of the meeting must be reg.37(4)
taken immediately.

▶ No notice need be given if the time and place are announced at the   reg.37(7),(8)
meeting, otherwise seven days' notice is required.

Quoted companies

Checklist

There are additional provisions which quoted companies must adhere to.

▶ A quoted company must publish on a website the results of any poll
votes including date of the meeting, text of the resolution and the   s.341
number of votes cast in favour of and against the resolution.

▶ Members representing at least 5% of the total voting rights or 100
members or more may request an independent report on a poll taken
or to be taken at a general meeting. The request may be in hard copy   s.342
or in electronic form, must identify the poll(s) to which it relates, must
be authenticated by all those members requesting it and must be
received by the company not later than one week after the date the
poll is taken.

▶ Where an independent assessor has been appointed, the company must publish on a website details of the appointment, the identity of the assessor, the text of the resolution(s) and a copy of the independent assessor's report.

s.351

Procedure

▶ An announcement should be drafted for the chair, which can be read out if a poll is demanded, to inform members of the procedure to be followed, or, if the poll is to take place at a later date, of the date and time for the taking of the poll and the procedure to be followed.

▶ It may be appropriate for the chair to suggest that since proxies already lodged are overwhelmingly in favour of the resolution, the person or persons requesting the poll may decide to withdraw their demand.

▶ If the demand for a poll is not withdrawn, the validity of the demand should be checked by confirming that those who have demanded it are, in fact, members or proxies or, for example, if only one member is demanding it, that he or she holds not less than one-tenth of the total voting rights. It is usually the scrutineers' responsibility to check the validity of the demand for the poll.

▶ If the scrutineers advise that the poll has not been properly demanded, the chair will make a statement to this effect and the meeting will usually proceed to its next business after having put the matter on which the poll was requested to the vote by a show of hands (if this had not already been done at the time the poll was demanded). Polls on procedural resolutions should take place immediately.

▶ If the demand for the poll is valid and is not withdrawn, the chair will advise the meeting to this effect. If the chair did not advise the meeting as to the proxy position when the poll was first demanded, this could now be done. Assuming the poll is still not withdrawn, the chair will read the statement announcing the time for holding of the poll (e.g. either immediately, at the conclusion of the meeting or at a later date). It is usual practice for the poll to be held at the end of the meeting and for it to be kept open for one hour. The meeting then proceeds to its next business until the conclusion of the business of the meeting.

▶ At the end of the meeting, the chair declares the meeting closed and informs the members as to the procedure for the conduct of the poll. The chair should explain that those who have appointed a proxy need not complete a ballot paper unless they wished to alter their vote.

▶ Stewards then distribute ballot papers to those present. These are collected by staff after completion by the members and proxy holders, and handed to the scrutineers.

▶ The scrutineers, especially if they are the company's auditors, have their own instructions with regard to the checking of the ballot papers, verification of the holdings, and preparation of a report and final certificate of the result of the poll. This is handed to the chair, who then declares the results of the poll. In the case of a listed company, or a company whose shares are traded on AIM or NEX, the result of the poll is notified to the Stock Exchange or NEX as appropriate.

Filing requirement

None.

Notes

▶ As procedures can vary from company to company, it is essential that the articles of association are checked to ensure the correct procedure is followed.

▶ In order for a demand for a poll to be valid, it must be called for before or immediately on the declaration by the chair of the result of the vote on a show of hands.

More information

▶ *Company Secretary's Handbook*, Chapter 8

Powers of Attorney – corporate

A corporate Power of Attorney is an appointment by a company of a person or persons to act on its behalf as set out in the document creating the Power of Attorney. Attorneys are usually appointed by companies to act on their behalf overseas, although an attorney may be appointed within the UK.

Although the Powers of Attorney Act 1971 (PAA1971) sets out a pro forma short-form Power of Attorney used to confer wide powers on the attorney, this is unlikely to be used by a company, as a corporate Power of Attorney is more likely to be for a specific purpose and would therefore be in a longer form, setting out the precise details of the Powers of Attorney. A long-form Power of Attorney would need to be used by a Scottish or Northern Ireland company, as the PAA 1971 does not apply in those countries.

PAA 1971 s. 10 & Sch. 1

The Power of Attorney need not be given under seal, provided it is stated as being executed as a deed on behalf of the company.

The directors' authority to delegate their authority to an attorney is contained in the articles of association.

reg. 5(b) schs 1 and 3, SI 2009/3229

Checklist

▶ Check the articles of association to ensure directors may delegate their authority to an attorney.

Procedure

▶ Convene a directors' meeting to approve the terms of the attorney's appointment. Ensure valid quorum is present.

▶ The document creating the Power of Attorney is to be executed in accordance with the articles of association, usually any two directors, one director and the company secretary or by a sole director duly witnessed.

▶ Any changes required to be made to an existing Power of Attorney will require a variation to the original agreement.

Filing requirement

None.

Notes

None.

Powers of Attorney – member

Individuals may give either a general or specific power of attorney under the provisions of the Powers of Attorney Act 1971 or a lasting power of attorney (LPA) under the Mental Capacity Act 2005. The LPA has replaced the enduring power of attorney given under the Powers of Attorney Act 1971, although an enduring power of attorney created prior to 1 October 2007 remains valid provided, in the case of a donor who has become mentally incapable, the enduring power of attorney has been registered under MCA2005 with the public guardian.

Checklist

▶ The document received for registration must be the original document, bearing a stamp duty impression if granted prior to 26 March 1985, or an authenticated copy of it.

▶ Care must be taken to ensure that the person granting the power of attorney is indeed a member of the company and holds the appropriate number of shares. It may be that the power of attorney is being granted by a member who has only recently acquired shares either by allotment, by renunciation of bonus or rights issue, or by transfer.

Procedure

Where a power of attorney is received for registration, the following procedure should be maintained:

▶ The company should retain a copy of the power of attorney for its records.

▶ The terms of the power of attorney must be checked to see whether one attorney is being appointed or more than one. In the case of more than one attorney, it will be necessary to check whether one attorney acting on his or her own has power to effect transfers, or whether all attorneys must act together.

▶ The power of attorney may change the registered address for the shareholder and the matter of to whom any future dividends must be made.

▶ If the power of attorney is in order, the company's registration stamp should be affixed to the original document and returned to the person giving the power of attorney.

▶ On every occasion that documents are executed by the attorney, this should be cross-referenced with the copy of the power of attorney retained by the company to ensure that the terms of the power of attorney have been complied with.

▶ Neither the name in the register of members nor the original share certificate requires amendment, since the beneficial owner is not changing and, indeed, as the register of members is a public document, the appointment of a power of attorney should not be noted on it.

▶ A power of attorney can be revoked or changed by the person giving the power of attorney at any time or, alternatively, the power of attorney may be given for a specific occasion or for a specific length of time.

Filing requirement

None.

Notes

None.

More information

▶ *Company Secretary's Handbook*, Chapter 18

Pre-emption rights – allotment

Any new equity securities (ordinary shares or rights to convert securities into or subscribe for ordinary shares) to be issued by a company must first be offered to existing members in proportion to the number of shares they already hold. An ordinary share is defined as a share without restriction on their entitlement to participate in dividends or return of capital. This provision safeguards members, as their holding of shares can only be diluted if they do not take up shares. **s.561** **s.560**

However, private companies may forgo these provisions in their articles of association and either substitute 'tailor-made' pre-emption provisions or delete pre-emption provisions entirely or may exclude the provisions by special resolution. **s.567**

Public companies may only relax these provisions by special resolution. Many private companies are incorporated with articles of association that remove the statutory pre-emption rights and substitute alternative provisions. Commonly the first allotment following incorporation is exempt from any pre-emption provisions. **s.569**

Where directors have been given authority to issue shares under s. 551 either generally or by special resolution, they may be given power either in the articles or by special resolution to allot shares as if s. 561 did not apply. **ss.570,571**

Listed companies and those whose shares are traded on AIM or NEX will usually seek an annual renewal of a limited waiver of pre-emption rights to enable ad hoc share issues during the year.

These pre-emption provisions also apply to the sale of any treasury shares held by a limited company. **ss.573,724**

Checklist

▶ Do the articles exclude or vary the statutory pre-emption provisions of s. 567 (private companies only)?

▶ Is any previous waiver still valid or has that authority been used by previous share issues or time expired?

▷ If the company has only a small number of shareholders, it may be more practical to arrange for the shareholders to waive their pre-emption rights by notice in writing or written resolution, as otherwise a general meeting will be required.

▷ If there is a shareholders' investment or similar agreement, this may contain pre-emption provisions that override the articles of association.

Procedure

▷ Convene a directors' meeting to recommend appropriate special resolution to waive pre-emption provisions to members and to seek members' approval by written resolution (private companies only) or at a general meeting. Ensure valid quorum is present.　　　　s.307

　　　　s.297

▷ Issue notice, signed by director or company secretary, on 14 clear days' notice (21 days if to be put to a public company's AGM) for members to consider resolution.

▷ Enclose with the notice a form of proxy if desired. Listed companies must enclose a three-way form of proxy (see page 200).

▷ If the meeting is to be convened on short notice, the company secretary should arrange for agreement to short notice to be signed by each of the shareholders.

▷ Hold general meeting. Ensure valid quorum is present. Resolution put to vote either by show of hands or by poll and to be passed by appropriate majority (special resolution by 75% majority).

▷ Where circulated as a written resolution by a private company, the requisite majority must be achieved within 28 days of circulation.　　s.29

▷ Amend articles of association if necessary.　　s.26

Filing requirement

▷ Copy of resolution within 15 days.

▷ Amended copy of articles of association if appropriate.

Notes

▷ It is not necessary to waive pre-emption rights for a rights, bonus or capitalisation issue as these are *pro rata* issues except where overseas shareholders are excluded. For example, many rights issues of publicly traded companies exclude overseas territories where to participate in the offer would require an offer document prepared under local laws to be registered in that overseas territory.

▷ Where there is more than one class of shares, each class may have different pre-emption rights.

▶ Listed companies will follow the recommendations of the Pre-Emption Group. This was set up in 2005 to produce a Statement of Principles to be taken into account when considering the case for disapplying pre-emption rights. This Statement of Principles was revised in 2015 with further clarification issued in 2016. The group's members represent listed companies, investors and intermediaries (www.pre-emptiongroup.org.uk).

More information

▶ *Company Secretary's Handbook*, Chapter 13

Pre-emption rights – transfer

There are no statutory pre-emption rights on the transfer of shares. However, many private companies and some public companies will have pre-emption rights embodied within their articles of association. Although the provisions usually stipulate a strict procedure to follow when shares are to be transferred, these provisions are frequently waived in circumstances where the transfer is agreed by all the shareholders. The provisions would, however, not be used in a contentious transfer. In such circumstances the pre-emption provisions must be followed strictly.

Checklist

▶ Check the articles of association to see whether pre-emption rights apply to the transfer.

▶ If the share transfer is not contentious, it may be appropriate for the existing shareholders to waive their rights of pre-emption by notice in writing.

▶ Alternatively, the transfer may be non-contentious but due to the large number of shareholders, the rights of pre-emption may best be waived by special resolution at a general meeting.

Procedure

▶ Where the transfer is likely to be contentious or it is deemed inappropriate or impractical to request members waive their rights of pre-emption, it will be necessary to follow strictly the pre-emption procedure, as set down in the articles. This procedure will often take a number of weeks to complete and may require the company's auditor or accountant to certify the fair value for the shares.

Filing requirement

None.

Notes

▶ Where a company's articles of association do contain pre-emption rights on transfer, there may be special dispensations for transfers between family members or group companies.

▶ Where shares are to be transferred following the death of a shareholder, the pre-emption provisions may be deemed to have been brought into effect and the shares offered to the existing shareholders even if the appropriate notice has not been given by the executor(s).

More information

▶ *Company Secretary's Handbook*, Chapter 18

Proxies

Members unable to attend a meeting can appoint one or more proxies to attend and vote in their place. A proxy need not be a member of the company.

s.324

A proxy can vote on a poll or on a show of hands. Proxies are entitled to exercise all of their appointors rights to speak at the meeting, including the right to call or join in a demand for a poll.

ss.282(4), 283(5), 284(2)(b)

Companies need not appoint a proxy, as they may appoint a representative who may attend on their behalf with the same rights as if they were a shareholder in their own right. However, where a corporation wishes to appoint multiple appointees, making such appointments as proxies gives greater flexibility, as where multiple corporate representatives are appointed by the same corporate member, only one of them can exercise the voting rights.

s.323(1)

s.323(3)

Proxies can either be appointed with specific instructions on how to vote or left to use their discretion. If the proxy is instructed how to vote, they must vote in accordance with those instructions.

The notice convening a members' meeting must disclose the members' rights to appoint proxies under s. 324 or any more extensive rights contained in the company's articles of association.

s.325

Checklist

▶ Where a company issues proxy forms, they must be sent to all members entitled to vote at the meeting.

s.326

▶ Normally proxies must be registered with the company not less than 48 hours prior to the meeting and it is unlawful for the company to require that these be lodged more than 48 hours prior to the meeting excluding any day that is not a business day.

s.327(2)

Filing requirement

None.

Notes

▷ Public companies listed on the Stock Exchange or AIM must issue three-way proxies.   **LR 9.3.6**

▷ Most companies will word the proxy form to appoint the chair as proxy by default unless another person is specified.

▷ Members can attend and vote in person even if they have lodged a proxy form and attendance will often automatically revoke the appointment of a proxy. Accordingly a check should be made at the meeting to discard any proxies received from those attending.

▷ Even if the form of proxy lodged with the company contains instructions on how the proxy must vote on the resolution(s), those votes can only be counted if the person appointed as the proxy attends the meeting and votes.

More information

▷ *Company Secretary's Handbook*, Chapter 8

Purchase of own shares – out of capital

It is possible, under certain circumstances, for a private company to purchase its own shares out of capital provided that the purchase is not restricted or prohibited by the company's articles of association. Additionally, there are restrictions on the company's ability to use its reserves to purchase its own shares and care must be taken to ensure that any profits available are utilised first as purchases out of capital can only be made (whether in whole or in part) if there are no distributable reserves available.

ss.690,709

s.710

Checklist

▶ Is the company a private company? **s.709(1)**

▶ Has the company no distributable reserves or will the purchase use up all available distributable reserves? **s.710(1)**

▶ Check articles to ensure company is not prohibited from purchasing its own shares.

▶ Accounts must be drawn up to a date within three months of the date of the directors' statement made under s. 714 and must be used to calculate the permissible capital payment. **ss.712(6),(7)**

▶ If the company's accounts are not audited, an auditor must be appointed.

▶ Will the directors be able to confirm the company's ability to pay its debts immediately after the payment and for the following 12 months, and will the auditor be able to confirm that such a statement is reasonable? **ss.714(3),(6)**

Procedure

▶ Convene a directors' meeting to approve the making of a statement specifying the permissible capital payment and confirming the company's ability to meet its debts, recommending the purchase to members and either to convene a general meeting or to circulate a written resolution to obtain members' approval. Ensure valid quorum is present. **s.714**

▷ Issue notice, signed by director or company secretary, on 14 clear
days' notice or circulate written resolution for members to consider
special resolution(s). Included with the notice or written resolution
must be an auditors' report and the terms of the purchase. The special
resolution must be approved within one week of the date of the
directors' statement made under s. 714.

ss.716,718

s.714

▷ Enclose with the notice a form of proxy if desired.

▷ A copy of the agreement, or a written schedule of its terms if the
contract is not in writing, must be made available for inspection by
the members of the company at the company's registered office for
not less than 15 days prior to the meeting and at the meeting itself.
The schedule of the terms must include the names of any members
holding shares which it is proposed be purchased and, if the written
contract does not show these names, a schedule must be attached
showing the names and the number of shares to which the contract
relates. Where a previously approved contract is being varied,
the terms of the variation must be available for inspection by the
members.

ss.693,696(2)

▷ This requirement for the documents to be made available for
inspection to the members prior to the meeting restricts the ability
of the company to hold the meeting at shorter notice than 15 days.
Where the resolutions are to be passed by written resolution of
the members, a copy of the contract and/or any schedule must be
supplied to the members no later than the date upon which they
receive a copy of the written resolution for signature.

s.696(2)(b)

▷ Directors to make the statutory declaration specifying the permissible
capital payment within one week before the date of the meeting.

s.714

▷ Hold general meeting. Ensure valid quorum is present. Resolution
put to vote either by show of hands or by poll and to be passed by
appropriate majority (special resolution by 75% majority).

s.716

▷ Within one week of the passing of the special resolution, the company
must publish a notice in the *London Gazette* giving details of the
proposed payment and notify creditors either individually or by
newspaper advertisement published within one week of the passing
of the resolution. Creditors may make application to the court to
cancel the resolution, provided such application is made within five
weeks of the date of approval of the special resolution.

s.719

s.721

▷ If an application is made, the court will decide whether to cancel the
resolution, reject the application or make such modification to the
proposed purchase as it deems appropriate.

s.721(4)

▷ If no objections are received, the payment may be made at the end
of the five-week period and must be made within seven weeks of the
date of approval of the special resolution.

s.723(1)

▷ Once the company has purchased the shares, a return on form SH03
must be submitted to the Registrar, stating the number of shares and
the class of shares, together with the nominal value of the shares and

s.707

the date on which they were repurchased. The purchase of shares by a company is subject to stamp duty where the amount payable exceeds £1,000, the duty being payable on the consideration and not the nominal value at the rate of 0.5% (rounded up to the nearest £5).

▷ Issue consideration cheques and cancel share certificates relating to shares purchased. Update register of members.

Filing requirement

▷ Copy of special resolution within 15 days.   **s.30**

▷ Amended copy of articles of association, if amended.   **ss.26,714**

▷ Directors' and auditors' statement.

▷ Notification in *London Gazette* of proposed payment.   **s.719(1)**

▷ Advertisement in appropriate newspapers or notice given to all   **s.719(2)**
creditors.

▷ Stamped form SH03 within 28 days.   **s.707**

Notes

▷ The resolution will be invalid if any member of the company holding
shares which it is proposed be repurchased exercises the voting rights   **s.695**
attaching to those shares, and the resolution would not have been
passed if those shares had not been voted.

▷ Copies of the contracts must be retained for 10 years.   **s.702(3)**

More information

▷ *Company Secretary's Handbook*, Chapter 14

Purchase of own shares – out of profit

It is possible under certain circumstances for public and private companies to purchase their own fully paid shares, provided that the purchase is not restricted or prohibited by the company's articles of association. Additionally, there are restrictions on the company's ability to use its reserves to purchase its own shares and care must be taken to ensure that the company has sufficient distributable reserves for the purpose. It may also be possible for the company to issue new shares to fund the redemption.

ss. 690, 691

s. 692(2)

Shares may be purchased as an off-market purchase in pursuance of a purchase contract approved in advance by members or by a market purchase on a recognised investment exchange.

s. 693(1)

Checklist

▷ Does the company have sufficient distributable reserves to fund the purchase?

▷ Check articles to ensure company is permitted to purchase its own shares.

Procedure – off-market purchase

▷ Convene a directors' meeting to recommend the purchase to members and to convene a general meeting or circulate a written resolution in the case of a private company. Ensure valid quorum is present.

▷ Issue notice, signed by director or company secretary, on 14 clear days' notice for members to consider resolution(s). Where approval is being sought by written resolution, a copy of the purchase contract or the terms of the purchase must be circulated with the written resolution.

ss. 694, 696(2(a))

▷ Enclose with the notice a form of proxy if desired. Listed companies must enclose a three-way form of proxy (see page 200).

▶ A copy of the agreement, or a written schedule of its terms if the contract is not in writing, must be made available for inspection by the members of the company at the company's registered office for not less than 15 days prior to the meeting and at the meeting itself. The schedule of the terms must include the names of any members holding shares which it is proposed be purchased and, if the written contract does not show these names, a schedule must be attached showing the names and the number of shares to which the contract relates. Where a previously approved contract is being varied, the terms of the variation must be available for inspection by the members.   **s.696(2)(b)**

▶ This requirement for the documents to be made available for inspection to the members prior to the meeting restricts the ability of the company to hold the meeting at shorter notice than 15 days.

▶ Hold general meeting. Ensure valid quorum is present. Resolution put to vote either by show of hands or by poll and to be passed by appropriate majority (ordinary resolution by 50% majority).

▶ Once the company has purchased the shares, a return on form SH03 must be submitted to the Registrar, stating the number of shares and the class of shares, together with the nominal value of the shares and the date on which they were repurchased. The repurchase of shares by a company is subject to stamp duty, the duty being payable on any consideration in excess of £1,000 and not the nominal value at the rate of 0.5% (rounded up to the nearest £5).

▶ Issue consideration cheques and cancel share certificates relating to shares purchased. Update register of members.

Procedure – market purchase

▶ A company may only make a market purchase of its own shares if the purchase has been approved in advance by ordinary resolution.   **s.701(1)**

▶ The resolution may be a general authorisation or limited to the purchase of shares of a particular class or description and may also be an unconditional authority or conditional.   **s.701(2)**

▶ The authority must specify the maximum number of shares that may be purchased, the maximum and minimum process that may be paid, and the date not more than five years from the date of the resolution when the authority lapses.   **s.701(3),(5)**

Filing requirement

▶ Copy of special resolution within 15 days.   **s.30**

▶ Amended copy of articles of association, if amended.   **s.26**

▶ Stamped form SH03 within 28 days.   **s.707**

Notes

▶ In the case of a public company, the resolution must state the date upon which the authority is to lapse, being not more than five years from the date of the resolution.

s.694(5)

▶ The resolution will be invalid if any member of the company holding shares which it is proposed be repurchased exercises the voting rights attaching to those shares, and the resolution would not have been passed if those shares had not been voted.

s.695

▶ Where a contract for an off-market purchase of shares has been approved, a copy of the contract or, if not in writing, a written memorandum of its terms must be kept at the registered office or another specified place for at least 10 years commencing on the date the purchase of shares was completed or the contract otherwise determines.

s.702

More information

▶ *Company Secretary's Handbook*, Chapter 14

Quorum – directors' meetings

The quorum for a meeting is the minimum number of directors that must be present and entitled to vote in order to constitute a valid meeting. The articles will normally stipulate the quorum. Unless modified, the default quorum established by the model articles for both private and public companies is two directors. They also provide for the directors to change the quorum as they see fit; however, any resolution to raise or lower the quorum must be taken at a directors' meeting at which a quorum is present.

reg. 11 sch. 1, reg. 10
sch. 3, SI 2008/3229

If the articles are silent on the question of a quorum and specifically preclude the provisions of the model articles, then the quorum will default to a majority of the directors in office from time to time.

The quorum must be maintained during the course of a meeting. If the number of directors present falls below the quorum, the meeting must stand adjourned until a quorum (not necessarily the same directors) is present. This can be difficult where directors are interested in the business before the meeting and excluded from voting and from being counted in the quorum.

Checklist

▶ Is a quorum present?

▶ Is a quorum maintained and present for each item of business, especially in circumstances where one or more directors may have a conflict of interests?

▶ If a director is also an alternate for another director, he or she will not count as 'two' people for the purposes of determining whether a quorum is present unless there is specific power in the articles.

▶ Directors 'present' by telephone/video conferencing etc will be included in the quorum.

Filing requirement

None.

Notes

None.

More information

▶ *Company Secretary's Handbook*, Chapter 9

Quorum – shareholders' meetings

The quorum for a meeting is the minimum number of members that must be present and entitled to vote in order to constitute a valid meeting. In the absence of any provisions in the articles of association, the default quorum is two members or, where the company has only one member, the quorum is reduced to one.

s.318

None of the model articles specifies a quorum.

The model articles for both private and public companies waive the quorum requirement on any resolution to appoint a chair for the meeting.

reg. 38 sch. 1, reg. 30 sch. 3, SI 2008/3229

The model articles require the quorum to be present within half an hour of the time at which the meeting was due to start and if not, the chair must adjourn the meeting. When adjourning a meeting, the chair must stipulate either the time and place to which it is adjourned or state that the meeting will continue at a time and place fixed by the directors.

reg. 41 sch. 1, reg. 33 sch. 3, SI 2008/3229

Occasionally the articles will stipulate that at the adjourned meeting those members attending, if any, shall constitute a valid quorum.

Checklist

▶ Check articles to establish quorum.

▶ Is a quorum present at the time the meeting has been convened to be held?

▶ If not present, is a quorum present within half an hour?

▶ Is a quorum maintained throughout the meeting?

Filing requirement

None.

Notes

None.

More information

▷ *Company Secretary's Handbook*, Chapter 8

Rectification of records at Companies House

Although Companies House staff do check certain documents to ensure they comply with the Act's requirements in terms of disclosures, statements and signatures they do not check, and often are not in a position to be able to check, that the information is correct or even that the document(s) require filing at all.

Introduced in 2015 by SBEEA2015 the Act permits Companies to make voluntary filings of information they would like placed on the public record.

s.1048A

As a result the records for any particular company, in addition to correctly filed documents, might also contain documents that are incorrect, that were filed voluntarily, contain unnecessary material or were filed accidently.

Depending on the nature of the document and the circumstances of its filing the document may be capable of being amended and replaced or removed.

Checklist

▷ Was the document one that was not required to be filed and not filed with due authority – if yes, eligible for removal on application to the Registrar.

S.1074

▷ If a document registering a charge appears to be incomplete or inconsistent it may be capable of informal correction by the Registrar.

s.1075

▷ Is there an error or omission on the document that requires amending or it contains unnecessary information and is the form one of the following qualifying forms.

S.1076, 1093

S.1095

▷ Was consent to the appointment as a director, notified on form AP01, not obtained?

▷ Was authority to use an address notified as the company's registered office on form AD01 not obtained?

S.1096

Procedure

Removal on application to Registrar

Write to the Registrar setting out detail of the document to be removed and the circumstances of the filing and justification for the removal.

s. 1094

Informal correction

This process is only available to correct inconsistencies or to complete an incomplete charge registration document. This process can only be used where the person submitting the form has included their own contact details. Provided the applicant or authenticator of the document can satisfy the Registrar that they may authorise any corrections the Registrar can make those corrections and the filing date will be the date those corrections are applied to the document.

s. 1096

Filing capable of correction

File form RP01 or RP02a giving details of the correction together with the replacement, corrected form.

s. 1095

Form RP01 is required to replace a form previously filed but not meeting the requirements for proper delivery.

Form RP02A can only be used to correct information filed on one of the following forms: IN01, IN01c (director or secretary details sections), AP01, AP01c, AP02, AP02c, AP03, AP03c, AP04, AP04c, CH01, CH01c, CH02, CH02c, CH03, CH03c, CH04, CH04c, TM01, TM01c,TM02 & TM02c.

Form RP04 is required to accompany a corrected form where the original form was properly delivered but contained inaccurate information. The form can only be used in support of a second filing of the following forms: AP01, AP02, AP03, AP04, CH01, CH02, CH03, CH04, TM01, TM02, SH01, AR01, CS01, PSC01, PSC02, PSC03, PSC04, PSC05, PSC06, PSC07, PSC08 & PSC09.

Form RP CH01 may be used to correct the date of birth shown on a form IN01.

To correct an inconsistency the Registrar may request an additional filing is made. (For example if a notice of termination is received for a person in circumstances where the original appointment was not notified.)

Rectification by court order

On application of the company the court may order the removal of documents that the court declares to be invalid or ineffective, done without due authority, factually inaccurate or derived from something inaccurate or forged. The court order must specify what is to be removed and where on the register it is located.

ss. 1096 & 1097

Disputed director appointment

Form RP06 can be used by any person disputing the appointment as a director of themself or a person they are applying on behalf of. In order to justify the appointment of the director whose appointment is disputed the company will need to provide evidence that the person consented to act. Failure to provide such evidence will result in the appointment being struck out.

s. 1095(4A)

Registered office address

Form RP07 can be used by any person to request a change of registered office in a case where the use of a particular address is disputed.

s. 1097A

In order to justify the use of a particular address as its registered office, which use is disputed, the company will need to provide evidence that it has consent or permission to use that address. Failure to provide such evidence will result in the address being removed and the registered office change to the Companies House address in its country of registration pending a new registered office location being notified.

s. 1095

Companies may file a form RP02B to remove a form AD02 purporting to change the registered office address that has been filed without due authority or fraudulently.

Filing requirement

Form RP01, RP02A, RP02B, RP03, RP04, RP CH01, RP06 or RP07 as necessary.

Notes

Use of the RP forms can only be used to correct errors and inaccuracies in forms originally filed under the Companies At 2006 on or after 1 October 2009.

More information

▶ Companies House Guidance GP6 – Registrar's rules and powers

Reduction of capital – by court order

The Act provides for public and private companies to reduce their share capital by special resolution of the members and subject to confirmation by the court. No specific authority is required in the articles of association. A private company will only use this process in circumstances where the directors are unable to provide a solvency statement.

s.641

Application to the court comprises three key dates:

▷ application made to the court;

▷ the directions hearing; and

▷ court hearing.

It is common practice to agree the application date in advance so that the application and accompanying documents can be filed immediately following the conclusion of the general meeting.

The claim form sets out details of the capital structure following the reduction, relevant details from the articles and financial position, as well as details of the resolution approved by the shareholders.

Details of the proposed reduction can be notified direct to creditors as well as by national advertisement.

Reduction of capital proceedings are rarely opposed and confirmation will be given unless:

▷ the court is not satisfied that creditors are safeguarded;

▷ the court is not satisfied that the reduction is fair and equitable to shareholders;

▷ the necessary formalities have not been completed adequately; or

▷ the reduction is intended solely for the avoidance of tax.

Checklist

▷ Check articles to ensure no restriction on reduction of capital.

▷ Where the reduction is part of a scheme of arrangement, it is possible to reduce the share capital to zero followed by an immediate issue of shares.

s.641(2)

▷ If the company is a PLC, will the reduction result in the issued capital falling below the minimum share capital requirement?

▷ There must remain at least one issued share following completion of the reduction of capital.

▷ Will all directors sign the declaration of solvency?

Procedure

▷ Convene a directors' meeting to recommend the reduction of capital to members and either to convene a general meeting or to circulate a written resolution (private companies only) to obtain members' approval. Ensure valid quorum is present.

▷ Issue notice, signed by director or company secretary, on 14 clear days' notice or circulate written resolution for members to consider special resolution(s).

▷ Enclose with the notice a form of proxy if desired.

▷ Hold general meeting or circulate written resolution. Ensure valid quorum is present. Resolution put to vote either by show of hands or by poll and to be passed by appropriate majority (special resolution by 75% majority).

▷ Within 15 days of the passing of the resolution, file a copy of the special resolution with Companies House.

▷ Application must be made to the court to approve the special resolution.

▷ Provided the court is satisfied that the proposed reduction meets all the jurisdictional and procedural requirements, it will make an order confirming the reduction.

▷ A copy of the court order and a statement of capital on form SH19 and the filing fee (£10) must be filed at Companies House.

▷ The reduction becomes effective upon registration of the documents by the Registrar of Companies. The Registrar must certify the registration of the court order.

▷ Issue consideration cheques if appropriate and cancel share certificates relating to shares reduced. Update register of members. Issue balancing share certificates if appropriate.

Filing requirement

▷ Copy of special resolution.

▷ Court order.

▷ Form SH19.

▷ Filing fee £10.

Notes

None.

More information

▷ *Company Secretary's Handbook*, Chapter 14

Reduction of capital – simplified process

Private companies proposing to make small value purchases of shares may take advantage of a simplified process.

Checklist

▶ Check articles to ensure no restriction on reduction of capital.

▶ The aggregate purchase consideration in any financial year must not exceed the lower of £15,000 or 5% of fully paid share capital, at the beginning of the financial year.

▶ The articles of association must contain authority for the company to purchase its own shares.

▶ The purchase must be made out of capital.   **s.692(1ZA)**

▶ There must remain at least one issued share following completion of the reduction of capital.

Procedure

▶ Convene a directors' meeting to recommend the reduction of capital   **s.694(2)**
to members and either to convene a general meeting or to circulate
a written resolution to obtain members' approval to the terms of the
proposed purchase contract. Ensure valid quorum is present.

▶ Ensure a copy of the proposed contract of purchase (or a written
memorandum of its terms if it is not in writing) is made available for
inspection by members of the company at the company's registered   **s.696**
office for not less than 15 days prior to the meeting and is available for
inspection at the meeting.

▶ Issue notice, signed by director or company secretary, on 14 clear
days' notice or circulate written resolution for members to consider
special resolution(s).

▶ Enclose with the notice a form of proxy if desired.

▶ Hold general meeting or circulate written resolution. Ensure valid
quorum is present. Resolution put to vote either by show of hands or
by poll and to be passed by appropriate majority (ordinary resolution
by 50% majority).

▷ The votes of any member whose shares are being repurchased should be disregarded for the purposes of establishing whether there is the necessary majority in favour of the resolution.

▷ The reduction becomes effective upon registration of the documents by the Registrar of Companies.

▷ Issue consideration cheques if appropriate and cancel share certificates relating to shares reduced. Update register of members. Issue balancing share certificates if appropriate.

Filing requirement

▷ Copy of ordinary resolution.

▷ Form SH19.

▷ Filing fee £10.

Notes

▷ The purchase may also be made under a contingent purchase whereby a company becomes entitled or obliged to purchase its own shares, provided this has been authorised by ordinary resolution. Authorities may be varied, revoked or renewed by an ordinary resolution. If the articles do not contain authority for the company to purchase its own shares, the articles should be amended by special resolution of the members.

▷ The memorandum of terms made available for inspection must include the names of the members holding the shares to which the contract relates. If it is the contract itself that is available for inspection, it must have annexed to it a written memorandum specifying the names if they do not appear in the contract itself. Similar arrangements must be made in the case of the variation of an existing contract, which also has to be approved by an ordinary resolution.

▷ A private company may authorise the purchase of its own shares by written resolution under s. 288. To be valid, a copy of the proposed contract or a memorandum of its terms must be made available to each member no later than the date on which the written resolution is forwarded to them for approval and signature. In practice, it is normal to circulate a copy of the contract or the memorandum of its terms, together with the written resolution for signature and return.

More information

▷ *Company Secretary's Handbook*, Chapter 14

Reduction of capital – supported by solvency statement

The Act provides for private companies to reduce their share capital by special resolution of the members, provided the resolution is supported by a solvency statement. No specific authority is required in the articles of association.

s.642

The solvency statement must be declared by the directors not more than 15 days prior to the date of the resolution and this must be registered at Companies House within 15 days, together with a statement of revised capital on form SH19, confirmation of the date of the solvency statement and the special resolution of the members.

s.644

The solvency statement requires each director to confirm that, in his or her opinion, there are no grounds at the date of the statement that the company could not meets its debts and that during the period of 12 months following the statement, the company will be able to pay its debts as they fall due.

Checklist

▶ Check articles to ensure no restriction on reduction of capital.

▶ There must remain at least one issued share following completion of the reduction of capital.

▶ Will all directors sign the declaration of solvency?

Procedure

▶ Convene a directors' meeting to approve giving of the solvency statement, recommending the reduction of capital to members and either to convene a general meeting or to circulate a written resolution to obtain members' approval. Ensure valid quorum is present.

▶ Issue notice, signed by director or company secretary, on 14 clear days' notice or circulate written resolution for members to consider special resolution(s). Included with the notice or written resolution must be a copy of the solvency statement. The special resolution must be approved within 15 days of the date of the directors' solvency statement made under s. 642.

▷ Enclose with the notice a form of proxy if desired.

▷ Hold general meeting or circulate written resolution. Ensure valid quorum is present. Resolution put to vote either by show of hands or by poll and to be passed by appropriate majority (special resolution by 75% majority).

▷ Within 15 days of the passing of the resolution, file a copy of the special resolution, solvency statement, statement confirming the solvency statement made within 15 days prior to the resolution and circulated to members and form SH19 with Companies House, together with filing fee of £10.

▷ The reduction becomes effective upon registration of the documents by the Registrar of Companies.

▷ Issue consideration cheques if appropriate and cancel share certificates relating to shares reduced. Update register of members. Issue balancing share certificates if appropriate.

Filing requirement

▷ Copy of special resolution.

▷ Solvency statement.

▷ Statement by directors that solvency statement made within 15 days prior to general meeting.

▷ Form SH19.

▷ Filing fee £10.

Notes

▷ The purchase may also be made under a contingent purchase whereby a company becomes entitled or obliged to purchase its own shares, provided this has been authorised by ordinary resolution. Authorities may be varied, revoked or renewed by an ordinary resolution. If the articles do not contain authority for the company to purchase its own shares, they should be amended by special resolution of the members.

▷ The memorandum of terms made available for inspection must include the names of the members holding the shares to which the contract relates. If it is the contract itself that is available for inspection, it must have annexed to it a written memorandum specifying the names if they do not appear in the contract itself. Similar arrangements must be made in the case of the variation of an existing contract, which also has to be approved by a special resolution.

▷ A private company may authorise the purchase of its own shares by written resolution under s. 288. To be valid, a copy of the proposed contract or a memorandum of its terms must be made available to each member no later than the date on which the written resolution is forwarded to them for approval and signature. In practice, it is normal to circulate a copy of the contract or the memorandum of its terms, together with the written resolution for signature and return.

More information

▶ *Company Secretary's Handbook*, Chapter 14

Register of charges

Companies are no longer required to keep a register of charges for charges created on or after 6 April 2013. In place of this requirement, copies of charges (and any amendments to them) and instruments creating a charge (if applicable) must be made available for inspection at either the company's registered office or SAIL address.

ss. 859(P) and (Q)

In practice, companies will still need to maintain a record in order to monitor outstanding charges, and it is likely that some sort of register will be maintained. Such a register or record is not required to be made available for public inspection.

The requirement to keep and maintain a register of charges remains in place for charges created before 6 April 2013.

Checklist

▶ Does the change relate to a charge created before 6 April 2013?

▷ If yes, note satisfaction, in full or part in register of charges.

▷ If no, then no entries need be made in the register of charges.

Filing requirement

Pre-6 April 2013 charge
▶ Form MR05 or MR06 as appropriate.

Post-6 April 2013 charges
▶ Form MR01, MR02, MR03, MR06, MR08, MR09 or MR10 to register a new, modified or satisfied charge as appropriate.

▶ Filing fee for new charges £15 electronic, £23 paper.

Notes

▶ Registration of new charges must be completed with 21 days of the creation of the charge.

▶ Copies of charges and any instruments creating a charge must be kept available for inspection at the registered office or SAIL address.

More information

▶ *Company Secretary's Handbook*, Chapters 7 and 20

▶ Companies House Guidance booklet GP3

Register of directors

All companies are required to maintain a register of directors and this must be available for inspection at the registered office or SAIL address.

s.162

Private companies may elect to keep their register of directors on the central register. When an election is in place there is no requirement for access to be provided to the register of directors previously maintained by the company.

s.167A

It is important to note that when such an election is in place, a director's full date of birth will be freely accessible to anyone searching the company's record at Companies House.

s.1136

Checklist

▷ Is an election under s. 167A in force?

Procedure

▷ Where the company maintains its register of directors, the following information must be recorded:

  ▷ For a director who is a natural person, his or her current and any former name(s) (within the previous 20 years), service address, nationality, business occupation and date of birth.

s.163

  ▷ For a corporate director, corporate name, registered or principal office, in the case of an EAA registered company, details of the state and register in which the company is registered and its registered number, for a non-EAA company, details of the legal form of the company and law by which it is governed and, if applicable, details of the register in which the company is registered and its registered number.

s.164

Filing requirement

▷ Form AD03 or AD04 as appropriate.

▷ Form EH01 if an election under s. 167A is made.

Notes

▶ If the company maintains its register of directors, this must be kept at either its registered office or its SAIL address.   **s.162(3)**

▶ Unless the register of directors has always been kept at the company's registered office, details of its location must be notified to Companies House.   **s.162(4)**

More information

▶ *Company Secretary's Handbook*, Chapters 6 and 7

▶ Companies House Guidance – Company registers

Register of directors' usual residential addresses

All companies are required to maintain a register of directors' usual residential addresses in respect of all its directors that are natural persons. This register should not be made available for inspection.

s. 165

s. 1136

Private companies may elect to keep their register of directors' usual residential addresses on the central register. It is important to note that when such an election is in place, a director's residential address information will be freely accessible to anyone searching the company's record at Companies House.

s. 167A

A director can apply to have their usual residential address suppressed from disclosure where the address is contained in documents or registers available for public inspection by the Registrar or by the Company.

ss. 240-246

Checklist

▷ Is an election under s. 167A in force?

Procedure

▷ Where the company maintains its register of directors' usual residential addresses, the following information must be recorded:

▷ Each director's usual residential address unless this is the same address as recorded in the register of directors as his or her service address, in which case the register need only contain an entry to that effect.

s. 165

Filing requirement

▷ Form EH02 if an election under s. 167A is made.
▷ Form SR01 to apply to suppress an address.

Notes

None.

More information

▷ *Company Secretary's Handbook*, Chapters 6 and 7

▷ FCA Listing Rules

Register of members

All companies are required to maintain a register of members and this must be available for inspection at the registered office or SAIL address.

ss. 112, 114
s. 1136

Private companies may elect to keep their register of members on the central register. It is important to note that when such an election is in place, a member's address information will be freely accessible to anyone searching the company's record at Companies House.

s. 128A -128k

Checklist

▶ Is an election under s. 128A in force?

Procedure

▶ Where the company maintains its register of members, the following information must be recorded:

  ▷ Name and address of each member and names of all joint holders.

  ▷ The date on which each member was registered as a member.

  ▷ The date each member ceased to be a member.

▶ Companies that have a share capital must also record:

  ▷ the number of shares held by each member including any distinguishing numbers, if any, and the class of share where there is more than one; and

  ▷ the amount paid or agreed to be paid on the shares.

Filing requirement

▶ Form EH05 if an election under s. 128A is made.

Notes

▶ If the company maintains its register of members, this must be kept at either its registered office or its SAIL address.

▷ Unless the register of members has always been kept at the company's registered office, details of its location must be notified to Companies House.

▷ Records relating to former members may be deleted 10 years after they ceased to be a member.

More information

▷ *Company Secretary's Handbook,* Chapters 7 and 18

Register of members – rectification

The Act does not contain specific authority for a company to rectify the register of members. The courts may order rectification of the register of members by the removal or addition of a person from or to the register. Original Orders will bear the seal of the court or, alternatively, a duly authenticated office copy of the Order may be registered.

s. 125

In practice, however, minor clerical errors are informally corrected on the register under the authority of a responsible officer following receipt by the company or its registrar of a duly completed form of request for rectification of transferee details following the registration of a transfer of shares.

Where there is a substantial difference between the registered details and the rectification request (e.g. a completely different name and address), great care must be taken and unless there has been a patent error, a court order should be obtained.

Checklist

▷ The Order should be checked to ensure that the holding referred to corresponds with a registered shareholding in the company. Identification will be facilitated by returning the relevant share certificate.

Procedure

▷ The amendments authorised in the Order should be made to the register of members, and the date of the Order and its registration should be entered as the authority for the amendment.

▷ The existing share certificate may be endorsed as appropriate, although it is preferable that a new share certificate be prepared.

▷ The company's registration stamp should be affixed to the Order, which should be returned to the sender together with the endorsed or replacement share certificate.

▷ If a dividend mandate is currently in force, it may be appropriate for this to be amended, cancelled or renewed.

Filing requirement

None.

Notes

None.

More information

▶ *Company Secretary's Handbook*, Chapter 18

Register of people with significant control

The register of people with significant control (the PSC Register) was introduced under SBEE2015 to provide greater transparency of ownership of UK companies. Up until its introduction, the majority of UK companies needed to disclose details only of the registered holder of their shares and not of beneficial ownership. The new sections in the Act are supported by the Register of People with Significant Control Regulations 2016 (SI 2016/339) (the PSC Regs).

ss.790A-790ZG

All companies other than those qualifying for exemption are required to keep a PSC Register. Listed companies are exempt from the PSC requirements since they are required under the Listing Rules to disclose all interests in their shares of 3% or more.

s.790B

As noted above, the purpose of the PSC Register is to increase transparency in ownership and accordingly the register is of natural persons. As a result, where the immediate ownership is through another corporate entity or a trust, companies are required to move up to the next layer of ownership until the ultimate owner(s) are identified.

Procedure

▶ If the company does not have a PSC or has been unable to obtain confirmed details of their PSCs, one of a number of permitted statements must be entered into the PSC Register and updated as required.

s.790E

▶ It may be perfectly obvious who the beneficial owner(s) is and no further steps are needed to identify them. For instance, for a private company with a sole shareholder and director, no investigation will be required. However, where the share structure is more complex or where there are trust or corporate members, it may be necessary for enquiries to be made of those members to establish beneficial ownership.

s.790D

▶ The PSC Register can never be blank and in circumstances where beneficial ownership has not yet been established, there are a number of permitted statements to describe the position, which will require updating as the enquiries continue.

s.790M

▷ These permitted statements are as follows:

Part 4 PSC
Regs 2016

  ▷ The company knows or has reasonable cause to believe that there is no registrable person or registrable relevant legal entity in relation to the company.

  ▷ The company knows or has reasonable cause to believe that there is a registrable person in relation to the company but it has not identified the registrable person.

  ▷ The company has identified a registrable person in relation to the company, but all of the required particulars of that person have not been confirmed.

  ▷ The company has not yet completed taking reasonable steps to find out if there is anyone who is a registrable person or a registrable relevant legal entity in relation to the company.

  ▷ The company has given a notice under section 790D of the Act which has not been complied with.

  ▷ The addressee has failed to comply with a notice given by the company under section 790E of the Act.

  ▷ The company has issued a restrictions notice under paragraph 1 of Schedule 1B to the Act.

▷ Although in general, it is details of individual ownership that must be recorded in the PSC Register, there are two other types of entity that are permitted. Accordingly there are three types of ownership structure whose details must be entered into a company's PSC Register. The categories are individual, registrable relevant legal entity (RLE) and other registrable person.

▷ The information to be registered about each category of ownership is as follows:

s. 790K(1)

  ▷ For an individual person:

    – the date the individual became a registrable person;

    – name;

    – country/state of residence;

    – nationality;

    – service address;

    – usual residential address (this is not shown on the public record);

    – date of birth (only the month and year are shown on the public record); and

    – the nature of their control over the company.

  ▷ For a registrable relevant legal entity (RLE) (such as a company):

    – the date that they became a registrable RLE;

- corporate name;
- address;
- legal form of the corporate body;
- governing law under which the RLE was registered;
- place of registration (if applicable);
- registration number (if applicable); and
- the nature of their control over the company.

▷ For another registrable person (such as a corporation sole or local authority):

- the date on which they became a registrable person in relation to the company in question;
- name;
- principal office;
- the legal form of the person;
- law by which they are governed; and
- the nature of their control over the company.

Checklist

▶ A PSC is anyone in the company who meets at least one of the four conditions set out in the Register of People with Significant Control Regulations 2016 (SI 339/2016). Some companies will have no PSCs while others may have several. The majority of companies will have one PSC, reflecting that the majority of companies have a sole shareholder.

▶ A PSC is a person who:

Sch. 2 PSC Regs

▷ holds, directly or indirectly, more than 25% of the shares;

▷ holds, directly or indirectly, more than 25% of the voting rights;

▷ holds the right, directly or indirectly, to appoint or remove a majority of directors;

▷ otherwise has the right to exercise, or actually exercises, significant influence or control over the company; and

▷ has the right to exercise, or actually exercises, significant influence or control over the activities of a trust or firm that is not a legal person, the trustees or members of which would satisfy any of the four conditions above.

▶ There are prescribed statements to be used to describe the nature of control in respect of each of the five conditions, and these are set out in Schedule 2 of the Register of People with Significant Control Regulations 2016.

▷ Once a PSC, RLE or other registrable person has been identified, in addition to updating their PSC Register, notice must be filed at Companies House.

Filing requirement

▷ Form EH04 if an election under s. 790X is made.

s. 790G

▷ Form PSC01, PSC02 or PSC03 to disclose identity of PSC, RLE or other registrable person, as relevant.

s. 790H

Notes

▷ Where a company issues a request to a member requesting details of beneficial ownership, the member has a duty to supply the requested information and to update the company in the event of any changes to that information.

More information

▷ *Company Secretary's Handbook*, Chapter 7

▷ Companies House Guidance – Company records, PSC requirements for companies and limited liability partnerships

Register of secretaries

All companies are required to maintain a register of secretaries and this must be available for inspection at the registered office or SAIL address.

s. 275(1)

Private companies may elect to keep their register of secretaries on the central register. When an election is in place, there is no requirement for access to be provided to the register of secretaries previously maintained by the company.

s. 279A

s. 1136

Checklist

▶ Is an election under s. 279A in force?

Procedure

▶ Where the company maintains its register of secretaries, the following information must be recorded:

▷ For a company secretary that is a natural person: his or her current and any former name(s) (within the previous 20 years) and service address.

s. 277

▷ For a corporate company secretary: corporate name, registered or principal office, in the case of an EAA registered company, details of the state and register in which the company is registered and its registered number, for a non-EAA company, details of the legal form of the company and law by which it is governed and, if applicable, details of the register in which the company is registered and its registered number.

s. 278

Filing requirement

▶ Form AD03 or AD04 as appropriate.

▶ Form EH03 if an election under s. 279A is made.

s. 276(3)

s. 276(4)

Notes

▶ If the company maintains its register of secretaries, this must be kept at either its registered office or its SAIL address.

▶ Unless the register of secretaries has always been kept at the company's registered office, details of its location must be notified to Companies House.

More information

▶ *Company Secretary's Handbook*, Chapters 1 and 7

▶ Companies House Guidance – Company registers

Registered office

All companies must have an address at which legal documents can be served. This is known as the registered office. On incorporation, the first registered office will be the address detailed on form IN01. Any change in registered office must be notified to Companies House on form AD01 to be effective. The registered office must be situated in the country of registration.

s. 86

s. 87

The registered office address must be shown on the company's business stationery, emails and its website(s) (see page 137).

s. 82
reg. 24 SI 2015/17

Checklist

▶ Is the proposed registered office address in the country of incorporation?

s. 9(2)(b)

▶ Is the proposed address a physical building? (PO Box addresses are not permitted.)

▶ Headed stationery must show the (new) registered office address within 14 days of any change.

s. 87(2)

▶ The company's name must be displayed at the registered office.

reg. 21 SI 2015/17

▶ Are the statutory registers kept at the registered office? If the registered office is changed, have the statutory registers been moved to the new location?

▶ If the registers are not/no longer kept at the registered office, notify Companies House (forms AD02, AD03).

Procedure

▶ Convene a directors' meeting to approve change in registered office address. Ensure valid quorum is present.

▶ File form AD01.

s. 87

Filing requirement

▶ Form AD01 within 14 days.

Notes

▷ Notify bankers, auditors, solicitors, HM Revenue & Customs (corporation tax, PAYE, share schemes, VAT) and other interested persons.

▷ The change does not become effective until the form is received and accepted as valid by the Registrar of Companies.

s.87(2)

▷ Documents delivered to the old address within 14 days of the date of change are validly served on the company.

s.87(3)

▷ The company's headed stationery must show the new registered office address not later than 14 days after the date that the notice was accepted by the Registrar of Companies.

s.87(3)

More information

▷ *Company Secretary's Handbook*, Chapter 7

▷ Companies House Guidance booklet GP3

Registered office – objection to use of address

The Small Business, Enterprise and Employment Act 2015 introduced a new procedure under which an objection may be made to the use by a company of an address as its registered office without consent. This situation can often occur where a company uses the address of one of its professional advisers or a service agent but does not then change the address when the company no longer uses that firm's services.

s. 1097A

If the objection is upheld, the Registrar has power to change the company's registered address to the Companies House office in the jurisdiction of the company, the 'default address'.

s. 1097A(2)(h)

Checklist

▷ Application will normally be made by or on behalf of the person whose address is being misused but may be made by any person.

Procedure

▷ The applicant or someone on their behalf must complete and file form RP07 setting out their name and address, identity of the company concerned, the address being used as the registered office and the grounds for the application.

▷ On receipt of the application the Registrar will consider the merits of the application. If there is little or no chance of success the application will be dismissed. Alternatively, the Registrar may decide, or have already started the process, to strike off the company, in which case the application is superfluous and will be dismissed.

▷ If the Registrar accepts the application they will send a notice to all directors and company secretary, if any, at their service and residential addresses and to the company at its registered office giving notice of the objection and that the registered office address will be changed unless, within 28 days, the company voluntarily changes it, an objection is received or the applicant withdraws the application.

▷ Provided no objection is received the Registrar will change the registered office to the default address and notify the company and the applicant.

▶ To object, the company need only provide evidence of proprietary rights in the address, written agreement entitling the company to use the address or a utility bill addressed to the company at that address within the previous six months.

Filing requirement

▶ Form RP07.

Notes

▶ If the default address is imposed on the company, documents may be validly served on the company at that address, but there is no obligation on the Registrar to open any mail received by them.

▶ Officers of the company may make application to the Registrar to collect any mail received.

More information

▶ *Company Secretary's Handbook*, Chapter 1

▶ Companies House Guidance – Registrar's rules and powers

Registration of charges

Particulars of every charge to which the Companies Act 2006 applies, created by a company registered in England and Wales, Scotland or Northern Ireland, should, within 21 days of its creation, be delivered for registration to Companies House together with a certified copy of any instrument creating or evidencing the charge.

s.859A

It is the duty of the company that creates a charge, or acquires property that is subject to a charge, to deliver to the Registrar the prescribed particulars of the charge within 21 days of the charge's creation, or the acquisition, as the case may be, using form MR01. A filing fee (currently £15 (online) or £23 (paper)) is payable. Although the obligation of registration is placed on the company, any interested party may effect this and it is, in practice, usual for the chargee, debenture holder or trustees to deal with the registration to ensure that their position is fully protected.

s.859A(4)

On receipt, the Registrar of Companies will enter details of the charge in the register kept for each company for the purpose and will also issue a certificate of registration, which states the amount thereby secured and is conclusive evidence that the registration requirements have been complied with. A copy of the certificate of registration must be endorsed by the company on every debenture or certificate of debenture stock secured by the registered charge.

s.859I

Checklist

▷ Charge must be registered within 21 days of creation by the company or the person to whom the charge is entrusted.

s.859A(4)

▷ Check articles of association to ensure the company's capacity to create a charge on its assets is not restricted in any way. Many listed companies will have the borrowing powers restricted to a multiple of their balance sheet value.

Procedure

▷ Convene a directors' meeting to approve the creation of a charge over some or all of the company's assets. Ensure valid quorum is present.

▷ Certified copies of the security document must be delivered to Companies House for registration within 21 days of the date of creation of the security. The security document must be accompanied by 'the prescribed particulars of the charge', set out on form MR01 for most forms of charge, form MR03 for a series of debentures and form MR02 where property is acquired subject to an existing mortgage or charge. **s.859D**

▷ If the security relates to real property, the security document or particulars of the security should also be sent to the Land Registry or the appropriate charge registered at the Land Charges Registry.

▷ A copy of every instrument creating a charge requiring registration must be kept at the registered office or a specified place of inspection. **ss.859P and Q**

Filing requirement

▷ Certified copy security document within 21 days.

▷ Form MR01, MR02, MR03, MR06, MR07, MR08, MR09 or MR10 as appropriate within 21 days.

▷ Filing fee £15 (online) or £23 (paper).

Notes

▷ If a charge is not properly registered with the Registrar of Companies, any security on the company's property or undertaking conferred by the charge is void against the liquidator or administrator and any creditor of the company, but not the company itself. **s.859H**

▷ The court has power under the Companies Act 2006, on the application of a company or any interested person, to extend the time for registration of the charge or to rectify an omission or misstatement of any particular relating to a charge. **s.859F**

More information

▷ *Company Secretary's Handbook*, Chapter 20

▷ Companies House Guidance booklet GP3

Re-registration – limited company as unlimited

Provided that all members consent, a private limited company may be re-registered as an unlimited company.

s.102

In practice this is seldom done; however, companies may choose to do so to keep their financial affairs secret, as unlimited companies do not need to file their accounts. Additionally, prior to dissolution, conversion to unlimited status can facilitate the return of funds to shareholders that may not be possible as a limited company, due to the constraints on distribution of profit and return of capital.

Checklist

▷ If the company has previously re-registered from unlimited to limited, this cannot be reversed.

s.102(2)

▷ Will all members consent to the change?

s.102(1)(a)

▷ Change company's stationery to reflect new status (see page 137).

Procedure

▷ Convene a directors' meeting to recommend appropriate resolutions to members and to convene a general meeting or circulate a written resolution. Additionally, resolutions to make certain amendments to the articles will be required to reflect the company's new status. Ensure valid quorum is present.

s.302

▷ Where a general meeting is to be held, issue notice, signed by director or company secretary, on 14 clear days' notice for members to consider resolutions.

s.307(1)

▷ Enclose with the notice a form of proxy if desired.

▷ If the meeting is to be convened on short notice, the company secretary should arrange for agreement to short notice to be signed by each of the members.

s.307(5)

▷ Hold general meeting. Ensure valid quorum is present. Resolution put to vote either by show of hands or by poll and to be passed by unanimous consent of all members.

s.102(1)(a)

▷ Where a written resolution is circulated the requisite majority must be obtained within 28 days of the circulation date of the proposed resolution(s).

▷ Application is then made to the Registrar of Companies on form RR05 within 15 days, together with a copy of the resolution detailing the alterations to the articles of association appropriate for an unlimited company and an amended copy of the articles, together with a fee (currently £20, or £50 same-day). **ss. 26, 103**

▷ Each member of the company must confirm in writing on form RR05 that they wish the company to be re-registered as an unlimited company, together with a statement of compliance by the directors that every member has agreed to the re-registration, either personally or by their duly authorised agent. **s. 103(4)**

▷ If the application is accepted, the Registrar issues a new certificate of incorporation stating the company's unlimited status, whereupon the alterations to the articles of association set out in the application take effect. There is no need for the members to pass a special resolution approving these amendments. **s. 104**

Filing requirement

▷ Form RR05.

▷ Filing fee £20 (same-day fee £50).

▷ Copy of resolution. **s. 103**

▷ Amended copy of memorandum and articles of association. **s. 26**

Notes

▷ Unlimited companies do not normally need to file a copy of their accounts with the Registrar of Companies.

▷ Once the Registrar has issued the certificate of re-registration, it will be necessary to obtain new headed stationery, and a new company seal where the company has a seal.

▷ Arrange for the name of the company's bank accounts to be changed.

▷ Notify the company's suppliers and customers of the change of name, HM Revenue & Customs for corporation tax, PAYE and VAT, pension scheme, title deeds, trademark registrations, data protection registration, insurers, etc. Signs at the company's premises and/or on the company's cars, vans and lorries will also require amendment.

More information

▷ *Company Secretary's Handbook*, Chapter 2

▷ Companies House Guidance booklet GP3

Re-registration – private company as public

Provided that a private limited company can satisfy five conditions it can, by special resolution of the members, re-register as a public limited company.

ss. 90-96

Shares recently issued for a non-cash consideration may need to have the consideration valued.

s. 93

Checklist

▶ Does the company have share capital?

s. 90(2)(a)

▶ The issued share capital of the company must have a nominal value of at least £50,000 or the prescribed euro equivalent, and each share must be paid up to at least 25% of its nominal value together with all of any premium.

ss. 90(2)(b), 91, 763, reg. 2, SI 2008/729

▶ The application for re-registration must be received by the Registrar of Companies within seven months of its year-end and a copy of an audited balance sheet must be filed on or before the date of application for re-registration. Normally the balance sheet is taken from the latest audited accounts; however, a balance sheet may be submitted made up to an appropriate date not more than seven months prior to the application.

ss. 90(2)(c), 92

▶ The company's auditors must give a statement to the effect that the net assets of the company are not less than its called-up share capital and undistributable reserves and, where the audit report to the audited accounts is qualified, that the subject of their qualification is not material for determining that the assets are greater than the called-up share capital and undistributable reserves.

s. 92

▶ If shares have been issued otherwise than for cash during the period between the balance sheet date and the date of application for re-registration, the provisions of s. 593 must be complied with. These require an independent valuer to value the consideration received by the company. These provisions do not apply to a share exchange or proposed merger with another company.

s. 90(2)(d)

s. 593

s. 93(2)(b)

▷ The company must not previously have been re-registered as an unlimited company.   **s.90(2)(e)**

▷ If the company does not have one, a company secretary must be appointed.   **s.271**

Procedure

▷ Convene a directors' meeting to recommend an appropriate special resolution to members and to convene a general meeting or circulate a written resolution. Additionally, resolutions to make certain amendments to the articles will be required to reflect the company's new status. Ensure valid quorum is present.   **s.302**

▷ Issue notice, signed by director or company secretary, on 21 clear days' notice for members to consider resolution.   **s.307(1)**

▷ Enclose with the notice a form of proxy if desired.

▷ If the meeting is to be convened on short notice, the company secretary should arrange for agreement to short notice to be signed by each of the shareholders.   **s.307(5)**

▷ Hold general meeting. Ensure valid quorum is present. Resolution put to vote either by show of hands or by poll and to be passed by appropriate majority (special resolution by 75% majority).

▷ Where a written resolution is circulated the requisite majority must be obtained within 28 days of the circulation date of the proposed resolution(s).   **s.30**

▷ File all necessary documents, as set out below, with Companies House within 15 days of passing the resolutions.   **s.96**

▷ If the application is accepted, the Registrar issues a new certificate of incorporation stating the company's PLC status, whereupon the alterations to the memorandum and articles of association set out in the application take effect. There is no need for the members to pass a special resolution approving these amendments.

Filing requirement

▷ Form RR01.

▷ A copy of the relevant balance sheet.

▷ A copy of the audit report.

▷ A copy of the auditors' statement.

▷ A copy of the amended articles of association.

▷ A copy of the special resolutions.

▷ Re-registration fee (currently £20; same-day fee £50).

Notes

▶ A company that has been re-registered as unlimited cannot subsequently be re-registered as a public company.

s.90(2)(e)

▶ If the company has insufficient share capital, additional shares must be issued. This is often achieved by a bonus issue, as a company seeking re-registration will normally have adequate reserves.

s.763

▶ There is no obligation for a public company's shares to be quoted. Many private companies re-register for the marketing advantages of being a PLC.

▶ The regulations governing PLCs, the actions of their directors and the preparation of accounts are more onerous than for private companies.

▶ Once the Registrar has issued the certificate of re-registration, it will be necessary to obtain new headed stationery, and a new company seal where the company has a seal.

▶ Arrange for the name of the company's bank accounts to be changed.

▶ Notify the company's suppliers and customers of the change of name: HM Revenue & Customs for corporation tax, PAYE and VAT, pension scheme, title deeds, trademark registrations, data protection registration, insurers, etc. Signs at the company's premises and/or on the company's cars, vans and lorries will also require amendment.

More information

▶ *Company Secretary's Handbook*, Chapter 2

Re-registration – public company as private

This procedure is becoming more common as more stringent and restrictive provisions for public companies, in particular accounting provisions, continue to increase their scope and effect.

There are no particular qualifying criteria and all public companies, subject to any other regulatory requirements such as FCA, UKLA, etc, could be re-registered as private companies. **s.97**

A public company can be registered as a private company limited by shares or guarantee, or as a private unlimited company. **s.89(b),(e)**

Procedure – change to private limited

▶ Convene a directors' meeting to recommend appropriate special resolution to members and to convene a general meeting. Additionally, resolutions to make certain amendments to the articles will be required to reflect the company's new status. Ensure valid quorum is present. **ss.97,302**

▶ Issue notice, signed by director or company secretary, on 14 clear days' notice for members to consider resolution, or 21 days' notice if the resolution(s) are to be put at an annual general meeting. **s.307(1)**

▶ Enclose with the notice a form of proxy if desired.

▶ If the meeting is to be convened on short notice, the company secretary should arrange for agreement to short notice to be signed by each of the shareholders. **s.307(5**

▶ Hold general meeting. Ensure valid quorum is present. Resolution put to vote either by show of hands or by poll and to be passed by appropriate majority (special resolution by 75% majority).

▶ File all necessary documents with Companies House within 15 days of passing the resolutions. **s.30**

▶ Within 28 days of the passing of the resolution, an application may be made to the court for the cancellation of the resolution. This application may be made only by a holder or holders of at least 5% of the issued share capital of the company (or of any class of shares) **s.98** or by not fewer than 50 of the company's members. If such an application is made, the court may confirm or cancel the resolution, or impose certain conditions on its approval. The company must file a copy of any order made by the court with the Registrar within 15 days of the making of the order or within such period as may be determined by the court.

▷ If no application is made to the court within 28 days of the passing of the resolution, an application for re-registration as a private company should be submitted to the Registrar on form RR02, signed by a director or secretary, together with a copy of the amended articles of association. If all shareholders voted in favour of the resolution, form RR02 may be filed immediately.

s.97(1)(c),(2)

▷ If accepted, the Registrar issues a new certificate of incorporation stating the company's limited status, whereupon the alterations to the memorandum and articles of association set out in the application take effect. There is no need for the members to pass a special resolution approving these amendments.

s.101

Procedure – change to private unlimited

The procedure for a re-registration as a private unlimited company are the same as for re-registering as a private limited company, except as follows:

▷ The resolution to re-register requires consent of all members entitled to vote.

s.109(1)(a)

▷ The company must not previously have been re-registered as a private limited or unlimited company.

s.109(2)

▷ The application form is form RR07.

s.110

Filing requirement

▷ Copy of special resolution.

▷ Form RR02 or RR07.

▷ Copy of amended articles of association.

▷ Statement of compliance.

▷ Copy of the court order, if appropriate.

▷ Re-registration fee (currently £20; same-day fee £50).

Notes

▷ Once the Registrar has issued the certificate of re-registration, it will be necessary to obtain new headed stationery and a new company seal, where the company has a seal.

▷ Arrange for the name of the company's bank accounts to be changed.

▷ Notify the company's suppliers and customers of the change of name: HM Revenue & Customs for corporation tax, PAYE and VAT, pension scheme, title deeds, trademark registrations, data protection registration, insurers, etc. Signs at the company's premises and/or on the company's cars, vans and lorries will also require amendment.

▷ In addition to the voluntary re-registration as a private company, a public company may be *required* to re-register by the court where its issued share capital is below the authorised minimum. This would normally only occur on a reduction of capital or redemption of redeemable shares. In such an event, the court may authorise the re-registration to be effective without a special resolution being passed and may specify in the order the amendments to be made to the memorandum and articles of association.

s.650

More information

▷ *Company Secretary's Handbook,* Chapter 2

▷ Companies House Guidance booklet GP3

Resolutions – filing requirements

A copy of the following resolutions must be filed with the Registrar of Companies within 15 days of approval.

s.30

Checklist

▶ Special resolutions:

▷ Resolutions or agreements that have been agreed to by all the members of a company, but that, if not so agreed to, would not have been effective for their purpose unless (as the case may be) they had been passed as special resolutions. Resolutions or agreements that have been agreed to by all the members of some class of shareholders but that, if not so agreed to, would not have been effective for their purpose unless they had been passed by some particular majority or otherwise in some particular manner, and all resolutions or agreements that effectively bind all the members of any class of shareholders, though not agreed to by all those members.

s.29

▷ A resolution passed by the directors of a company in compliance with a direction to change name by Secretary of State.

s.67

▷ A resolution of a company to give, vary, revoke or renew an authority to the directors for allotment of relevant securities.

ss.550,551

▷ A resolution conferring, varying, revoking or renewing authority for market purchase of company's own shares.

s.701

▷ A resolution for voluntary winding up.

s.84 IA1986

▷ A directors' resolution to amend the Articles of Association of the company to allow title to securities to be transferred through CREST.

▷ Forms IC01 or IC02: notification of intention to carry on business or cease to carry on business as an investment company.

Procedure

None.

Notes

Failure to file copies of resolutions can lead to prosecution of the company and any officers in default and they are liable to a fine if convicted.

s.30(2)

More information

▶ *Company Secretary's Handbook*, Chapter 7

▶ Companies House Guidance booklet GP3

Resolutions – majority

The majorities required to pass resolutions are as follows:

Checklist

▶ Ordinary resolutions: simple majority.   **s. 282**

▶ Special resolutions: 75% majority.   **s. 283**

Procedure

None.

Filing requirement

None.

Notes

▶ The majority for type of resolution is of those members entitled to
attend and vote and who are present and voting at a general meeting
in person or by proxy.

▶ At a meeting on a show of hands, each member or their proxy has one   **ss. 282(3), 283(4)**
vote.

▶ On a poll vote, each member or their proxy has one vote per share.   **ss. 282(4), 283(5)**

▶ For a written resolution of a private company, the majority is   **ss. 282(2), 283(2)**
calculated by reference to each member's total voting rights.

▶ Many forms of proxy now include the option to instruct the proxy to
abstain. It should be noted however that an abstention is not a vote in
law and does not count as a vote cast.

More information

▶ *Company Secretary's Handbook*, Chapter 7

▶ FCA Listing Rules

Resolutions – written: private companies

A private company may, by written resolution of members, pass resolutions that would otherwise require a general meeting to be held.

ss. 282, 283, 288

Checklist

▷ Is the company a private company?

▷ Are sufficient members available to sign the written resolution?

Procedure

▷ Written resolutions must be approved with members representing sufficient voting rights to meet the simple or 75% majority required for ordinary and special resolutions, respectively.

ss. 282(2), 283(2)

▷ The signatures need not all appear on the same document, provided that all the signed documents are in the same form; the resolution is effective and dated when signed by or on behalf of the last member to sign.

▷ If the appropriate majority has not been reached within 28 days of the date of circulation, the resolution lapses.

s. 297

▷ The original signed copies of a written resolution should be inserted in the company's minute book in the normal manner.

▷ As the majority of resolutions for a private company may now be passed by written resolution, certain changes have been necessitated to the circulation of documentation to shareholders. Accordingly, documents that are required to be circulated to shareholders with a notice of a general meeting or that are to be made available at the company's registered office for inspection prior to the meeting must, where a written resolution is to be used, be circulated to each member before or at the same time as the resolution is supplied for signature. Such documents include:

   ▷ a written statement to be given by directors pursuant to a special resolution, waiving the rights of pre-emption on the allotment of shares;

s. 571(6)

▷ a copy of the purchase contract, or written memorandum of its terms relating to the off-market purchase or contingent purchase by a company of its own shares;

s.701

▷ a declaration of compliance and the auditors' report relating to the purchase by a company of its own shares out of capital;

s.718

▷ a solvency statement by directors in support of a non-court reduction of capital;

s.641

▷ a written memorandum setting out the terms of a proposed director's service contract for a term of more than two years; and

s.188(5)

▷ disclosure of matters relating to the approval of a director's expenditure to enable him or her to perform their duties properly.

s.203(3)

Filing requirement

▶ Copy of resolution signed by all shareholders within 15 days.

s.30

Notes

▶ There are two resolutions that cannot be passed by a written resolution under any circumstances:

▷ the removal of a director before the expiration of their period of office; and

▷ the removal of an auditor before the expiration of his or her period of office.

▶ Where any particular member is interested in the matter to be approved by written resolution and would not be eligible to vote at a general meeting, he or she is similarly barred from voting by written resolution on the same matter.

More information

▶ *Company Secretary's Handbook*, Chapter 7

Restoration – administrative

Where a company has been struck off the Register and dissolved using the procedures set out in ss. 1000 or 1001, the former directors or former members may apply to the Registrar to have the company restored to the Register. Such application must be made within six years of the date of dissolution of the company.

s. 1024(1),(2)

s. 1024(4)

It should be noted that where a company has been wound up and dissolved, any application for restoration must made to the court (see page 259).

s. 1029

Prior to restoration, it will be necessary to bring the company's statutory records up to date. This will normally involve the completion of all outstanding confirmation statements and the preparation of accounts as well as any changes in shareholdings, officers or other statutory details of the company to be filed and obtaining the consent of the relevant Crown Representative if any property has vested *bona vacantia*.

s. 1025

Checklist

▷ If dissolved under ss. 1000 or 1001, restoration application must be within six years.

s. 1024(4)

▷ The company must have been carrying on business or have been in operation at the time of dissolution.

s. 1025(2)

▷ The Crown Representative, usually the Treasury Solicitor, must consent in writing to the restoration where any property has vested *bona vacantia*.

s. 1025(3)

▷ All documents required to bring the company's record at Companies House up to date must be delivered to the Registrar together with payment of any filing penalties outstanding at the date of dissolution.

s. 1025(5)

Procedure

▷ Ensure conditions of s. 1025 have been met and all appropriate documents lodged with the Registrar.

s. 1026(1)

▷ File form RT01 together with a statement of compliance that the requirements for administrative restoration are met.

s. 1026(2)

▷ If the Registrar decides that the application is successful, written confirmation is issued to the applicant and the company's name is restored to the Register of companies together with publication of that fact in the *Gazette*.

s.1027

Filing requirement

▷ All necessary forms, confirmation statements and accounts to bring the company's records up to date.

▷ Late filing penalties as appropriate.

▷ Restoration fee, currently £100.

Notes

▷ In addition to the restoration fee payable to the Registrar of Companies, the company will also be required to pay the costs of the Crown Representative, if any, and the penalties for late submission of accounts, as appropriate. Where late filing penalties were levied in respect of accounts required to be filed prior to dissolution, these are at the minimum statutory penalty rate.

▷ In practice, restoration is often required where a company has been dissolved by the Registrar (for failure to file returns and/or accounts) or at the request of the directors/shareholders and it is subsequently found that the company has valuable assets. In these circumstances, it is necessary for the company to be restored to the Register for the assets to be reclaimed, as the assets of a dissolved company automatically attach to the Crown. It is becoming increasingly common for a company with assets to be dissolved as a result of oversight on the part of directors: either neglect in filing statutory documents, or requesting the Registrar to strike off the company without properly checking that the company has no assets. For example, particular care should be taken when requesting the dissolution of a subsidiary that the legal ownership of property has passed to its holding company or fellow subsidiary. It is not uncommon for the appropriate book entries to be made, for example, transferring the lease of a property to another group company without ensuring that the legal transfer of title is also effected.

More information

▷ *Company Secretary's Handbook*, Chapter 22

▷ Companies House Guidance – Strike off, dissolution and restoration

Restoration – by court order

Application to the court may be made to restore a company dissolved:

▷ under the Insolvency Acts;   **s. 1029(1)**

▷ at the conclusion of an administration; or

▷ either by the registrar under ss. 1000 or 1001, or under the voluntary
  dissolution procedures under s. 1003.   **s. 1024(4)**

Application is made to the High Court, usually the Registrar of Companies
Court in London. Cases can also be heard in District Registries or County
Courts that have authority to wind up a company. For companies
incorporated in Scotland, application is made to the Court of Session or,
where the issued capital does not exceed £120,000, to the Sheriff Court
in the Sheriffdom where the registered office was located. Companies
incorporated in Northern Ireland should apply to the Royal Court of
Justice in Belfast.

Application may be made by any person having an interest in the   **s. 1029(2)**
company including the Secretary of State, former directors or members,
any creditor, former liquidator, persons with contractual arrangements
with the company, managers or trustees of pension funds, etc.

Prior to restoration, it will be necessary to bring the company's statutory
records up to date. This will normally involve the completion of all
outstanding confirmation statements and the preparation of audited
accounts as well as any changes in shareholdings, officers or other
statutory details of the company to be filed.

Checklist

▷ Restoration to pursue personal injury claims may be made at any time.   **s. 1030(1)**

▷ Except as noted below, in all other cases application must be made   **s. 1030(4)**
  within six years of the date of dissolution of the company.

▷ The exception is where a company was dissolved under ss. 1000 or
  1001 and an application for administrative restoration under s. 1024
  has been rejected. In such circumstances, an application to court must   **s. 1030(5)**
  be made within 28 days of the notice of the decision by the Registrar
  to reject the application under s. 1024.

Procedure

▶ The restoration process requires an application to the court and accordingly the services of a solicitor are required. In the circumstances, the procedure is not detailed here.

Filing requirement

▶ All necessary forms, confirmation statements and accounts to bring the company's records up to date.

▶ Late filing penalties as appropriate.

Notes

▶ In addition to the restoration fee payable to the Registrar of Companies (currently £100), the company will also be required to pay the legal costs of the Registrar (currently between £250 and £300) and the penalties for late submission of accounts, as appropriate. Where late filing penalties are levied in respect of accounts required to be filed prior to restoration, these are at the minimum statutory penalty rate.

▶ In practice, restoration is often required where a company has been dissolved by the Registrar (for failure to file returns and/or accounts) or at the request of the directors/shareholders and it is subsequently found that the company has valuable assets. In these circumstances, it is necessary for the company to be restored to the Register for the assets to be reclaimed, as the assets of a dissolved company automatically attach to the Crown. It is becoming increasingly common for a company with assets to be dissolved as a result of oversight on the part of directors: either neglect in filing statutory documents, or requesting the Registrar to strike off the company without properly checking that the company has no assets. For example, particular care should be taken when requesting the dissolution of a subsidiary that the legal ownership of property has passed to its holding company or fellow subsidiary. It is not uncommon for the appropriate book entries to be made, for example, transferring the lease of a property to another group company without ensuring that the legal transfer of title is also effected.

▶ Occasionally, a company that has been dissolved will be found to have a large outstanding creditor. In such circumstances, the creditor may apply to the court to have the company restored to the Register at the company's cost, to enable the claim to be pursued.

More information

▶ *Company Secretary's Handbook*, Chapter 22

▶ Companies House Guidance – Strike off, dissolution and restoration

Rights issue

A rights issue is an issue of shares to the existing shareholders *pro rata* to their existing holdings.

Rights issues are used by companies to obtain additional funding from the company's shareholders rather than obtaining working capital by borrowing from banks or other financial institutions.

Checklist

▶ Check the articles to ensure there is no restriction on the maximum number of shares that may be issued. If not, it will be necessary to increase or remove that restriction (see page 37).

▶ Check the articles of association to ensure the directors have authority in terms of ss. 550 or 551 to issue shares. If not, a resolution to renew the authority will be required (see page 37).

▶ If the company has overseas shareholders, it may be necessary to exclude them from the rights issue due to securities legislation in their country, in which case the company must have sufficient waiver of pre-emption rights in terms of ss. 567–571.

▶ If the rights issue is to be made by way of renounceable letters of allotment, the articles of association must be checked to ensure that no pre-emption rights on allotment are infringed.

Procedure

▶ Convene a directors' meeting to approve resolutions declaring the rights issue and resolve to issue the provisional allotment letters to the company's shareholders. Ensure valid quorum is present.

▶ If it is intended that the existing members may renounce their entitlement to third parties, these letters include letters of renunciation.

▶ Once the closing date for the acceptance of the allotment letters has been reached, the directors will meet to allot those shares taken up.

▶ The company secretary should ensure that appropriate share certificates are prepared and issued to the shareholders and that form SH01 is filed with the Registrar of Companies within 15 days. **s.555**

▶ The company secretary should ensure that the register of members is written up to reflect the issue of shares.

Filing requirement

▶ Form SH01.

▶ Copies of any ordinary and special resolutions, as necessary. **s.30**

More information

▶ *Company Secretary's Handbook*, Chapter 13

Sensitive words

Certain words and phrases ('sensitive' words) require the consent of the Secretary of State for the Department for Business, Energy and Industrial Strategy before their use is allowed in a company name. Alternatively, the Secretary of State may require that appropriate authority be obtained from a relevant body.

ss. 54-56

The sensitive words that require the consent of the Secretary of State for Business, Energy and Industrial Strategy are:

SI 2014/3140

▷ words that imply pre-eminence or a particular status or function;

▷ words that imply a connection with the UK Government, a devolved administration, local authority or specified public authorities;

▷ words that represent regulated activities; and

▷ words whose use could be an offence.

For a company to use one or more of these sensitive words in its name, the use must be justified.

The Registrar of Companies has issued guidelines giving details of the criteria to be used, and these are set out below. It should be noted, however, that these are not definitive criteria and in every case the decision on whether or not to allow a particular name to be used will rest with the Secretary of State for the Department for Business, Energy and Industrial Strategy.

Checklist

Guidance GP1

▷ **Words and expressions specified for the purposes of sections 55(1) and 1194(1) of the 2006 Act:** Accredit, Accreditation, Accredited, Accrediting, Adjudicator, Association, Assurance, Assurer, Audit office, Auditor General, *Banc, Bank, Banking, Benevolent, *Breatainn, *Breatannach, *Brenhiniaeth, *Brenhinol, *Brenin, Britain, British, Chamber of commerce, Charitable, Charity, Charter, Chartered, Child maintenance, Child support, *Coimisean, *Comhairle, *Comisiwn, Commission, Co-operative, Council, *Cyngor, Dental, Dentistry, *Diùc, *Dug, Duke, Ei Fawrhydi, England, English, Federation, Foundation, Friendly Society, Fund, Government, *Gwasanaeth iechyd, Health centre, Health service, Health visitor, His Majesty, HPSS, HSC, Inspectorate, Institute, Institution, Insurance,

Insurer, Judicial appointment, King, Licensing, *Llywodraeth, Medical centre, Midwife, Midwifery, *Mòrachd, Mutual, NHS, Northern Ireland, Northern Irish, Nurse, Nursing, Oifis sgrùdaidh, *Oilthigh, Ombudsman, *Ombwdsmon, *Parlamaid, Parliament, Parliamentarian, Parliamentary, Patent, Patentee, Police, Polytechnic, Post office, *Prifysgol, Prince, *Prionnsa, *Prydain, *Prydeinig, Queen, Reassurance, Reassurer, Registrar, Regulator, Reinsurance, Reinsurer, *Riaghaltas, *Rìgh, Rìoghachd Aonaichte, Rìoghail, Rìoghalachd, Royal, Royalty, Scotland, Scottish, Senedd, Sheffield, Siambr fasnach, Social service, Society, Special school, Standards, Stock exchange, Swyddfa archwilio, *Teyrnas Gyfunol, *Teyrnas Unedig, Trade union, Tribunal, Trust, *Tywysog, Underwrite, Underwriting, University, Wales, Welsh, Windsor.

* in the case of the words and expressions which are marked with an asterisk, the grammatically mutated forms of those words and expressions

▶ **Words and expressions specified for the purposes of section 55(1) of the 2006 Act:** Alba, Albannach, *Cymraeg, *Cymreig, *Cymru, Na h-Alba.

* in the case of the words and expressions which are marked with an asterisk, the grammatically mutated forms of those words and expressions

▶ **List of government departments and other bodies whose views must be sought**

Part 1: Applications where situation of registered office or principal place of business is irrelevant

Word or expression specified under regulation 3	*Specified government department or other body whose view must be sought*
Accredit	Department for Business, Energy and Industrial Strategy
Accreditation	Department for Business, Energy and Industrial Strategy
Accredited	Department for Business, Energy and Industrial Strategy
Accrediting	Department for Business, Energy and Industrial Strategy
Assurance	Financial Conduct Authority
Assurer	Financial Conduct Authority
Banc	Financial Conduct Authority
Bank	Financial Conduct Authority
Banking	Financial Conduct Authority
Brenhiniaeth	The Welsh Assembly Government
Brenhinol	The Welsh Assembly Government
Brenin	The Welsh Assembly Government
Child maintenance	Department for Work and Pensions
Child support	Department for Work and Pensions
Dental	General Dental Council
Dentistry	General Dental Council
Diùc	The Scottish Government
Dug	The Welsh Assembly Government
Ei Fawrhydi	The Welsh Assembly Government
Friendly Society	Financial Conduct Authority
Fund	Financial Conduct Authority

Gwasanaeth iechyd	The Welsh Assembly Government
Health visitor	Nursing & Midwifery Council
HPSS	Department of Health, Social Services and Public Safety
HSC	Department of Health, Social Services and Public Safety
Word or expression specified under regulation 3	*Specified government department or other body whose view must be sought*
Insurance	Financial Conduct Authority
Insurer	Financial Conduct Authority
Judicial appointment	Ministry of Justice
Llywodraeth	The Welsh Assembly Government
Medical centre	Department of Health, Social Services and Public Safety
Midwife	Nursing & Midwifery Council
Midwifery	Nursing & Midwifery Council
Mòrachd	The Scottish Government
Mutual	Financial Conduct Authority
NHS	Department of Health
Nurse	Nursing & Midwifery Council
Nursing	Nursing & Midwifery Council
Oifis sgrùdaidh	Audit Scotland
Oilthigh	The Scottish Government
Parlamaid	The Scottish Parliamentary Corporate Body
Parliament	The Corporate Officer of the House of Lords and the Corporate Officer of the House of Commons
Parliamentarian	The Corporate Officer of the House of Lords and the Corporate Officer of the House of Commons
Parliamentary	The Corporate Officer of the House of Lords and the Corporate Officer of the House of Commons
Patent	The Patent Office
Patentee	The Patent Office
Polytechnic	Department for Business, Energy and Industrial Strategy
Prifysgol	The Welsh Assembly Government
Prionnsa	The Scottish Government
Reassurance	Financial Conduct Authority
Reassurer	Financial Conduct Authority
Reinsurance	Financial Conduct Authority
Reinsurer	Financial Conduct Authority
Riaghaltas	The Scottish Government
Rìgh	The Scottish Government
Rìoghail	The Scottish Government
Rìoghalachd	The Scottish Government
Senedd	The National Assembly for Wales
Sheffield	The Company of Cutlers in Hallamshire
Swyddfa archwilio	Auditor General for Wales
Tywysog	The Welsh Assembly Government
Underwrite	Financial Conduct Authority
Underwriting	Financial Conduct Authority

▶ **Applications where situation of registered office or principal place of business is relevant**

Word or expression specified under regulation 3 *Specified government department or other body whose view must be sought under regulation*

	6(a)	6(b)	6(c)	6(d)
Audit office	Comptroller & Auditor General	Auditor General for Wales	Audit Scotland	Audit Office Northern Ireland
Charitable Charity	The Charity Commission	The Charity Commission	Office of the Scottish Charity Regulator	The Charity Commission
Duke His Majesty King Prince Queen Royal Royalty	Ministry of Justice	The Welsh Assembly Government	The Scottish Government	Ministry of Justice
Health centre Health service	Department of Health	The Welsh Assembly Government	The Scottish Government	Department of Health, Social Services and Public Safety
Police	The Home Office	The Home Office	The Scottish Government	Department of Justice in Northern Ireland
Special school	Department for Education	The Welsh Assembly Government	The Scottish Government	Department for Education
University	Department for Business, Innovation and Skills	The Welsh Assembly Government	The Scottish Government	Department for Employment and Learning

Procedure

▶ Where any word or phrase requires the consent of the Secretary of State or from a relevant body, advice should be sought from Companies House as to the form of the authority required. Companies House guidance 'Incorporation and names' sets out details of the relevant body that must provide approval and an overview of the circumstances in which approval will be given.

Filing requirement

None.

Notes

None.

More information

▶ *Company Secretary's Handbook*, Chapter 4, Appendix

▶ Companies House Guidance – Incorporation and names

Share certificate – duplicates

Share certificates are evidence of title and so care must be taken when issuing duplicate certificates.

Checklist

▶ Check that there is no difference between the identity of the registered shareholder and the person requesting the duplicate.

Procedure

In the event of a shareholder losing his or her share certificate, the following procedure should be carried out.

▶ The shareholder should be sent a form of indemnity in respect of the issue of a duplicate certificate. This is to protect the company should the original share certificate fall into the wrong hands and an attempt be made to transfer the shares fraudulently.

▶ The form of indemnity should be signed by the shareholder and, for most quoted public limited companies, it will be necessary for the indemnity to be guaranteed by a bank or insurance company.

▶ On receipt by the company of a completed indemnity form, a duplicate share certificate should be prepared and issued to the shareholder.

▶ If the original share certificate is found, it should be returned to the company and cancelled.

Filing requirement

None.

Notes

None.

More information

▶ *Company Secretary's Handbook*, Chapter 18

Shareholders – probate

Where a shareholder dies, the shares form part of their estate; their executors can give valid instructions in respect of those shares. In circumstances where the deceased shareholder left a will, the executors will apply for a grant of probate which gives them the authority to deal with the deceased's affairs. A company should accept for registration any grant of probate for confirmation, or a properly validated copy, provided that it bears the court seal. If there is no will, the document will be Letters of Administration.

Checklist

▷ A careful check must be made to ensure that the details shown on the grant of probate correspond with the entry in the register of members. If there is any doubt as to whether the deceased is indeed a shareholder of the company, then the company should obtain a declaration of identity from the executors. This will usually be given by the solicitors acting for the estate, although the deceased's bankers can also give a declaration of identity.

s.774

Procedure

▷ The date of death and the date of registration of the probate, together with the name(s) and address(es) of the executor(s), should be noted in the register of members and the register should be amended to show the word 'deceased' after the shareholder's name. The postal address for correspondence should be amended to that of the executor and should be addressed to the 'Executor of [shareholder's name] deceased'.

▷ The share certificates should be endorsed with the fact and date of death, the date of registration of probate and the name(s) and address(es) of the executor(s). The endorsement should be validated with the company's security seal.

▷ The company's security seal should be impressed on the probate, and this probate, together with the amended share certificate, should be returned to the person who lodged them. A new dividend mandate form may also be enclosed, as any existing mandate will have been revoked on the death of the shareholder.

Filing requirement

None.

Notes

▶ The company may request that the executor(s) transfer the shares to themselves, as this simplifies further requests and the need to validate instructions no longer applies. This transfer may, however, invoke the pre-emption provisions contained in the articles of association.

More information

▶ *Company Secretary's Handbook*, Chapter 18

Shares – application and allotment

Checklist

▶ Prior to any allotment of shares, the directors should ensure that they have sufficient authority to allot shares and that the statutory pre-emption provisions on the allotment of shares or, if different, any provisions contained in the company's articles of association are not infringed or, to the extent that they are, that the necessary waivers have been received from the members, either in writing or in general meeting.

ss. 550, 551

s. 561

▶ If the company's articles restrict the aggregate number of issued shares, it will be necessary to convene a general meeting or circulate a written resolution in the case of a private company to remove the restriction to increase the directors' authority to allot shares and to waive any pre-emption rights as necessary (see below).

Procedure

▶ A form of application should be made available for those persons wishing to subscribe for shares. Private companies must take care when drafting an application letter to ensure that it is not regarded as an invitation to the public to subscribe for shares. Only public companies can issue shares to the public.

s. 112

ss. 755, 756

▶ Those persons wishing to subscribe for the shares will complete the application form and return this to the company together with a cheque in full or part payment for the shares, as appropriate.

▶ Once the application forms and remittances have been received, the remittance cheques should be banked as soon as possible.

▶ Convene a directors' meeting to approve the applications, issue of shares, issue of share certificates and updating of the register of members. Ensure valid quorum is present.

s. 554

▶ File form SH01 with Companies House within one month.

▶ As soon as possible, share certificates should be issued to the applicants, and in any event not more than two months from the date of allotment.

s. 769

▶ Companies whose shares are publicly traded may have their shares held in uncertificated form in CREST.

▶ Within one month of the date of allotment, a return of allotments (form SH01) should be filed with the Registrar of Companies.

s.555

▶ If the shares are all fully paid, it will not be necessary for them to have distinguishing numbers.

Filing requirement

▶ Form SH01 within one month.

Notes

▶ Under certain circumstances, fully paid and partly paid shares of the same class may be regarded as two different classes of shares.

More information

▶ *Company Secretary's Handbook*, Chapter 18

Shares – consolidation

Occasionally, it will be necessary to consolidate the share capital of the company into shares of a greater nominal value. For instance, a consolidation of 4,000 25p shares into £1.00 shares will result in the authorised share capital being 1,000 shares of £1.00 each.

s.618

Occasionally, a quoted public limited company will consolidate its shares into shares of a higher nominal value where the shares have a very low market price. The consolidation of the shares will effectively increase the market price and make it easier to trade in the shares.

Alternatively, consolidation of shares will be used in capital reconstruction or capital reduction schemes. For instance, a company may decide to reduce its capital from £1.00 shares to 50p shares and then consolidate the shares into £1.00 shares, thus achieving a 50% capital reduction while retaining a nominal value of £1.00 for the shares.

Procedure

▷ Convene a directors' meeting to recommend an appropriate ordinary resolution to members and to convene a general meeting or circulate a written resolution in the case of a private company. Ensure valid quorum is present.

s.302

▷ Issue notice, signed by director or company secretary, on 14 clear days' notice for members to consider resolution.

s.307

▷ Enclose with the notice a form of proxy if desired.

▷ If the meeting is to be convened on short notice, the company secretary should arrange for agreement to short notice to be signed by each of the shareholders.

s.307(5)

▷ Hold general meeting. Ensure valid quorum is present. Resolution put to vote either by show of hands or by poll and to be passed by appropriate majority (ordinary resolution by 50% majority).

▷ File copy of resolution and form SH02 at Companies House.

ss.30,619

▷ The register of members will require amendment to show details of the new number of shares and nominal value of the shares currently held, and any distinguishing numbers will require reallocation.

▷ If there are any fractions of shares arising on the consolidation, these should be sold for the benefit of the members concerned or, alternatively, occasionally new shares can be issued, credited as fully paid, to round their holding up to the nearest whole number.

▷ All existing share certificates should be recalled, either for amendment or cancellation, and new share certificates should be issued.

Filing requirement

▷ Form SH02 within one month.

Notes

None.

More information

▷ *Company Secretary's Handbook*, Chapter 12

Shares – convertible

As the name implies, these are shares that can be converted from one class to another, either at some specific time in the future, on the occurrence of a specific event or at the option of the company or the shareholder.

ss. 549, 550, 551

Convertible shares will often be issued so that the company can attract additional funds, with the shares being issued with enhanced dividend rights. After a period of time, the shares would be converted to ordinary shares, thus reducing the dividends payable by the company.

The issue of convertible shares is similar to loans to the company, but with repayment of the loan at the end of its term being replaced by conversion to ordinary shares.

Checklist

The following points should be considered when convertible shares are being created:

▷ whether the shares could carry pre-emption rights on allotment or transfer;

▷ the amount, if any, of dividend and whether this should be preferential;

▷ whether the shares should carry voting rights;

▷ whether the shares should carry a preferential right to the return of capital on any winding up or distribution and whether the shares should participate in any surplus;

▷ the terms of conversion, including whether conversion should be at the option of the company, the shareholder or both, or at predetermined dates, and the basis of conversion to ordinary shares;

▷ creation of the shares will require alterations to the articles of association and must be authorised by the shareholders by ordinary and special resolutions at a general meeting or by written resolution in the case of a private company; and

▷ once the shares have been created, any further changes to the articles of association may require approval of the holders of the convertible shares at a separate class meeting, whether or not they are voting shares.

Procedure

▶ The procedure to be followed on conversion of the shares is the same as that to be followed on the conversion of convertible loan stock (see page 160).

Filing requirement

▶ Form SH01 on issue of shares.

Notes

The rights attaching to the convertible shares should be set out in the articles of association or in a memorandum of terms and conditions which should be appended to the form SH01 when the shares are issued.

More information

▶ *Company Secretary's Handbook*, Chapters 12 and 13

Shares – cumulative

The dividend payable on such shares is 'cumulative' – that is, any dividend not paid on the shares in one year will be accumulated and paid in succeeding years.

As dividends can be paid only out of distributable profits available for the purpose, the dividend may not be paid in a particular year as the company has insufficient distributable profit. In these circumstances, the unpaid dividend will accumulate until such time as the company has sufficient distributable profit to pay a dividend and any arrears to date.

It would be unusual for cumulative shares not to have a fixed dividend, as the directors would only declare a discretionary dividend in circumstances where the company has profits available for distribution.

Checklist

The following points should be considered when cumulative shares are being created:

▷ whether the shares should carry pre-emption rights on allotment or transfer;

▷ whether the shares will have a preferential right to the return of capital and whether this should be limited to the amounts paid up or credited as paid up on the shares, or whether they should participate in any surplus;

▷ whether the shares should be voting shares;

▷ the amount of the fixed dividend and any preferential payment terms, i.e. before or after any dividend to be declared on any other class of shares;

▷ the creation of the shares will require alterations to the articles of association of the company. If the shares are to be created after the incorporation of the company, the creation of the shares will require the consent of the shareholders by ordinary and special resolutions at a general meeting or by written resolution in the case of a private company;

▶ any subsequent alteration to the articles may also require approval of the holders of any cumulative shares if the alteration changes their class rights. This approval will be required at a separate class meeting and is required even where the particular class of shares are non-voting; and

▶ whether or not the shares should be redeemable or convertible at some future date.

Procedure

None.

Filing requirement

None.

Notes

None.

More information

▶ *Company Secretary's Handbook*, Chapter 12

Shares – redeemable

A limited company having a share capital may, if authorised by its articles of association, issue shares that are redeemable or that are liable to be redeemed at the option of the company or the shareholder. The articles of a public company must include specific authority for the issue of redeemable shares.

s.684

s.684(3)

Checklist

▷ At the time of issue of redeemable shares, there must be in issue shares that are not redeemable. This is to ensure that the issued share capital of the company cannot all be redeemed, leaving the company with no shareholders.

s.684(4)

▷ Redeemable shares can only be redeemed if they are fully paid.

s.686(1)

▷ The terms of redemption may provide for payment in cash on a date later than redemption, failing which they must be paid for on redemption.

s.686(2),(3)

▷ Public companies may only redeem shares out of the distributable profits or out of the proceeds of a fresh issue of shares made for that purpose. Under certain circumstances, private companies may redeem shares out of capital.

s.687

▷ Redeemed shares are treated as cancelled on redemption, the amount of the issued share capital being reduced by the nominal value of the shares.

s.688

Procedure

▷ The process for the redemption of shares is identical to that for purchase of shares by the company (see pages 202–207).

Filing requirement

▷ Form SH02 within one month.

Notes

None.

More information

▶ *Company Secretary's Handbook*, Chapter 14

Shares – transfer

The transfer of shares in a company are governed by the provisions of the company's articles of association and ss. 770–782 of the Act.

Companies adopting either of the model articles will not have any restrictions on the transferability of shares; however, many private companies will adopt pre-emption provisions on the transfer of shares.

Public companies whose shares are publicly traded are not permitted to restrict the transfer of shares except in a few specified circumstances, such as transfers to more than four joint holders or transfer of shares over which the company has a lien.

Checklist

▷ Is the transferee a shareholder?

▷ Is the stock transfer form completed correctly and signed by the transferor?   **s.770(1)(a)**

▷ Is the form stamped or certified as exempt?   **s.770(1)(b)**

▷ Is the form accompanied by share certificates evidencing title to at least the number of shares being transferred?

Procedure

▷ The transferor should complete a stock transfer form giving details of the shares to be transferred, their own name and address as transferor, and the name and address of the transferee. The form should be signed by the transferor and, where the shares are partly paid, by the transferee.

▷ Prior to registration by the company, it will be necessary for the stock transfer form to be stamped by HM Revenue & Customs (see page 139) unless the transfer is exempt from duty and has been signed and certified on the reverse. Stamp duty is payable by the purchaser of the shares. Duty is due on transfers with a consideration of more than £1,000. The current rate for stamp duty is 0.5%, rounded up to the nearest £5, of the consideration paid or payable (whether or not the consideration is cash).

▶ The stamped stock transfer form, together with the original share certificate, should be forwarded to the company or its registrar (as appropriate) for registration.

▶ Upon receipt of a stock transfer form, the company should check that the details of the transferor are correct and that the share certificate is valid. If the original share certificate has been mislaid, it will be necessary for the transferor to complete an indemnity in respect of this lost certificate.

▶ Many private companies have detailed pre-emption provisions on the transfer of shares and care must be taken to ensure that these are followed. Alternatively, the pre-emption rights may be waived by the remaining shareholders.

▶ The transfer of shares requires approval from the board of directors, who should also authorise the issue of a share certificate to the transferee and of any balancing certificate to the transferor.

▶ Details of the transfer must be entered in the register of members.

▶ Transfers must be processed or rejected within two months of receipt. Where they are rejected, the reasons for refusal must be provided. **s.771(1)**

Filing requirement

▶ Share transfers are not notified to Companies House; however, details of the transfers of shares in non-traded companies must be shown on the company's next confirmation statement. **s.856(3)(b)**

More information

▶ *Company Secretary's Handbook*, Chapter 7

Shares – transmission

Transmission is the process by which title to shares is transferred by operation of law rather than a sale or transfer by a shareholder. The most common form of transmission of shares is on the death of a shareholder.

Checklist

▷ Is the transferee a shareholder?

▷ Is the stock transfer form completed correctly and signed by the executor or personal representative?   **s.770(1)(a)**

▷ Is the form stamped or certified as exempt?   **s.770(1)(b)**

▷ Is the form accompanied by share certificates evidencing title to at least the number of shares being transferred?

Procedure

▷ A stock transfer form should be completed giving details of the shares to be transferred, the name and address of the registered holder as transferor and the name and address of the transferee. The form should be signed by the person lodging the form together with documentary evidence of their authority, such as a grant of probate.

▷ Prior to registration by the company, it will be necessary for the stock transfer form to be stamped by HM Revenue & Customs (see page 139), unless the transfer is exempt from duty and has been signed and certified on the reverse. Most transmissions of shares are not liable to stamp duty and the form should be certified accordingly.

▷ The stamped stock transfer form, together with the original share certificate, should be forwarded to the company or its registrar (as appropriate) for registration.

▷ Upon receipt of a stock transfer form, the company should check that the details of the transferor are correct and that the share certificate is valid. If the original share certificate has been mislaid, it will be necessary for the transferor to complete an indemnity in respect of this lost certificate.

▷ Many private companies have detailed pre-emption provisions on the transfer of shares and care must be taken to ensure that these are followed. Alternatively, the pre-emption rights may be waived by the remaining shareholders.

▷ The transfer of shares requires approval from the board of directors, who should also authorise the issue of a share certificate to the transferee and of any balancing certificate to the transferor. For quoted companies with an external share registrar the share registrar is usually given delegated authority to approve share transfers.

▷ Details of the transfer must be entered in the register of members.

▷ Transfers must be processed or rejected within two months of receipt.

▷ Where they are rejected, the reasons for refusal must be provided.

Filing requirement

▷ Share transfers are not notified to Companies House; however, details of the transfer of shares in non-traded companies must be shown on the company's next confirmation statement.

Notes

None.

More information

▷ *Company Secretary's Handbook*, Chapter 7

Single alternative inspection location (SAIL) address

There are particular requirements with regard to the place where various statutory records or registers are kept and where they may be inspected. As an alternative to the registered office address, companies can choose to keep and make available for inspection some or all of the records and registers at a single alternative inspection location, also referred to as the SAIL address.

Checklist

▷ Any, or all, of the registers or documents that must be kept available for inspection by members or the public may be kept at the SAIL address (see page 153).

▷ There can only be one alternative inspection address, and this must be in the same part of the United Kingdom in which the company is registered.

▷ Ensure that there are adequate processes in place at the SAIL address to facilitate the upkeep and inspection of the registers.

Procedure

▷ The directors should formally agree the transfer of register(s) to the SAIL address or their return to the registered office.

▷ Notify Companies House using forms AD02, AD03 and AD04 as appropriate.

▷ Transfer relevant records to SAIL address.

Filing requirement

▷ Forms AD02, AD03 and AD04 as appropriate.

Notes

▷ For companies using the services of a share registrar due to the
requirement that there can only be one SAIL address and that will
be the address where the register of members can be inspected, the
remaining registers will need to be located at the registered office.

More information

▷ *Company Secretary's Handbook*, Chapter 7

▷ Companies House Guidance booklet GP3

Substantial property transactions

Where a director or a person 'connected' with a director acquires a substantial non-cash asset from the company, or disposes of such an asset to the company, in most instances, shareholder approval must be sought. **s.190(1)**

A substantial transaction is one with a value of more than £5,000 and that exceeds the lower limit of £100,000, or 10% of the company's net assets. **s.191(2)**

If the director or the connected person is also a director of the company's holding company, then approval of the members of the holding company must also be sought. **s.190(2)**

Procedure

▶ Convene a directors' meeting to recommend an appropriate special resolution to members and to convene a general meeting or seek approval by written resolution in the case of a private company. Ensure valid quorum is present.

▶ Issue notice signed by director or company secretary, on 14 clear days' notice for members to consider resolution. **s.307**

▶ Enclose with the notice a form of proxy if desired.

▶ If the meeting is to be convened on short notice, the company secretary should arrange for agreement to short notice to be signed by each of the shareholders. **s.307(5)**

▶ Hold general meeting. Ensure valid quorum is present. Resolution put to vote either by show of hands or by poll and to be passed by appropriate majority (ordinary resolution by 50% majority). **s.282**

Filing requirement

None.

Notes

▶ Transactions between companies of a wholly owned group do not require approval.   **s. 192**

▶ Where a transaction has not received approval of the members, the transaction will usually be voidable by the company.   **s. 195**

▶ Where a transaction was not approved in advance, it may be affirmed by members within a reasonable period.   **s. 196**

▶ Transactions undertaken on behalf of the director or connected person on a recognised Stock Exchange by an 'independent' broker do not require approval.

▶ Where a director acquires a non-cash asset by virtue of being a member of the company, approval is not required.   **s. 192**

▶ Any arrangements entered into which have not received prior or retrospective approval between a director, connected person or holding company and the company make that director or connected person liable to the company for any gain arising out of the transaction or any losses suffered by the company.   **s. 195**

More information

▶ *Company Secretary's Handbook*, Chapter 6

Statutory forms and filing periods

Type	Description	CA2006 section(s)	Form code	Filing period	Web filing available
Accounts					
	Change of accounting reference date	392	AA01	Effective on registration	Yes
	Dormant company accounts (DCA)	441	AA02	9 months	Yes
	Notice of resolution removing auditors from office	512	AA03	14 days	
	Statement of guarantee by a parent undertaking of a subsidiary company	394A, 448A, 479A	AA06	On submission of unaudited subsidiary accounts	
Change of constitution					
	Notice of restriction on the company's articles	23	CC01	Effective on registration	
	Notice of removal of restriction on the company's articles	23	CC02	Effective on registration	
	Statement of compliance where amendment of articles restricted	24	CC03	Effective on registration	
	Statement of company's objects	31	CC04	Effective on registration	
	Change of constitution by enactment	34	CC05	Effective on registration	
	Change of constitution by order of court or other authority	35	CC06	Effective on registration	

Type	Description	CA2006 section(s)		Filing period	Web filing available
Change of name					
	Exemption from requirement as to use of 'limited' or 'cyfyngedig' on change of name	60	NE01	On application	
	Notice of change of name by resolution	78	NM01	On application	Yes
	Notice of change of name by conditional resolution	78	NM02	On application	
	Notice confirming satisfaction of the conditional resolution for change of name	78	NM03	On application	
	Notice of change of name by means provided for in the articles	79	NM04	On application	
	Notice of change of name by resolution of directors	64 or 1033	NM05	On application	
	Request to seek comments of government department or other specified body on change of name	56	NM06	On application	
Change of registered office					
	Change of registered office address	87	AD01	Effective on registration	Yes
	Notice to change the situation of an England and Wales company or a Welsh company	88	AD05	Effective on registration	
Company records					
	Notification of single alternative inspection location (SAIL)	114. 162, 228, 237, 275, 358, 702, 805, 809, 877, 859Q, 892	AD02	Effective on registration	Yes

Type	Description	CA2006 section(s)		Filing period	Web filing available
	Change of location of the company records to the single alternative inspection location (SAIL)	114, 128D, 162, 228, 237, 275, 358, 702, 720, 743, 790N, 790Z, 805, 809, 859Q, 877, 892	AD03	Effective on registration	Yes
	Change of location of the company records to the registered office	114, 128D, 162, 228, 237, 275, 358, 702, 720, 743, 790N, 790Z, 805, 809, 859Q, 877, 892	AD04	Effective on registration	Yes
	Election to keep information from register of directors on the central (public) register	167A	EH01	Effective on registration	Yes
	Election to keep information from register of directors on the central (public) register	167A	EH02	Effective on registration	Yes
	Election to keep information from register of directors on the central (public) register	279A	EH03	Effective on registration	Yes
	Election to keep information from register of people with significant control (PSC) on the central (public) register	790X	EH04	Effective on registration	Yes
	Election to keep information from register of members on the central (public) register	128B	EH05	Effective on registration	Yes
	Update to members' information held on the central (public) register	128E	EH06	As soon as possible once obligation to notify commences	

Type	Description	CA2006 section(s)	Form code	Filing period	Web filing available
	Withdrawal of election to keep information from register of directors on the central (public) register	167E	EW01	Effective on registration	Yes
	Withdrawal of election to keep information from register of directors' usual residential addresses on the central (public) register	167E	EW02	Effective on registration	Yes
	Withdrawal of election to keep information from register of secretaries on the central (public) register	279E	EW03	Effective on registration	Yes
	Withdrawal of election to keep information from register of people with significant control (PSC) on the central (public) register	790ZD	EW04	Effective on registration	Yes
	Withdrawal of election to keep members' information on the central (public) register	128J	EW05	Effective on registration	Yes
Confirmation statement					
	Confirmation statement	853A	CS01	14 days	Yes
Directors and secretaries					
	Appointment of director	167, 167D	AP01	14 days	Yes
	Appointment of corporate director	167, 167D	AP02	14 days	Yes
	Appointment of secretary	276, 279D	AP03	14 days	Yes
	Appointment of corporate secretary	276, 279D	AP04	14 days	Yes
	Change of director's details	167, 167D	CH01	14 days	Yes
	Change of corporate director's details	167, 167D	CH02	14 days	Yes
	Change of secretary's details	276, 279D	CH03	14 days	Yes

Type	Description	CA2006 section(s)		Filing period	Web filing available
	Change of corporate secretary's details	276	CH04	14 days	Yes
	Termination of appointment of director	167, 167D	TM01	14 days	Yes
	Termination of appointment of secretary	276, 279D	TM02	14 days	Yes
Incorporation					
	Application to register a company	9	IN01	On application	Yes
Investment companies					
	Notice of intention to carry on business as an investment company	833(1)	IC01	Effective on registration	
	Notice that a company no longer wishes to be an investment company	833(4)	IC02	Effective on registration	
Mortgage					
	Particulars of an instrument of alteration to a floating charge created by a company registered in Scotland	ss. 410, 466 CA1985	466 (Scot)	21 days	
	Particulars of a charge	859A, 859J	MR01	21 days	Yes
	Particulars of a charge subject to which property or undertaking has been acquired	859C, 859J	MR02	Effective on registration	Yes
	Particulars for the registration of a charge to secure a series of debentures	859B, 859J	MR03	21 days	
	Statement of satisfaction in full or in part of a charge	859L	MR04	Effective on registration	Yes
	Statement that part or the whole of the property charged (a) has been released from the charge, (b) no longer forms part of the company's property or undertaking	859L	MR05	Effective on registration	

Type	Description	CA2006 section(s)		Filing period	Web filing available
	Statement of company acting as a trustee	859J	MR06	Effective on registration	
	Particulars of alteration of a charge (particulars of a negative pledge)	859O	MR07	Effective on registration	
	Particulars of a charge where there is no instrument	859A, 859J	MR08	21 days	
	Particulars of a charge subject to which property or undertaking has been acquired where there is no instrument	859C, 859J	MR09	Effective on registration	
	Particulars for the registration of a charge to secure a series of debentures where there is no instrument	859B, 859J	MR10	21 days	
Opening of overseas branch register					
	Notice of opening of overseas branch register	130	AD06	Effective on registration	
	Notice of discontinuance of overseas branch register	135	AD07	Effective on registration	
Other appointments					
	Appointment of a manager under s. 47 of the Companies (Audit, Investigations and Community Enterprise) Act 2004 or receiver and manager under s. 18 of the Charities Act 1993 or judicial factor (Scotland)	1154	AP05	14 days	
	Change of service address for manager appointed under s. 47 of the Companies (Audit, Investigations and Community Enterprise) Act 2004 or receiver and manager under s. 18 of the Charities Act 1993 or judicial factor (Scotland)	1154	CH05	14 days	

Type	Description	CA2006 section(s)		Filing period	Web filing available
	Termination of appointment of manager under s. 47 of the Companies (Audit, Investigations and Community Enterprise) Act 2004 or receiver and manager under s. 18 of the Charities Act 1993 or judicial factor (Scotland)	1154	TM03	14 days	
People with significant control (PSC)					
	Notice of individual person with significant control (PSC)	790K, 790ZA	PSC01	As soon as possible once obligation to notify arises	Yes
	Notice of relevant legal entity (RLE) with significant control	790K, 790ZA	PSC02	As soon as possible once obligation to notify arises	Yes
	Notice of other registrable person (ORP) with significant control	790K, 790ZA	PSC03	As soon as possible once obligation to notify arises	Yes
	Change of details of individual person with significant control (PSC)	790M, 790ZA	PSC04	As soon as possible once obligation to notify arises	Yes
	Change of details of relevant legal entity (RLE) with significant control	790M, 790ZA	PSC05	As soon as possible once obligation to notify arises	Yes
	Change of details of other registrable person (ORP) with significant control	790M, 790ZA	PSC06	As soon as possible once obligation to notify arises	Yes

Type	Description	CA2006 section(s)		Filing period	Web filing available
	Notice of ceasing to be an individual person with significant control (PSC), relevant legal entity (RLE), or other registrable person (ORP)	790M, 790ZA	PSC07	As soon as possible once obligation to notify arises	Yes
	Notification of PSC statements	790M, 790ZA	PSC08	As soon as possible once obligation to notify arises	Yes
	Update to PSC statements	790M, 790ZA	PSC09	As soon as possible once obligation to notify arises	
Receiver/Manager					
	Notice of appointment of an administrative receiver, receiver or manager	859K	RM01	7 days	
	Notice of ceasing to act as an administrative receiver, receiver or manager	859K	RM02	Effective on registration	
Registrar's powers					
	Replacement of document not meeting requirements for proper delivery	1076	RP01	As specified in request from Companies House	
	Application for rectification by the Registrar of Companies	1095 and regs 4, 5 Registrar of Companies and Applications for Striking off Regulations 2009	RP02A	On application	

Type	Description	CA2006 section(s)		Filing period	Web filing available
	Application for rectification of a registered office or UK establishment address by the Registrar of Companies	1095 and regs 4, 5 Registrar of Companies and Applications for Striking off Regulations 2009	RP02B	On application	
	Notice of an objection to a request for the Registrar of Companies to rectify the Register	1095 and regs 4, 5 Registrar of Companies and Applications for Striking off Regulations 2009	RP03	Within 28 days of application	
	Second filing of a document previously delivered		RP04	Effective on registration	
	Application for removal of material about directors who have not consented to act	1095(4A) and regs 4, 5 Registrar of Companies and Applications for Striking off Regulations 2009	RP06	Effective on registration	
	Application to change a company's disputed registered office address	The Companies (Address of Registered Office) Regulations 2016	RP07	Effective on registration	
	Correction of a director's date of birth which was incorrectly stated on incorporation	167	RPCH01	Effective on registration	

Type	Description	CA2006 section(s)		Filing period	Web filing available
	Certified voluntary translation of an original document that is or has been delivered to the Registrar of Companies	1106, reg 4 Companies (Cross-Border Mergers) Regulations 2007	VT01	Effective on registration	
Re-registration					
	Application by a private company for re-registration as a public company	94, 765(4)	RR01	15 days	
	Application by a public company for re-registration as a private limited company	100	RR02	15 days	
	Notice by the company of application to the court for cancellation of resolution for re-registration	99(2)	RR03	15 days	
	Notice by the applicants of application to the court for cancellation of resolution for re-registration	99(1)	RR04	On application to court	
	Application by a private limited company for re-registration as an unlimited company	103	RR05	15 days	
	Application by an unlimited company for re-registration as a private limited company	106	RR06	15 days	
	Application by a public company for re-registration as a private unlimited company	110	RR07	15 days	
	Application by a public company for re-registration as a private limited company following a court order reducing capital	651	RR08	15 days	

Type	Description	CA2006 section(s)		Filing period	Web filing available
	Application by a public company for re-registration as a private company following cancellation of shares	664	RR09	15 days	
	Statement of capital	108	SH19	15 days	
Restoration					
	Application for administrative restoration to the register	1024	RT01	On application	
Share capital					
	Notice to non-assenting shareholders	984(3)	984	1 month, to shareholders only	
	Notice to non-assenting shareholders	980(1)	980(1)	Within 3 months after the last day the offer can be accepted, or 6 months after the date of the offer where not governed by the Takeover Code	
	Statutory declaration relating to a notice to non-assenting shareholders	980(4)(b)	980dec	When offeror gives notice under s. 979	
	Notice of application to court to cancel share warrants	s. 5(5), sch 4 SBEEA 2015	NAC01	On application	
	Return of allotment of shares	555	SH01	1 month	Yes
	Notice of consolidation, sub-division, redemption of shares or re-conversion of stock into shares	619, 621, 689	SH02	1 month	

Type	Description	CA2006 section(s)		Filing period	Web filing available
	Return of purchase of own shares	707	SH03	28 days	
	Notice of sale or transfer of treasury shares	728	SH04	28 days	
	Notice of cancellation of treasury shares	730	SH05	28 days	
	Notice of cancellation of shares	708	SH06	28 days	
	Notice of cancellation of shares held by or for a public company	663	SH07	1 month	
	Notice of name or other designation of class of shares	636	SH08	1 month	
	Return of allotment by unlimited company allotting a new class of shares	556	SH09	1 month	
	Notice of particulars of variation of rights attached to shares	637	SH10	1 month	
	Notice of new class of members	638	SH11	1 month	
	Notice of particulars of variation of class rights	640	SH12	1 month	
	Notice of name or other designation of class of members	639	SH13	1 month	
	Notice of re-denomination	625	SH14	1 month	
	Notice of reduction of capital following redenomination	627	SH15	15 days	
	Notice by the applicants of application to court for cancellation of the special resolution approving a redemption or purchase of shares out of capital	722(1)	SH16	On application to court	

Type	Description	CA2006 section(s)		Filing period	Web filing available
	Notice by the company of application to court for cancellation of the special resolution approving a redemption or purchase of shares out of capital	722(2)	SH17	On receipt of notice that an application has been made	
	Statement of capital for reduction supported by solvency statement or court order	644, 649	SH19	15 days	
	Statement of capital on cancellation of share warrants	s. 7(2), sch 4 SBEEA 2015	SH19	15 days	
	Application for trading certificate for a public company	761 & 762	SH50	On application	
Strike off and dissolution					
	Striking off application by a company	1003	DS01	On application	
	Withdrawal of striking-off application by a company	1010	DS02	On application	Yes

Statutory registers and records

The Companies Act requires the following registers to be kept by all companies:

▶ register of members;   **s. 113**

▶ historic register of members;   **s. 128D**

▶ register of charges – pre-6 April 2013 charges;   **s.876 or s.891**

▶ minute books of the proceedings of meetings of the shareholders and its directors, and of any sub-committees of the directors;   **ss.355, 248**

▶ accounting records;   **s.386**

▶ register of directors;   **s.162**

▶ register of directors' usual residential addresses;   **s.165**

▶ copies of directors' service contracts or memorandum of terms;   **s.228**

▶ copies of any indemnity provisions for directors;   **s.237**

▶ register of secretaries;   **s.275**

▶ copies of contracts for market and off-market purchases of own shares;   **s.702**

▶ directors' and auditors' statements in relation to purchase of shares by a private company out of capital;   **s.720**

▶ although not required by the Act, if the company maintains a register of debenture holders, there are requirements laid down by the Act governing its maintenance and inspection;   **s.743**

▶ PSC Register;   **s.790M**

▶ historic PSC Register;   **s.790Z**

▶ reports into investigation of ownership of shares;   **s.805**

▶ if the company is a public company, register of interests in voting shares; and   **s.808**

▶ instruments creating charges.   **s.859Q**

Checklist

▶ Unless an election is made to use the central register to maintain the registers, where applicable, these must all be kept at the registered office or the companies SAIL address, details of which must be notified to Companies House on form AD02.

Procedure

None.

Notes

None.

Filing requirement

▶ Forms AD02, AD03 or AD04.

More information

▶ *Company Secretary's Handbook*, Chapter 7

Statutory registers – use of central registry

Introduced as a de-regulating measure by SBEE2015 private companies can elect to hold all or some of their statutory registers on the central registry maintained by the Registrar of Companies and not keep their own stand-alone registers. Although available to all private companies it was introduced primarily for the benefit of sole director/member companies.

Checklist

▶ Is the company a private company?

▶ Has the company already opted in to use the central registry?

Procedure

▶ Companies must opt in to make use of the central registry to keep all or some of their statutory registers and do so by opting in on the incorporation form IN01 or at any time after incorporation by submitting the requisite form to Companies House as follows:

▷ EH01   Register of directors

▷ EH02   Register of directors' usual residential addresses

▷ EH03   Register of secretaries

▷ EH04   PSC Register

▷ EH05   Register of members

▶ Companies may opt out of using the central registry to keep all or some of their statutory registers at any time and do so by opting out by submitting the requisite form to Companies House as follows:

▷ EW01   Register of directors

▷ EW02   Register of directors' usual residential addresses

▷ EW03   Register of secretaries

▷ EW04   PSC Register

▷ EW05   Register of members

▶ Any changes to the members' details must be separately notified to the Registrar using form EH06.

Filing requirement

▶ Form EH01, EH02, EH03, EH04 or EH05 as required to opt in.

▶ Form EH06 to record changes in the members details as required.

▶ Form EW01, EW02, EW03, EW04 or EW05 as required to opt out.

Notes

The register will maintain all the registers other than the register of members updated from the usual notification of changes such as form AP01, TM01 etc.

More information

▶ *Company Secretary's Handbook*, Chapter 7

▶ Companies House Guidance – Company registers
https://www.gov.uk/government/publications/company-registers/
company-registers

Treasury shares

Any company may acquire its own shares and hold these in treasury. Unlike the existing provisions relating to purchase of own shares (see page 202), shares purchased under the treasury shares provisions are not cancelled on purchase but may be retained, or sold.

s. 724 as amended by SI 2013/999

Checklist

▶ Will the shares be purchased out of distributable profit or the proceeds of a fresh issue or capital (private companies only)?

s. 724(2)

▶ Does the company have sufficient distributable profit?

s. 724(1)(b)

▶ Does the company have sufficient cash resources?

▶ Do the articles permit the purchase of its own shares by the company?

Procedure

▶ The general procedure for the purchase by a company of its own shares is set out on pages 202–207.

▶ Once the company has purchased the shares to be held in treasury, a return on form SH03 must be submitted to the Registrar, stating the number of shares and the class of shares, together with the nominal value of the shares and the date on which they were repurchased. The purchase of shares to be held in treasury by a company is subject to stamp duty, the duty being payable where the aggregate consideration exceeds £1,000 and not the nominal value at the rate of 0.5% (rounded up to the nearest £5).

s. 707

▶ If the shares are subsequently cancelled, sold or transferred, form SH04 or SH05 must be filed.

ss. 727, 728, 729

Filing requirement

▶ Copy of ordinary resolution.

▶ Form SH03.

▶ Form SH04 or SH05 within 28 days of cancellation, sale or transfer.

Notes

▶ Listed companies must comply with Chapter 13 of the Listing Rules.

▶ Shares held in treasury may be sold for cash, transferred to satisfy **s.727**
claims under employee share schemes or cancelled.

▶ Shares held in treasury have no voting or dividend rights, but may take **s.726**
up rights in respect of bonus issues and may be redeemed if the shares
are redeemable.

▶ There is no maximum number of shares that a company can hold **s.725(2),(3)**
in treasury provided it always has at least 1 share in issue and not in
Treasury.

More information

▶ *Company Secretary's Handbook*, Chapter 14

Types of trading entity

The majority of companies are private companies limited by shares. However, there are three types of private company, each with qualities better suited to certain activities than others. Additionally, rather than incorporating a company, entrepreneurs may prefer an unincorporated trading entity such as a partnership or sole trader, or a mix of the two in the form of an LLP.

The following table shows the more common factors to consider when assessing what form of trading entity to use.

	PLC	Ltd	Unltd	Guar	LLP	Uninc
Is the company to trade for profit?	✓	✓	✓		✓	✓
Is it to be a charitable or non-profit-making body such as an association?				✓		✓
Is the liability of the members to be:						
limited	✓	✓		✓	✓	
or unlimited?			✓			✓
(Some professional associations require their members to trade without limited liability.)						
Is financial information regarding the company to be kept confidential?						
Yes			✓			✓
No	✓	✓		✓	✓	
Are the profits of the business to be assessed for tax on:						
the owners					✓	✓
or the trading vehicle?	✓	✓	✓	✓		
Are shares in the business to be offered for subscription to:						
the public (>50 persons)	✓					
or a defined, restricted membership?		✓	✓	✓	✓	✓

KEY

PLC	Public limited company	Guar	Guarantee
Ltd	Limited	LLP	Limited liability partnership
Unltd	Unlimited	Uninc	Unincorporated

More information

▶ *Company Secretary's Handbook*, Chapter 2

Waiver of dividend

Occasionally, particularly with private family-owned companies, shareholders will elect to waive entitlement to receive dividends in respect of one or more financial years. This is commonly used where shares are held by a nominee to satisfy a minimum number of shareholder requirements in the articles and thus the nominee will elect not to receive dividends.

Checklist

▶ Waiver must pre-date date of declaration of dividend.

Procedure

▶ The shareholder will complete a formal letter of waiver under seal or witnessed and will lodge this with the company.

▶ Often waivers will be restricted to any dividends paid in respect of stated period rather than undated, as the waiver is irrevocable.

Filing requirement

None.

Notes

None.

More information

▶ *Company Secretary's Handbook*, Chapter 19

Appendix I – UK Corporate Governance Code
July 2018

Introduction

The first version of the UK Corporate Governance Code (the Code) was published in 1992 by the Cadbury Committee. It defined corporate governance as 'the system by which companies are directed and controlled. Boards of directors are responsible for the governance of their companies. The shareholders' role in governance is to appoint the directors and the auditors and to satisfy themselves that an appropriate governance structure is in place.' This remains true today, but the environment in which companies, their shareholders and wider stakeholders operate continues to develop rapidly.

Companies do not exist in isolation. Successful and sustainable businesses underpin our economy and society by providing employment and creating prosperity. To succeed in the long-term, directors and the companies they lead need to build and maintain successful relationships with a wide range of stakeholders. These relationships will be successful and enduring if they are based on respect, trust and mutual benefit. Accordingly, a company's culture should promote integrity and openness, value diversity and be responsive to the views of shareholders and wider stakeholders.

Over the years the Code has been revised and expanded to take account of the increasing demands on the UK's corporate governance framework. The principle of collective responsibility within a unitary board has been a success and – alongside the stewardship activities of investors – played a vital role in delivering high standards of governance and encouraging long-term investment. Nevertheless, the debate about the nature and extent of the framework has intensified as a result of financial crises and high-profile examples of inadequate governance and misconduct, which have led to poor outcomes for a wide range of stakeholders.

At the heart of this Code is an updated set of Principles that emphasise the value of good corporate governance to long-term sustainable success. By applying the Principles, following the more detailed Provisions and using the associated guidance, companies can demonstrate throughout their reporting how the governance of the company contributes to its long-term sustainable success and achieves wider objectives.

Achieving this depends crucially on the way boards and companies apply the spirit of the Principles. The Code does not set out a rigid set of rules; instead it offers flexibility through the application of Principles and through 'comply or explain' Provisions and supporting guidance. It is the responsibility of boards to use this flexibility wisely and of investors and their advisors to assess differing company approaches thoughtfully.

Reporting on the Code

The 2018 Code focuses on the application of the Principles. The Listing Rules require companies to make a statement of how they have applied the Principles, in a manner that would enable shareholders to evaluate how the Principles have been applied. The ability of investors to evaluate the approach to governance is important. Reporting should cover the application of the Principles in the context of the particular circumstances of the company and how the board has set the company's purpose and strategy, met objectives and achieved outcomes through the decisions it has taken.

It is important to report meaningfully when discussing the application of the Principles and to avoid boilerplate reporting. The focus should be on how these have been applied, articulating what action has been taken and the resulting outcomes. High-quality reporting will include signposting and cross-referencing to those parts of the annual report that describe how the Principles have been applied. This will help investors with their evaluation of company practices.

The effective application of the Principles should be supported by high-quality reporting on the Provisions. These operate on a 'comply or explain' basis and companies should avoid a 'tick-box approach'. An alternative to complying with a Provision may be justified in particular circumstances based on a range of factors, including the size, complexity, history and ownership structure of a company. Explanations should set out the background, provide a clear rationale for the action the company is taking, and explain the impact that the action has had. Where a departure from a Provision is intended to be limited in time, the explanation should indicate when the company expects to conform to the Provision. Explanations are a positive opportunity to communicate, not an onerous obligation.

In line with their responsibilities under the UK Stewardship Code, investors should engage constructively and discuss with the company any departures from recommended practice. In their consideration of explanations, investors and their advisors should pay due regard to a company's individual circumstances. While they have every right to challenge explanations if they are unconvincing, these must not be evaluated in a mechanistic way. Investors and their advisors should also give companies sufficient time to respond to enquiries about corporate governance.

Corporate governance reporting should also relate coherently to other parts of the annual report – particularly the Strategic Report and other complementary information – so that shareholders can effectively assess the quality of the company's governance arrangements, and the board's activities and contributions. This should include providing information that enables shareholders to assess how the directors have performed their duty under section 172 of the Companies Act 2006 (the Act) to promote the success of the company. Nothing in this Code overrides or is intended as an interpretation of the statutory statement of directors' duties in the Act.

The Code is also supported by the *Guidance on Board Effectiveness* (the Guidance). We encourage boards and companies to use this to support their activities. The Guidance does not set out the 'right way' to apply the Code. It is intended to stimulate thinking on how boards can carry out their role most effectively. The Guidance is designed to help boards with their actions and decisions when reporting on the application of the Code's Principles. The board should also take into account the Financial Reporting Council's *Guidance on Audit Committees and Guidance on Risk Management, Internal Control and Related Financial and Business Reporting*.

Application

The Code is applicable to all companies with a premium listing, whether incorporated in the UK or elsewhere. The new Code applies to accounting periods beginning on or after 1 January 2019.

For parent companies with a premium listing, the board should ensure that there is adequate co-operation within the group to enable it to discharge its governance responsibilities under the Code effectively. This includes the communication of the parent company's purpose, values and strategy.

Externally managed investment companies (which typically have a different board and company structure that may affect the relevance of particular Principles) may wish to use the Association of Investment Companies' Corporate Governance Code to meet their obligations under the Code. In addition, the Association of Financial Mutuals produces an annotated version of the Code for mutual insurers to use.

1   Board leadership and company purpose

Principles

A.   A successful company is led by an effective and entrepreneurial board, whose role is to promote the long-term sustainable success of the company, generating value for shareholders and contributing to wider society.

B.   The board should establish the company's purpose, values and strategy, and satisfy itself that these and its culture are aligned. All directors must act with integrity, lead by example and promote the desired culture.

C.   The board should ensure that the necessary resources are in place for the company to meet its objectives and measure performance against them. The board should also establish a framework of prudent and effective controls, which enable risk to be assessed and managed.

D.   In order for the company to meet its responsibilities to shareholders and stakeholders, the board should ensure effective engagement with, and encourage participation from, these parties.

E.   The board should ensure that workforce policies and practices are consistent with the company's values and support its long-term sustainable success. The workforce should be able to raise any matters of concern.

Provisions

1.   The board should assess the basis on which the company generates and preserves value over the long-term. It should describe in the annual report how opportunities and risks to the future success of the business have been considered and addressed, the sustainability of the company's business model and how its governance contributes to the delivery of its strategy.

2.   The board should assess and monitor culture. Where it is not satisfied that policy, practices or behaviour throughout the business are aligned with the company's purpose, values and strategy, it should seek assurance that management has taken corrective action. The annual report should explain the board's activities and any action taken. In addition, it should include an explanation of the company's approach to investing in and rewarding its workforce.

3.   In addition to formal general meetings, the chair should seek regular engagement with major shareholders in order to understand their views on governance and performance against the strategy. Committee chairs should seek engagement with shareholders on significant matters related to their areas of responsibility. The chair should ensure that the board as a whole has a clear understanding of the views of shareholders.

4.   When 20 per cent or more of votes have been cast against the board recommendation for a resolution, the company should explain, when announcing voting results, what actions it intends to take to consult shareholders in order to understand the reasons

behind the result. An update on the views received from shareholders and actions taken should be published no later than six months after the shareholder meeting. The board should then provide a final summary in the annual report and, if applicable, in the explanatory notes to resolutions at the next shareholder meeting, on what impact the feedback has had on the decisions the board has taken and any actions or resolutions now proposed.[1]

5. The board should understand the views of the company's other key stakeholders and describe in the annual report how their interests and the matters set out in section 172 of the Companies Act 2006 have been considered in board discussions and decision-making.[2] The board should keep engagement mechanisms under review so that they remain effective. For engagement with the workforce,[3] one or a combination of the following methods should be used:
   ▷ a director appointed from the workforce;
   ▷ a formal workforce advisory panel;
   ▷ a designated non-executive director.
   If the board has not chosen one or more of these methods, it should explain what alternative arrangements are in place and why it considers that they are effective.

6. There should be a means for the workforce to raise concerns in confidence and – if they wish – anonymously. The board should routinely review this and the reports arising from its operation. It should ensure that arrangements are in place for the proportionate and independent investigation of such matters and for follow-up action.

7. The board should take action to identify and manage conflicts of interest, including those resulting from significant shareholdings, and ensure that the influence of third parties does not compromise or override independent judgement.

8. Where directors have concerns about the operation of the board or the management of the company that cannot be resolved, their concerns should be recorded in the board minutes. On resignation, a non-executive director should provide a written statement to the chair, for circulation to the board, if they have any such concerns.

2 Division of responsibilities

Principles

F. The chair leads the board and is responsible for its overall effectiveness in directing the company. They should demonstrate objective judgement throughout their tenure and promote a culture of openness and debate. In addition, the chair facilitates constructive board relations and the effective contribution of all non-executive directors, and ensures that directors receive accurate, timely and clear information.

G. The board should include an appropriate combination of executive and non-executive (and, in particular, independent non-executive) directors, such that no one individual

---

1 Details of significant votes against and related company updates are available on the Public Register maintained by The Investment Association – www. theinvestmentassociation.org/publicregister.html

2 The Companies (Miscellaneous Reporting) Regulations 2018 require directors to explain how they have had regard to various matters in performing their duty to promote the success of the company in section 172 of the Companies Act 2006. The Financial Reporting Council's Guidance on the Strategic Report supports reporting on the legislative requirement.

3 See the Guidance on Board Effectiveness Section 1 for a description of 'workforce' in this context.

or small group of individuals dominates the board's decision-making. There should be a clear division of responsibilities between the leadership of the board and the executive leadership of the company's business.

H.   Non-executive directors should have sufficient time to meet their board responsibilities. They should provide constructive challenge, strategic guidance, offer specialist advice and hold management to account.

I.   The board, supported by the company secretary, should ensure that it has the policies, processes, information, time and resources it needs in order to function effectively and efficiently.

Provisions

9.   The chair should be independent on appointment when assessed against the circumstances set out in Provision 10. The roles of chair and chief executive should not be exercised by the same individual. A chief executive should not become chair of the same company. If, exceptionally, this is proposed by the board, major shareholders should be consulted ahead of appointment. The board should set out its reasons to all shareholders at the time of the appointment and also publish these on the company website.

10. The board should identify in the annual report each non-executive director it considers to be independent. Circumstances which are likely to impair, or could appear to impair, a non-executive director's independence include, but are not limited to, whether a director:

▶   is or has been an employee of the company or group within the last five years;

▶   has, or has had within the last three years, a material business relationship with the company, either directly or as a partner, shareholder, director or senior employee of a body that has such a relationship with the company;

▶   has received or receives additional remuneration from the company apart from a director's fee, participates in the company's share option or a performance-related pay scheme, or is a member of the company's pension scheme;

▶   has close family ties with any of the company's advisers, directors or senior employees;

▶   holds cross-directorships or has significant links with other directors through involvement in other companies or bodies;

▶   represents a significant shareholder; or

▶   has served on the board for more than nine years from the date of their first appointment.

Where any of these or other relevant circumstances apply, and the board nonetheless considers that the non-executive director is independent, a clear explanation should be provided.

11. At least half the board, excluding the chair, should be non-executive directors whom the board considers to be independent.

12. The board should appoint one of the independent non-executive directors to be the senior independent director to provide a sounding board for the chair and serve as an intermediary for the other directors and shareholders. Led by the senior independent director, the non-executive directors should meet without the chair present at least annually to appraise the chair's performance, and on other occasions as necessary.

13. Non-executive directors have a prime role in appointing and removing executive directors. Non-executive directors should scrutinise and hold to account the performance of management and individual executive directors against agreed performance objectives. The chair should hold meetings with the non-executive

directors without the executive directors present.

14. The responsibilities of the chair, chief executive, senior independent director, board and committees should be clear, set out in writing, agreed by the board and made publicly available. The annual report should set out the number of meetings of the board and its committees, and the individual attendance by directors.

15. When making new appointments, the board should take into account other demands on directors' time. Prior to appointment, significant commitments should be disclosed with an indication of the time involved. Additional external appointments should not be undertaken without prior approval of the board, with the reasons for permitting significant appointments explained in the annual report. Full-time executive directors should not take on more than one non-executive directorship in a FTSE 100 company or other significant appointment.

16. All directors should have access to the advice of the company secretary, who is responsible for advising the board on all governance matters. Both the appointment and removal of the company secretary should be a matter for the whole board.

3 Composition, succession and evaluation

Principles

J. Appointments to the board should be subject to a formal, rigorous and transparent procedure, and an effective succession plan should be maintained for board and senior management.[4] Both appointments and succession plans should be based on merit and objective criteria[5] and, within this context, should promote diversity of gender, social and ethnic backgrounds, cognitive and personal strengths.

K. The board and its committees should have a combination of skills, experience and knowledge. Consideration should be given to the length of service of the board as a whole and membership regularly refreshed.

L. Annual evaluation of the board should consider its composition, diversity and how effectively members work together to achieve objectives. Individual evaluation should demonstrate whether each director continues to contribute effectively.

Provisions

17. The board should establish a nomination committee to lead the process for appointments, ensure plans are in place for orderly succession to both the board and senior management positions, and oversee the development of a diverse pipeline for succession. A majority of members of the committee should be independent non-executive directors. The chair of the board should not chair the committee when it is dealing with the appointment of their successor.

18. All directors should be subject to annual re-election. The board should set out in the papers accompanying the resolutions to elect each director the specific reasons why their contribution is, and continues to be, important to the company's long-term sustainable success.

19. The chair should not remain in post beyond nine years from the date of their

4 The definition of 'senior management' for this purpose should be the executive committee or the first layer of management below board level, including the company secretary.

5 Which protect against discrimination for those with protected characteristics within the meaning of the Equalities Act 2010.

first appointment to the board. To facilitate effective succession planning and the development of a diverse board, this period can be extended for a limited time, particularly in those cases where the chair was an existing non-executive director on appointment. A clear explanation should be provided.

20. Open advertising and/or an external search consultancy should generally be used for the appointment of the chair and non-executive directors. If an external search consultancy is engaged it should be identified in the annual report alongside a statement about any other connection it has with the company or individual directors.

21. There should be a formal and rigorous annual evaluation of the performance of the board, its committees, the chair and individual directors. The chair should consider having a regular externally facilitated board evaluation. In FTSE 350 companies this should happen at least every three years. The external evaluator should be identified in the annual report and a statement made about any other connection it has with the company or individual directors.

22. The chair should act on the results of the evaluation by recognising the strengths and addressing any weaknesses of the board. Each director should engage with the process and take appropriate action when development needs have been identified.

23. The annual report should describe the work of the nomination committee, including:

> the process used in relation to appointments, its approach to succession planning and how both support developing a diverse pipeline;

> how the board evaluation has been conducted, the nature and extent of an external evaluator's contact with the board and individual directors, the outcomes and actions taken, and how it has or will influence board composition;

> the policy on diversity and inclusion, its objectives and linkage to company strategy, how it has been implemented and progress on achieving the objectives; and

> the gender balance of those in the senior management[6] and their direct reports.

4 Audit, risk and internal control

Principles

M. The board should establish formal and transparent policies and procedures to ensure the independence and effectiveness of internal and external audit functions and satisfy itself on the integrity of financial and narrative statements.[7]

N. The board should present a fair, balanced and understandable assessment of the company's position and prospects.

O. The board should establish procedures to manage risk, oversee the internal control framework, and determine the nature and extent of the principal risks the company is willing to take in order to achieve its long-term strategic objectives.

---

6 See footnote 4.

7 The board's responsibility to present a fair, balanced and understandable assessment extends to interim and other price-sensitive public records and reports to regulators, as well as to information required to be presented by statutory instruments.

Provisions

24. The board should establish an audit committee of independent non-executive directors, with a minimum membership of three, or in the case of smaller companies, two.[8] The chair of the board should not be a member. The board should satisfy itself that at least one member has recent and relevant financial experience. The committee as a whole shall have competence relevant to the sector in which the company operates.

25. The main roles and responsibilities of the audit committee should include:

  ▶ monitoring the integrity of the financial statements of the company and any formal announcements relating to the company's financial performance, and reviewing significant financial reporting judgements contained in them;

  ▶ providing advice (where requested by the board) on whether the annual report and accounts, taken as a whole, is fair, balanced and understandable, and provides the information necessary for shareholders to assess the company's position and performance, business model and strategy;

  ▶ reviewing the company's internal financial controls and internal control and risk management systems, unless expressly addressed by a separate board risk committee composed of independent non-executive directors, or by the board itself;

  ▶ monitoring and reviewing the effectiveness of the company's internal audit function or, where there is not one, considering annually whether there is a need for one and making a recommendation to the board;

  ▶ conducting the tender process and making recommendations to the board, about the appointment, reappointment and removal of the external auditor, and approving the remuneration and terms of engagement of the external auditor;

  ▶ reviewing and monitoring the external auditor's independence and objectivity;

  ▶ reviewing the effectiveness of the external audit process, taking into consideration relevant UK professional and regulatory requirements;

  ▶ developing and implementing policy on the engagement of the external auditor to supply non-audit services, ensuring there is prior approval of non-audit services, considering the impact this may have on independence, taking into account the relevant regulations and ethical guidance in this regard, and reporting to the board on any improvement or action required; and

  ▶ reporting to the board on how it has discharged its responsibilities.

26. The annual report should describe the work of the audit committee, including:

  ▶ the significant issues that the audit committee considered relating to the financial statements, and how these issues were addressed;

  ▶ an explanation of how it has assessed the independence and effectiveness of the external audit process and the approach taken to the appointment or reappointment of the external auditor, information on the length of tenure of the current audit firm, when a tender was last conducted and advance notice of any retendering plans;

  ▶ in the case of a board not accepting the audit committee's recommendation on the external auditor appointment, reappointment or removal, a statement from the audit committee explaining its recommendation and the reasons why the board has taken a different position (this should also be supplied in any papers recommending appointment or reappointment);

---

8 A smaller company is one that is below the FTSE 350 throughout the year immediately prior to the reporting year.

> ▶ where there is no internal audit function, an explanation for the absence, how internal assurance is achieved, and how this affects the work of external audit; and
> ▶ an explanation of how auditor independence and objectivity are safeguarded, if the external auditor provides non-audit services.

27. The directors should explain in the annual report their responsibility for preparing the annual report and accounts, and state that they consider the annual report and accounts, taken as a whole, is fair, balanced and understandable, and provides the information necessary for shareholders to assess the company's position, performance, business model and strategy.

28. The board should carry out a robust assessment of the company's emerging and principal risks.[9] The board should confirm in the annual report that it has completed this assessment, including a description of its principal risks, what procedures are in place to identify emerging risks, and an explanation of how these are being managed or mitigated. 29. The board should monitor the company's risk management and internal control systems and, at least annually, carry out a review of their effectiveness and report on that review in the annual report. The monitoring and review should cover all material controls, including financial, operational and compliance controls.

30. In annual and half-yearly financial statements, the board should state whether it considers it appropriate to adopt the going concern basis of accounting in preparing them, and identify any material uncertainties to the company's ability to continue to do so over a period of at least twelve months from the date of approval of the financial statements.

31. Taking account of the company's current position and principal risks, the board should explain in the annual report how it has assessed the prospects of the company, over what period it has done so and why it considers that period to be appropriate. The board should state whether it has a reasonable expectation that the company will be able to continue in operation and meet its liabilities as they fall due over the period of their assessment, drawing attention to any qualifications or assumptions as necessary.

5 Remuneration

Principles

P. Remuneration policies and practices should be designed to support strategy and promote long-term sustainable success. Executive remuneration should be aligned to company purpose and values, and be clearly linked to the successful delivery of the company's long-term strategy.

Q. A formal and transparent procedure for developing policy on executive remuneration and determining director and senior management[10] remuneration should be established. No director should be involved in deciding their own remuneration outcome.

---

9 Principal risks should include, but are not necessarily limited to, those that could result in events or circumstances that might threaten the company's business model, future performance, solvency or liquidity and reputation. In deciding which risks are principal risks companies should consider the potential impact and probability of the related events or circumstances, and the timescale over which they may occur

10 See footnote 4.

R. Directors should exercise independent judgement and discretion when authorising remuneration outcomes, taking account of company and individual performance, and wider circumstances.

Provisions

32. The board should establish a remuneration committee of independent non-executive directors, with a minimum membership of three, or in the case of smaller companies, two.[11] In addition, the chair of the board can only be a member if they were independent on appointment and cannot chair the committee. Before appointment as chair of the remuneration committee, the appointee should have served on a remuneration committee for at least 12 months.

33. The remuneration committee should have delegated responsibility for determining the policy for executive director remuneration and setting remuneration for the chair, executive directors and senior management.[12] It should review workforce[13] remuneration and related policies and the alignment of incentives and rewards with culture, taking these into account when setting the policy for executive director remuneration.

34. The remuneration of non-executive directors should be determined in accordance with the Articles of Association or, alternatively, by the board. Levels of remuneration for the chair and all non-executive directors should reflect the time commitment and responsibilities of the role. Remuneration for all non-executive directors should not include share options or other performance-related elements.

35. Where a remuneration consultant is appointed, this should be the responsibility of the remuneration committee. The consultant should be identified in the annual report alongside a statement about any other connection it has with the company or individual directors. Independent judgement should be exercised when evaluating the advice of external third parties and when receiving views from executive directors and senior management.[14]

36. Remuneration schemes should promote long-term shareholdings by executive directors that support alignment with long-term shareholder interests. Share awards granted for this purpose should be released for sale on a phased basis and be subject to a total vesting and holding period of five years or more. The remuneration committee should develop a formal policy for post-employment shareholding requirements encompassing both unvested and vested shares.

37. Remuneration schemes and policies should enable the use of discretion to override formulaic outcomes. They should also include provisions that would enable the company to recover and/or withhold sums or share awards and specify the circumstances in which it would be appropriate to do so.

38. Only basic salary should be pensionable. The pension contribution rates for executive directors, or payments in lieu, should be aligned with those available to the workforce. The pension consequences and associated costs of basic salary increases and any other changes in pensionable remuneration, or contribution rates, particularly for directors close to retirement, should be carefully considered when compared with workforce arrangements.

---

11 See footnote 8.

12 See footnote 4.

13 See the Guidance on Board Effectiveness Section 5 for a description of 'workforce' in this context.

14 See footnote 4.

39. Notice or contract periods should be one year or less. If it is necessary to offer longer periods to new directors recruited from outside the company, such periods should reduce to one year or less after the initial period. The remuneration committee should ensure compensation commitments in directors' terms of appointment do not reward poor performance. They should be robust in reducing compensation to reflect departing directors' obligations to mitigate loss.

40. When determining executive director remuneration policy and practices, the remuneration committee should address the following:

 ▶ **clarity** – remuneration arrangements should be transparent and promote effective engagement with shareholders and the workforce;

 ▶ **simplicity** – remuneration structures should avoid complexity and their rationale and operation should be easy to understand;

 ▶ **risk** – remuneration arrangements should ensure reputational and other risks from excessive rewards, and behavioural risks that can arise from target-based incentive plans, are identified and mitigated;

 ▶ **predictability** – the range of possible values of rewards to individual directors and any other limits or discretions should be identified and explained at the time of approving the policy;

 ▶ **proportionality** – the link between individual awards, the delivery of strategy and the long-term performance of the company should be clear. Outcomes should not reward poor performance; and

 ▶ **alignment to culture** – incentive schemes should drive behaviours consistent with company purpose, values and strategy.

41. There should be a description of the work of the remuneration committee in the annual report, including:

 ▶ an explanation of the strategic rationale for executive directors' remuneration policies, structures and any performance metrics;

 ▶ reasons why the remuneration is appropriate using internal and external measures, including pay ratios and pay gaps;

 ▶ a description, with examples, of how the remuneration committee has addressed the factors in Provision 40;

 ▶ whether the remuneration policy operated as intended in terms of company performance and quantum, and, if not, what changes are necessary;

 ▶ what engagement has taken place with shareholders and the impact this has had on remuneration policy and outcomes;

 ▶ what engagement with the workforce has taken place to explain how executive remuneration aligns with wider company pay policy; and

 ▶ to what extent discretion has been applied to remuneration outcomes and the reasons why.

Appendix 2 – Stewardship Code

Financial Reporting Council September 2012

Contents

Stewardship and the Code

1. Stewardship aims to promote the long term success of companies in such a way that the ultimate providers of capital also prosper. Effective stewardship benefits companies, investors and the economy as a whole.

2. In publicly listed companies responsibility for stewardship is shared. The primary responsibility rests with the board of the company, which oversees the actions of its management. Investors in the company also play an important role in holding the board to account for the fulfilment of its responsibilities.

3. The UK Corporate Governance Code identifies the principles that underlie an effective board. The UK Stewardship Code sets out the principles of effective stewardship by investors. In so doing, the Code assists institutional investors better to exercise their stewardship responsibilities, which in turn gives force to the 'comply or explain' system.

4. For investors, stewardship is more than just voting. Activities may include monitoring and engaging with companies on matters such as strategy, performance, risk, capital structure, and corporate governance, including culture and remuneration. Engagement is purposeful dialogue with companies on these matters as well as on issues that are the immediate subject of votes at general meetings.

5. Institutional investors' activities include decision-making on matters such as allocating assets, awarding investment mandates, designing investment strategies, and buying or selling specific securities. The division of duties within and between institutions may span a spectrum, such that some may be considered asset owners and others asset managers.

6. Broadly speaking, asset owners include pension funds, insurance companies, investment trusts and other collective investment vehicles. As the providers of capital, they set the tone for stewardship and may influence behavioural changes that lead to better stewardship by asset managers and companies. Asset managers, with day-to-day

responsibility for managing investments, are well positioned to influence companies' long-term performance through stewardship.

7. Compliance with the Code does not constitute an invitation to manage the affairs of a company or preclude a decision to sell a holding, where this is considered in the best interest of clients or beneficiaries.

Application of the Code

1. The UK Stewardship Code traces its origins to 'The Responsibilities of Institutional Shareholders and Agents: Statement of Principles,' first published in 2002 by the Institutional Shareholders Committee (ISC), and which the ISC converted to a code in 2009. Following the 2009 Walker Review of governance in financial institutions, the FRC was invited to take responsibility for the Code. In 2010, the FRC published the first version of the UK Stewardship Code, which closely mirrored the ISC code. This edition of the Code does not change the spirit of the 2010 Code.

2. The Code is directed in the first instance to institutional investors, by which is meant asset owners and asset managers with equity holdings in UK listed companies. Institutional investors may choose to outsource to external service providers some of the activities associated with stewardship. However, they cannot delegate their responsibility for stewardship. They remain responsible for ensuring those activities are carried out in a manner consistent with their own approach to stewardship. Accordingly, the Code also applies, by extension, to service providers, such as proxy advisers and investment consultants.

3. The FRC expects signatories of the Code to publish on their website, or if they do not have a website in another accessible form, a statement that:

   ▷ describes how the signatory has applied each of the seven principles of the Code and discloses the specific information requested in the guidance to the principles; or

   ▷ if one or more of the principles have not been applied or the specific information requested in the guidance has not been disclosed, explains why the signatory has not complied with those elements of the Code.

4. Disclosures under the Code should improve the functioning of the market for investment mandates. Asset owners should be better equipped to evaluate asset managers, and asset managers should be better informed, enabling them to tailor their services to meet asset owners' requirements.

5. In particular the disclosures should, with respect to conflicts of interest, address the priority given to client interests in decision-making; with respect to collective engagement, describe the circumstances under which the signatory would join forces with other institutional investors to ensure that boards acknowledge and respond to their concerns on critical issues and at critical times; and, with respect to proxy voting agencies, how the signatory uses their advice.

6. The statement of how the Code has been applied should be aligned with the signatory's role in the investment chain.

7. Asset owners' commitment to the Code may include engaging directly with companies or indirectly through the mandates given to asset managers. They should clearly communicate their policies on stewardship to their managers. Since asset owners are the primary audience of asset managers' public statements as well as client reports on stewardship, asset owners should seek to hold their managers to account for their stewardship activities. In so doing, they better fulfil their duty to their beneficiaries to exercise stewardship over their assets.

8. An asset manager should disclose how it delivers stewardship responsibilities on

behalf of its clients. Following the publication in 2011 of the Stewardship Supplement to Technical Release AAF 01/06, asset managers are encouraged to have the policies described in their stewardship statements independently verified. Where appropriate, asset owners should also consider having their policy statements independently verified.

9. Overseas investors who follow other national or international codes that have similar objectives should not feel the application of the Code duplicates or confuses their responsibilities. Disclosures made in respect of those standards can also be used to demonstrate the extent to which they have complied with the Code. In a similar spirit, UK institutions that apply the Code should use their best efforts to apply its principles to overseas equity holdings.

10. Institutional investors with several types of funds or products need to make only one statement, but are encouraged to explain which of their funds or products are covered by the approach described in their statements. Where institutions apply a stewardship approach to other asset classes, they are encouraged to disclose this.

11. The FRC encourages service providers to disclose how they carry out the wishes of their clients with respect to each principle of the Code that is relevant to their activities.

12. Signatories are encouraged to review their policy statements annually, and update them where necessary to reflect changes in actual practice.

13. This statement should be easy to find on the signatory's website, or if they do not have a website in another accessible form, and should indicate when the statement was last reviewed. It should include contact details of an individual who can be contacted for further information and by those interested in collective engagement. The FRC hosts on its website the statements of signatories without their own website.

14. The FRC retains on its website a list of asset owners, asset managers and service providers that have published a statement on their compliance or otherwise with the Code, and requests that signatories notify the FRC when they have done so, and when the statement is updated.

15. The FRC regularly monitors the take-up and application of the Code. It expects the content of the Code to evolve over time to reflect developments in good stewardship practice, the structure and operation of the market, and the broader regulatory framework. Unless circumstances change, the FRC does not envisage proposing further changes to the Code until 2014 at the earliest.

Financial Reporting Council
September 2012

Comply or Explain

1. As with the UK Corporate Governance Code, the UK Stewardship Code should be applied on a 'comply or explain' basis.

2. The Code is not a rigid set of rules. It consists of principles and guidance. The principles are the core of the Code and the way in which they are applied should be the central question for the institutional investor as it determines how to operate according to the Code. The guidance recommends how the principle might be applied.

3. Those signatories that choose not to comply with one of the principles, or not to follow the guidance, should deliver meaningful explanations that enable the reader to understand their approach to stewardship. In providing an explanation, the signatory should aim to illustrate how its actual practices contribute to good stewardship and promote the delivery of the institution's or its clients' investment objectives. They should provide a clear rationale for their approach.

4. The Financial Services Authority requires any firm authorised to manage funds, which is not a venture capital firm, and which manages investments for professional clients that

are not natural persons, to disclose 'the nature of its commitment' to the Code or 'where it does not commit to the Code, its alternative investment strategy' (under Conduct of Business Rule 2.2.3).

5.   The FRC recognises that not all parts of the Code are relevant to all signatories. For example, smaller institutions may judge that some of its principles and guidance are disproportionate in their case. In these circumstances, they should take advantage of the 'comply or explain' approach and set out why this is the case.

6.   In their responses to explanations, clients and beneficiaries should pay due regard to the signatory's individual circumstances and bear in mind in particular the size and complexity of the signatory, the nature of the risks and challenges it faces, and the investment objectives of the signatory or its clients.

7.   While clients and beneficiaries have every right to challenge a signatory's explanations if they are unconvincing, they should not evaluate explanations in a mechanistic way. Departures from the Code should not be automatically treated as breaches. A signatory's clients and beneficiaries should be careful to respond to the statements from the signatory in a manner that supports the 'comply or explain' process and bears in mind the purpose of good stewardship. They should put their views to the signatory and both parties should be prepared to discuss the position.

The Principles of the Code

So as to protect and enhance the value that accrues to the ultimate beneficiary, institutional investors should:

1.   publicly disclose their policy on how they will discharge their stewardship responsibilities;

2.   have a robust policy on managing conflicts of interest in relation to stewardship which should be publicly disclosed;

3.   monitor their investee companies;

4.   establish clear guidelines on when and how they will escalate their stewardship activities;

5.   be willing to act collectively with other investors where appropriate;

6.   have a clear policy on voting and disclosure of voting activity; and

7.   report periodically on their stewardship and voting activities.

The UK Stewardship Code

Principle 1: Institutional investors should publicly disclose their policy on how they will discharge their stewardship responsibilities.

Guidance

Stewardship activities include monitoring and engaging with companies on matters such as strategy, performance, risk, capital structure, and corporate governance, including culture and remuneration. Engagement is purposeful dialogue with companies on those matters as well as on issues that are the immediate subject of votes at general meetings.

The policy should disclose how the institutional investor applies stewardship with the aim of enhancing and protecting the value for the ultimate beneficiary or client.

The statement should reflect the institutional investor's activities within the investment chain, as well as the responsibilities that arise from those activities. In particular, the stewardship responsibilities of those whose primary activities are related to asset ownership may be different from those whose primary activities are related to asset management or other investment-related services.

Where activities are outsourced, the statement should explain how this is compatible with the proper exercise of the institutional investor's stewardship responsibilities and what steps the investor has taken to ensure that they are carried out in a manner consistent with the approach to stewardship set out in the statement.

The disclosure should describe arrangements for integrating stewardship within the wider investment process.

Principle 2: Institutional investors should have a robust policy on managing conflicts of interest in relation to stewardship which should be publicly disclosed.

Guidance

An institutional investor's duty is to act in the interests of its clients and/or beneficiaries.

Conflicts of interest will inevitably arise from time to time, which may include when voting on matters affecting a parent company or client.

Institutional investors should put in place, maintain and publicly disclose a policy for identifying and managing conflicts of interest with the aim of taking all reasonable steps to put the interests of their client or beneficiary first. The policy should also address how matters are handled when the interests of clients or beneficiaries diverge from each other.

Principle 3: Institutional investors should monitor their investee companies.

Guidance

Effective monitoring is an essential component of stewardship. It should take place regularly and be checked periodically for effectiveness.

When monitoring companies, institutional investors should seek to:

- ▷ keep abreast of the company's performance;
- ▷ keep abreast of developments, both internal and external to the company, that drive the company's value and risks;
- ▷ satisfy themselves that the company's leadership is effective;
- ▷ satisfy themselves that the company's board and committees adhere to the spirit of the UK Corporate Governance Code, including through meetings with the chairman and other board members;
- ▷ consider the quality of the company's reporting; and
- ▷ attend the General Meetings of companies in which they have a major holding, where appropriate and practicable.

Institutional investors should consider carefully explanations given for departure from the UK Corporate Governance Code and make reasoned judgements in each case. They should give a timely explanation to the company, in writing where appropriate, and be prepared to enter a dialogue if they do not accept the company's position.

Institutional investors should endeavour to identify at an early stage issues that may result in a significant loss in investment value. If they have concerns, they should seek to ensure that the appropriate members of the investee company's board or management are made aware.

Institutional investors may or may not wish to be made insiders. An institutional investor who may be willing to become an insider should indicate in its stewardship statement the willingness to do so, and the mechanism by which this could be done.

Institutional investors will expect investee companies and their advisers to ensure that information that could affect their ability to deal in the shares of the company concerned is not conveyed to them without their prior agreement.

Principle 4: Institutional investors should establish clear guidelines on when and how they will escalate their stewardship activities.

Guidance

Institutional investors should set out the circumstances in which they will actively intervene and regularly assess the outcomes of doing so. Intervention should be considered regardless of whether an active or passive investment policy is followed. In addition, being underweight is not, of itself, a reason for not intervening. Instances when institutional investors may want to intervene include, but are not limited to, when they have concerns about the company's strategy, performance, governance, remuneration or approach to risks, including those that may arise from social and environmental matters.

Initial discussions should take place on a confidential basis. However, if companies do not respond constructively when institutional investors intervene, then institutional investors should consider whether to escalate their action, for example, by:

- holding additional meetings with management specifically to discuss concerns;
- expressing concerns through the company's advisers;
- meeting with the chairman or other board members;
- intervening jointly with other institutions on particular issues;
- making a public statement in advance of General Meetings;
- submitting resolutions and speaking at General Meetings; and
- requisitioning a General Meeting, in some cases proposing to change board membership.

Principle 5: Institutional investors should be willing to act collectively with other investors where appropriate.

Guidance

At times collaboration with other investors may be the most effective manner in which to engage.

Collective engagement may be most appropriate at times of significant corporate or wider economic stress, or when the risks posed threaten to destroy significant value.

Institutional investors should disclose their policy on collective engagement, which should indicate their readiness to work with other investors through formal and informal groups when this is necessary to achieve their objectives and ensure companies are aware of concerns. The disclosure should also indicate the kinds of circumstances in which the institutional investor would consider participating in collective engagement.

Principle 6: Institutional investors should have a clear policy on voting and disclosure of voting activity.

Guidance

Institutional investors should seek to vote all shares held. They should not automatically support the board.

If they have been unable to reach a satisfactory outcome through active dialogue then they should register an abstention or vote against the resolution. In both instances, it is good practice to inform the company in advance of their intention and the reasons why.

Institutional investors should disclose publicly voting records.

Institutional investors should disclose the use made, if any, of proxy voting or other voting advisory services. They should describe the scope of such services, identify the providers and disclose the extent to which they follow, rely upon or use recommendations made by such services.

Institutional investors should disclose their approach to stock lending and recalling lent stock.

Principle 7: Institutional investors should report periodically on their stewardship and voting activities.

Guidance

Institutional investors should maintain a clear record of their stewardship activities.

Asset managers should regularly account to their clients or beneficiaries as to how they have discharged their responsibilities. Such reports will be likely to comprise qualitative as well as quantitative information. The particular information reported and the format used, should be a matter for agreement between agents and their principals.

Asset owners should report at least annually to those to whom they are accountable on their stewardship policy and its execution.

Transparency is an important feature of effective stewardship. Institutional investors should not, however, be expected to make disclosures that might be counterproductive. Confidentiality in specific situations may well be crucial to achieving a positive outcome.

Asset managers that sign up to this Code should obtain an independent opinion on their engagement and voting processes having regard to an international standard or a UK framework such as AAF 01/06. The existence of such assurance reporting should be publicly disclosed. If requested, clients should be provided access to such assurance reports.

Appendix 3 – Wates Principles for large private companies

PRINCIPLE ONE

PURPOSE AND LEADERSHIP

An effective board develops and promotes the purpose of a company, and ensures that its values, strategy and culture align with that purpose.

GUIDANCE

Purpose

A well developed and defined purpose will help companies of all sizes and structures articulate their business model and develop their strategy, operating practices, workforce, and approach to risk.

All directors should promote the success of the company. Boards should have a clear understanding of the views of shareholders including those with a minority interest. Directors should act with integrity and lead by example, setting the tone from the top, building positive relationships with all stakeholders, particularly the workforce.

Effective boards ensure that the company operates with a clear sense of purpose and collective vision. To promote this, boards will appreciate the importance of dialogue with the workforce and wider stakeholders around the company's stated purpose and be proactive in ensuring that it takes place. Effective boards are able to demonstrate how the sharing of this purpose has informed the decision-making process to achieve long-term sustainable success.

Values and Culture

A company's purpose and values should inform expected behaviours and practices throughout the organisation. The values should be explained and integrated into the different functions and operations of the business. This may include internal assurance, employment practices, risk management and compliance functions.

A healthy culture is critical to the company's competitive advantage, and vital to the creation and protection of long-term value. Culture can be defined as a combination of the values, attitudes and behaviours manifested by a company in its operations and relationships with its stakeholders. The board, shareholders and management must make and maintain a commitment to embedding the desired culture throughout the organisation.

Effective ways of monitoring culture include (but are not limited to) employee surveys, engagement with trade unions, absenteeism rates, exit interviews and board feedback sessions.

Strategy

An effective board develops a strategy and business model to generate long-term sustainable value. It is responsible for ensuring that its strategy is clearly articulated and implemented throughout the organisation, and that it, along with the company values, supports appropriate behaviours and practices.

The board should lead on the establishment of transparent policies in relation to raising concerns about misconduct and unethical practices; such polices should include effective review processes.

The board manages conflicts of interest and a balance should be struck between short-term targets or needs, and long-term aspirations.

PRINCIPLE TWO

BOARD COMPOSITION

Effective board composition requires an effective chair and a balance of skills, backgrounds, experience and knowledge, with individual directors having sufficient capacity to make a valuable contribution. The size of a board should be guided by the scale and complexity of the company.

GUIDANCE

Chair

The chair leads the board and is responsible for its overall effectiveness, promoting open debate and facilitating constructive discussion. The chair should ensure that all directors have appropriate information and sufficient time is made available for meaningful discussion.

Consideration should be given to separating the roles of the chair and chief executive to ensure a balance of power and effective decision-making.

Balance and diversity

A balanced board promotes effective decision-making and supports the delivery of a company's strategy.

An effective board has an appropriate combination of skills, backgrounds, experience and knowledge that promotes accountability and incorporates objective thought, which in turn provides constructive challenge to achieve effective decision-making.

The board should collectively demonstrate a high-level of understanding relevant to the company's business needs and stakeholder interests.

Appointments to the board should promote diversity in line with the protected characteristics within the Equalities Act 2010.7 An effective board should be able to demonstrate that there has been a considered effort to establish an appropriate balance of expertise, diversity and objectivity.

A policy on diversity and inclusion aligned to company strategy can support appointments to the board and succession planning. Such a policy should also consider targets and aspirations promoted by Government and industry initiatives or expert reviews.

Size and structure

A board should give careful consideration to its size and structure so that it is appropriate to meet the strategic needs and challenges of the organisation and enables effective decision-making.

Companies should consider the value of appointing independent non-executive directors to offer constructive challenge. Appointment of independent non-executive directors should be subject to a transparent procedure. Boards may wish to delegate some functions to committees which can consider specific issues such as risk or remuneration; however, this will be dependent on structure, complexity and size of the company.

Effectiveness

The closely held nature of ownership within many large private companies means directors are often required to maintain objectivity in complex situations, in particular when there is an influential shareholder.

Companies should demonstrate a commitment to the ongoing professional development of their board, and directors should embrace such opportunities and ensure that they have sufcient time to discharge their duties.

Regular evaluation of the board can help individual directors to contribute effectively and highlight the strengths and weaknesses of the board as a whole. The chair should act on the recommendations of such evaluations. This approach may be part of board refreshment and succession plans.

PRINCIPLE THREE

DIRECTOR RESPONSIBILITIES

The board and individual directors should have a clear understanding of their accountability and responsibilities.

The board's policies and procedures should support effective decision-making and independent challenge.

GUIDANCE

Accountability

An effective board should establish and maintain corporate governance practices that provide clear lines of accountability and responsibility to support effective decision-making.

Clear corporate governance policies, practices and company leadership, all working together, promote effective stewardship to deliver long-term value.

A company should set out policies and practices that govern the internal affairs of the company. These include matters relating to the authority, accountability, role and conduct of directors, and may include specific information relating to shareholders, such as shareholder agreements and protection of minority shareholders.

Conflicts of interest can arise and compromise objective decision-making.

In such cases the board should agree and set out how such conflicts should be identified and managed.

The chair and the company secretary should periodically review the governance processes to confirm that they remain fit for purpose and consider any initiatives which could strengthen the governance of the company. Transparent corporate governance policies and practices can clarify the relationship between the company and its owners, including that of a parent company and its subsidiary in order to deliver long-term sustainable success.

Committees

A board may make use of committees to help with the consideration of matters such as financial reporting, risk, succession and remuneration.

The terms of each committee should be set out including authorities delegated to it. A board retains responsibility for any final decisions.

The provision of independent challenge in board and committee decision-making should mitigate the risk of individuals having unfettered powers. Independent challenge encourages constructive problem-solving that benefits companies in the long-term.

Integrity of information

A board should establish formal and robust internal processes to ensure systems and controls are operating effectively, and that the quality and integrity of information provided to it is reliable, enabling directors to monitor and challenge the performance of the company, and make informed decisions.

A board may rely on a broad range of information sources, including, but not limited to:

▶ financial reporting;

▶ key performance indicators;

▶ workforce data;

▶ environmental data;

▶ stakeholder engagement feedback; and

▶ consumer data.

Board papers and supporting information should:

▶ be accurate, clear, comprehensive and up to date;

▶ contain a summary of the contents of any paper;

▶ inform the director what is expected of them on each issue; and

▶ be issued in good time.

PRINCIPLE FOUR

OPPORTUNITY AND RISK

A board should promote the long-term sustainable success of the company by identifying opportunities to create and preserve value, and establishing oversight for the identification and mitigation of risks.

GUIDANCE

Opportunity

A board should consider and assess how the company creates and preserves value over the long-term. This requires boards to consider both tangible and intangible sources of value, and the stakeholders that contribute to it.

This should include processes for the identification of future opportunities for innovation and entrepreneurship. Such opportunities may often be dependent on an agreed risk appetite and the company's long-term strategy and prospects. It may also include processes for ensuring that new business opportunities of a certain value are considered and approved at board level.

Risk

A board has responsibility for an organisation's overall approach to strategic decision-making and effective risk management (financial and non-financial), including reputational risk. This requires oversight of risk and how it is managed, and appropriate accountability to stakeholders.

The size and nature of the business will determine the internal control systems put in place to manage and mitigate both emerging and principal risks. Some companies may decide to delegate to a committee to oversee such matters.

Responsibilities

The board should establish an internal control framework with clearly defined roles and responsibilities for those involved. It should agree an approach to reporting, including frequency of reporting and the points at which decisions are made and escalated. Responsibilities may include:

▶ developing appropriate risk management systems that identify emerging and established risks facing the company and its stakeholders. Such systems should enable the board to make informed and robust decisions, including those associated with material environmental, social and governance matters, such as climate change, workforce relationships, supply chains, and ethical considerations;

▶ determining the nature and extent of the principal risks faced and those risks which the organisation is willing to take in achieving its strategic objectives (determining its 'risk appetite');

▶ agreeing how the principal risks should be managed or mitigated and over what timeframe to reduce the likelihood of their incidence or the magnitude of their impact;

▶ establishing clear internal and external communication channels on the identification of risk factors, both internally and externally; and

▶ agreeing a monitoring and review process.

PRINCIPLE FIVE

REMUNERATION
A board should promote executive remuneration structures aligned to the long-term sustainable success of a company, taking into account pay and conditions elsewhere in the company.

GUIDANCE

Setting remuneration

Appropriate and fair levels of remuneration help companies to secure and retain high-quality directors, senior management and their workforce. Remuneration for directors and senior managers should be aligned with performance, behaviours, and the achievement of company purpose, values and strategy. In setting director and senior manager remuneration consideration should be given to remuneration throughout the organisation to reinforce a sense of shared purpose.

Policies

The board should establish clear policies on remuneration structures and practices which should enable effective accountability to shareholders.

This should take account of the broader operating context, including the pay and conditions of the wider workforce and the company's response to matters such as any gender pay gap.

Such accountability can be supported by clear remuneration structures that are aligned with the company's purpose, values and culture, and the delivery of strategy to support long-term sustainable success. Policies may include robust consideration of the reputational and behavioural risks to the company that can result from inappropriate incentives and excessive rewards.

Boards should consider the benefits of greater transparency of remuneration structures and policies which will build trust from wider stakeholders. Additional transparency could extend to commenting on how executive remuneration reflects general practice within the sector or voluntary disclosure of pay ratios.

Delegating remuneration decisions

The establishment of a committee is a way some boards may wish to delegate responsibility for designing remuneration policies and structures for directors and senior management. Such a committee might benefit from the contribution of an independent non-executive director.

Subsidiary companies

In some companies, director pay will be controlled by a parent company, and in such circumstances the subsidiary should explain this and cross-refer to information available elsewhere which explains the policy in relation to the subsidiary.

Directors should foster effective stakeholder relationships aligned to the company's purpose. The board is responsible for overseeing meaningful engagement with stakeholders, including the workforce, and having regard to their views when taking decisions.

PRINCIPLE SIX

STAKEHOLDER RELATIONSHIPS AND ENGAGEMENT

GUIDANCE

External impacts

Large private companies create their own social, economic and environmental impact, but are also affected by changes to their operating environment. Sustainable business benefits wider society, and large private companies have a responsibility to create and sustain long-term value for their shareholders and stakeholders. This includes consideration of how a company's activities may impact both current and future stakeholders, which, for example, could include impacts on the environment.

Stakeholders

Dialogue with stakeholders helps boards understand the effects of company policies and practices, predict future developments and trends, and re-align strategy. A company should identify and prioritise stakeholder relationships for those affected by company operations and are integral to its ability to generate and preserve value. These are likely to vary dependent on the size and nature of the company.

Stakeholders include the workforce, customers and suppliers, but also other material stakeholders specific to company circumstances or sectors, such as regulators, Governments, pensioners, creditors and community groups.

The board should present to stakeholders a fair, balanced and understandable assessment of the company's position and prospects and make this available on an annual basis.

Boards should ensure that there are channels to receive appropriate feedback from discussions with stakeholders. When explaining impact on the community or environment, boards may want to refer to recognised international standards or frameworks that it follows.

Workforce

For many large private companies, their largest material stakeholder group is their workforce. Companies should develop a range of formal and informal channels that enable them to engage in meaningful two-way dialogue, enabling the workforce to share ideas and concerns with senior management. This might include engagement with trade unions, focus or consultative groups. Such forms of engagement provide useful feedback about business practices and can support the desired culture.

Workforce policies and practices should be aligned with the company's purpose and values. Such policies should establish clear procedures for raising concerns (for example, speak up and whistleblowing policies), and should be reviewed regularly to ensure that they are effective.

A board should demonstrate how the company has undertaken effective engagement with material stakeholders and how such dialogue has been considered in its decision-making.

Companies may also wish to comment on any good practice which may have emerged and contributed to the success of the company.

Explanations in support of applying this Principle will be closely aligned to other disclosure requirements of the Regulations (section 172 reporting, and reporting on workforce engagement). Additional guidance on how to meet these requirements can be found in the FRC's *Guidance on the Strategic Report*, including sections 8.14 - 8.22.

Appendix 4 – Model articles

Model Articles for a private company

Companies (Model Articles) Regulations 2008 Schedule 1
(SI 2008/3229)

PART I INTERPRETATION AND LIMITATION OF LIABILITY

Defined terms

1. In the articles, unless the context requires otherwise—
    "articles" means the company's articles of association;
    "bankruptcy" includes individual insolvency proceedings in a jurisdiction other than England and Wales or Northern Ireland which have an effect similar to that of bankruptcy;
    "chairman" has the meaning given in article 12;
    "chairman of the meeting" has the meaning given in article 39;
    "Companies Acts" means the Companies Acts (as defined in section 2 of the Companies Act 2006), in so far as they apply to the company;
    "director" means a director of the company, and includes any person occupying the position of director, by whatever name called;
    "distribution recipient" has the meaning given in article 31;
    "document" includes, unless otherwise specified, any document sent or supplied in electronic form;
    "electronic form" has the meaning given in section 1168 of the Companies Act 2006;
    "fully paid" in relation to a share, means that the nominal value and any premium to be paid to the company in respect of that share have been paid to the company;
    "hard copy form" has the meaning given in section 1168 of the Companies Act 2006;
    "holder" in relation to shares means the person whose name is entered in the register of members as the holder of the shares;
    "instrument" means a document in hard copy form;
    "ordinary resolution" has the meaning given in section 282 of the Companies Act 2006;
    "paid" means paid or credited as paid;
    "participate", in relation to a directors' meeting, has the meaning given in article 10;
    "proxy notice" has the meaning given in article 45;
    "shareholder" means a person who is the holder of a share;
    "shares" means shares in the company;
    "special resolution" has the meaning given in section 283 of the Companies Act 2006;
    "subsidiary" has the meaning given in section 1159 of the Companies Act 2006;

"transmittee" means a person entitled to a share by reason of the death or bankruptcy of a shareholder or otherwise by operation of law; and

"writing" means the representation or reproduction of words, symbols or other information in a visible form by any method or combination of methods, whether sent or supplied in electronic form or otherwise.

Unless the context otherwise requires, other words or expressions contained in these articles bear the same meaning as in the Companies Act 2006 as in force on the date when these articles become binding on the company.

Liability of members

2. The liability of the members is limited to the amount, if any, unpaid on the shares held by them.

PART 2 DIRECTORS

DIRECTORS' POWERS AND RESPONSIBILITIES

Directors' general authority

3. Subject to the articles, the directors are responsible for the management of the company's business, for which purpose they may exercise all the powers of the company.

Shareholders' reserve power

4.— (1) The shareholders may, by special resolution, direct the directors to take, or refrain from taking, specified action.

(2) No such special resolution invalidates anything which the directors have done before the passing of the resolution.

Directors may delegate

5.— (1) Subject to the articles, the directors may delegate any of the powers which are conferred on them under the articles—

(a) to such person or committee;

(b) by such means (including by power of attorney);

(c) to such an extent;

(d) in relation to such matters or territories; and

(e) on such terms and conditions;

as they think fit.

(2) If the directors so specify, any such delegation may authorise further delegation of the directors' powers by any person to whom they are delegated.

(3) The directors may revoke any delegation in whole or part, or alter its terms and conditions.

Committees

6.— (1) Committees to which the directors delegate any of their powers must follow procedures which are based as far as they are applicable on those provisions of the articles which govern the taking of decisions by directors.

(2) The directors may make rules of procedure for all or any committees, which prevail over rules derived from the articles if they are not consistent with them.

DECISION-MAKING BY DIRECTORS

Directors to take decisions collectively

7.— (1)   The general rule about decision-making by directors is that any decision of the directors must be either a majority decision at a meeting or a decision taken in accordance with article 8.

(2)   If—

(a)   the company only has one director, and

(b)   no provision of the articles requires it to have more than one director, the general rule does not apply, and the director may take decisions without regard to any of the provisions of the articles relating to directors' decision-making.

Unanimous decisions

8.— (1)   A decision of the directors is taken in accordance with this article when all eligible directors indicate to each other by any means that they share a common view on a matter.

(2)   Such a decision may take the form of a resolution in writing, copies of which have been signed by each eligible director or to which each eligible director has otherwise indicated agreement in writing.

(3)   References in this article to eligible directors are to directors who would have been entitled to vote on the matter had it been proposed as a resolution at a directors' meeting.

(4)   A decision may not be taken in accordance with this article if the eligible directors would not have formed a quorum at such a meeting.

Calling a directors' meeting

9.— (1)   Any director may call a directors' meeting by giving notice of the meeting to the directors or by authorising the company secretary (if any) to give such notice.

(2)   Notice of any directors' meeting must indicate—

(a)   its proposed date and time;

(b)   where it is to take place; and

(c)   if it is anticipated that directors participating in the meeting will not be in the same place, how it is proposed that they should communicate with each other during the meeting.

(3)   Notice of a directors' meeting must be given to each director, but need not be in writing.

(4)   Notice of a directors' meeting need not be given to directors who waive their entitlement to notice of that meeting, by giving notice to that effect to the company not more than 7 days after the date on which the meeting is held. Where such notice is given after the meeting has been held, that does not affect the validity of the meeting, or of any business conducted at it.

Participation in directors' meetings

10.—(1)   Subject to the articles, directors participate in a directors' meeting, or part of a directors' meeting, when—

(a)   the meeting has been called and takes place in accordance with the articles, and

(b)   they can each communicate to the others any information or opinions they have on any particular item of the business of the meeting.

(2)   In determining whether directors are participating in a directors' meeting, it is irrelevant where any director is or how they communicate with each other.

(3)   If all the directors participating in a meeting are not in the same place, they may decide that the meeting is to be treated as taking place wherever any of them is.

Quorum for directors' meetings

11.—(1)   At a directors' meeting, unless a quorum is participating, no proposal is to be voted on, except a proposal to call another meeting.

(2)   The quorum for directors' meetings may be fixed from time to time by a decision of the directors, but it must never be less than two, and unless otherwise fixed it is two.

(3)   If the total number of directors for the time being is less than the quorum required, the directors must not take any decision other than a decision—

(a)   to appoint further directors, or

(b)   to call a general meeting so as to enable the shareholders to appoint further directors.

Chairing of directors' meetings

12.—(1)   The directors may appoint a director to chair their meetings.

(2)   The person so appointed for the time being is known as the chairman.

(3)   The directors may terminate the chairman's appointment at any time.

(4)   If the chairman is not participating in a directors' meeting within ten minutes of the time at which it was to start, the participating directors must appoint one of themselves to chair it.

Casting vote

13.—(1)   If the numbers of votes for and against a proposal are equal, the chairman or other director chairing the meeting has a casting vote.

(2)   But this does not apply if, in accordance with the articles, the chairman or other director is not to be counted as participating in the decision-making process for quorum or voting purposes.

Conflicts of interest

14.—(1)   If a proposed decision of the directors is concerned with an actual or proposed transaction or arrangement with the company in which a director is interested, that director is not to be counted as participating in the decision-making process for quorum or voting purposes.

(2)   But if paragraph (3) applies, a director who is interested in an actual or proposed transaction or arrangement with the company is to be counted as participating in the decision-making process for quorum and voting purposes.

(3)   This paragraph applies when—

(a   )the company by ordinary resolution disapplies the provision of the articles which would otherwise prevent a director from being counted as participating in the decision-making process;

(b)   the director's interest cannot reasonably be regarded as likely to give rise to a conflict of interest; or

(c)   the director's conflict of interest arises from a permitted cause.

(4) For the purposes of this article, the following are permitted causes—

    (a) a guarantee given, or to be given, by or to a director in respect of an obligation incurred by or on behalf of the company or any of its subsidiaries;

    (b) subscription, or an agreement to subscribe, for shares or other securities of the company or any of its subsidiaries, or to underwrite, sub-underwrite, or guarantee subscription for any such shares or securities; and

    (c) arrangements pursuant to which benefits are made available to employees and directors or former employees and directors of the company or any of its subsidiaries which do not provide special benefits for directors or former directors.

(5) For the purposes of this article, references to proposed decisions and decision-making processes include any directors' meeting or part of a directors' meeting.

(6) Subject to paragraph (7), if a question arises at a meeting of directors or of a committee of directors as to the right of a director to participate in the meeting (or part of the meeting) for voting or quorum purposes, the question may, before the conclusion of the meeting, be referred to the chairman whose ruling in relation to any director other than the chairman is to be final and conclusive.

(7) If any question as to the right to participate in the meeting (or part of the meeting) should arise in respect of the chairman, the question is to be decided by a decision of the directors at that meeting, for which purpose the chairman is not to be counted as participating in the meeting (or that part of the meeting) for voting or quorum purposes.

Records of decisions to be kept

15. The directors must ensure that the company keeps a record, in writing, for at least 10 years from the date of the decision recorded, of every unanimous or majority decision taken by the directors.

Directors' discretion to make further rules

16. Subject to the articles, the directors may make any rule which they think fit about how they take decisions, and about how such rules are to be recorded or communicated to directors.

APPOINTMENT OF DIRECTORS

Methods of appointing directors

17.—(1) Any person who is willing to act as a director, and is permitted by law to do so, may be appointed to be a director—

    (a) by ordinary resolution, or

    (b) by a decision of the directors.

(2) In any case where, as a result of death, the company has no shareholders and no directors, the personal representatives of the last shareholder to have died have the right, by notice in writing, to appoint a person to be a director.

(3) For the purposes of paragraph (2), where 2 or more shareholders die in circumstances rendering it uncertain who was the last to die, a younger shareholder is deemed to have survived an older shareholder.

Termination of director's appointment

18. A person ceases to be a director as soon as—

(a) that person ceases to be a director by virtue of any provision of the Companies Act 2006 or is prohibited from being a director by law;

(b) a bankruptcy order is made against that person;

(c) a composition is made with that person's creditors generally in satisfaction of that person's debts;

(d) a registered medical practitioner who is treating that person gives a written opinion to the company stating that that person has become physically or mentally incapable of acting as a director and may remain so for more than three months;

(e) by reason of that person's mental health, a court makes an order which wholly or partly prevents that person from personally exercising any powers or rights which that person would otherwise have;

(f) notification is received by the company from the director that the director is resigning from office, and such resignation has taken effect in accordance with its terms.

Directors' remuneration

19.—(1) Directors may undertake any services for the company that the directors decide.

(2) Directors are entitled to such remuneration as the directors determine—

(a) for their services to the company as directors, and

(b) for any other service which they undertake for the company.

(3) Subject to the articles, a director's remuneration may—

(a) take any form, and

(b) include any arrangements in connection with the payment of a pension, allowance or gratuity, or any death, sickness or disability benefits, to or in respect of that director.

(4) Unless the directors decide otherwise, directors' remuneration accrues from day to day.

(5) Unless the directors decide otherwise, directors are not accountable to the company for any remuneration which they receive as directors or other officers or employees of the company's subsidiaries or of any other body corporate in which the company is interested.

Directors' expenses

20. The company may pay any reasonable expenses which the directors properly incur in connection with their attendance at—

(a) meetings of directors or committees of directors,

(b) general meetings, or

(c) separate meetings of the holders of any class of shares or of debentures of the company, or otherwise in connection with the exercise of their powers and the discharge of their responsibilities in relation to the company.

PART 3 SHARES AND DISTRIBUTIONS

SHARES

All shares to be fully paid up

21.—(1) No share is to be issued for less than the aggregate of its nominal value and any premium to be paid to the company in consideration for its issue.

(2) This does not apply to shares taken on the formation of the company by the subscribers to the company's memorandum.

Powers to issue different classes of share

22.—(1) Subject to the articles, but without prejudice to the rights attached to any existing share, the company may issue shares with such rights or restrictions as may be determined by ordinary resolution.

(2) The company may issue shares which are to be redeemed, or are liable to be redeemed at the option of the company or the holder, and the directors may determine the terms, conditions and manner of redemption of any such shares.

Company not bound by less than absolute interests

23. Except as required by law, no person is to be recognised by the company as holding any share upon any trust, and except as otherwise required by law or the articles, the company is not in any way to be bound by or recognise any interest in a share other than the holder's absolute ownership of it and all the rights attaching to it.

Share certificates

24.—(1) The company must issue each shareholder, free of charge, with one or more certificates in respect of the shares which that shareholder holds.

(2) Every certificate must specify—

(a) in respect of how many shares, of what class, it is issued;

(b) the nominal value of those shares;

(c) that the shares are fully paid; and

(d) any distinguishing numbers assigned to them.

(3) No certificate may be issued in respect of shares of more than one class.

(4) If more than one person holds a share, only one certificate may be issued in respect of it.

(5) Certificates must—

(a) have affixed to them the company's common seal, or

(b) be otherwise executed in accordance with the Companies Acts.

Replacement share certificates

25.—(1) If a certificate issued in respect of a shareholder's shares is—

(a) damaged or defaced, or

(b) said to be lost, stolen or destroyed, that shareholder is entitled to be issued with a replacement certificate in respect of the same shares.

(2) A shareholder exercising the right to be issued with such a replacement certificate—

(a) may at the same time exercise the right to be issued with a single certificate or separate certificates;

(b)   must return the certificate which is to be replaced to the company if it is damaged or defaced; and

(c)   must comply with such conditions as to evidence, indemnity and the payment of a reasonable fee as the directors decide.

Share transfers

26.—(1)   Shares may be transferred by means of an instrument of transfer in any usual form or any other form approved by the directors, which is executed by or on behalf of the transferor.

(2)   No fee may be charged for registering any instrument of transfer or other document relating to or affecting the title to any share.

(3)   The company may retain any instrument of transfer which is registered.

(4)   The transferor remains the holder of a share until the transferee's name is entered in the register of members as holder of it.

(5)   The directors may refuse to register the transfer of a share, and if they do so, the instrument of transfer must be returned to the transferee with the notice of refusal unless they suspect that the proposed transfer may be fraudulent.

Transmission of shares

27.—(1)   If title to a share passes to a transmittee, the company may only recognise the transmittee as having any title to that share.

(2)   A transmittee who produces such evidence of entitlement to shares as the directors may properly require—

(a)   may, subject to the articles, choose either to become the holder of those shares or to have them transferred to another person, and

(b)   subject to the articles, and pending any transfer of the shares to another person, has the same rights as the holder had.

(3)   But transmittees do not have the right to attend or vote at a general meeting, or agree to a proposed written resolution, in respect of shares to which they are entitled, by reason of the holder's death or bankruptcy or otherwise, unless they become the holders of those shares.

Exercise of transmittees' rights

28.—(1)   Transmittees who wish to become the holders of shares to which they have become entitled must notify the company in writing of that wish.

(2)   If the transmittee wishes to have a share transferred to another person, the transmittee must execute an instrument of transfer in respect of it.

(3)   Any transfer made or executed under this article is to be treated as if it were made or executed by the person from whom the transmittee has derived rights in respect of the share, and as if the event which gave rise to the transmission had not occurred.

Transmittees bound by prior notices

29.   If a notice is given to a shareholder in respect of shares and a transmittee is entitled to those shares, the transmittee is bound by the notice if it was given to the shareholder before the transmittee's name has been entered in the register of members.

DIVIDENDS AND OTHER DISTRIBUTIONS

Procedure for declaring dividends

30.—(1) The company may by ordinary resolution declare dividends, and the directors may decide to pay interim dividends.

(2) A dividend must not be declared unless the directors have made a recommendation as to its amount. Such a dividend must not exceed the amount recommended by the directors.

(3) No dividend may be declared or paid unless it is in accordance with shareholders' respective rights.

(4) Unless the shareholders' resolution to declare or directors' decision to pay a dividend, or the terms on which shares are issued, specify otherwise, it must be paid by reference to each shareholder's holding of shares on the date of the resolution or decision to declare or pay it.

(5) If the company's share capital is divided into different classes, no interim dividend may be paid on shares carrying deferred or non-preferred rights if, at the time of payment, any preferential dividend is in arrear.

(6) The directors may pay at intervals any dividend payable at a fixed rate if it appears to them that the profits available for distribution justify the payment.

(7) If the directors act in good faith, they do not incur any liability to the holders of shares conferring preferred rights for any loss they may suffer by the lawful payment of an interim dividend on shares with deferred or non-preferred rights.

Payment of dividends and other distributions

31.—(1) Where a dividend or other sum which is a distribution is payable in respect of a share, it must be paid by one or more of the following means—

(a) transfer to a bank or building society account specified by the distribution recipient either in writing or as the directors may otherwise decide;

(b) sending a cheque made payable to the distribution recipient by post to the distribution recipient at the distribution recipient's registered address (if the distribution recipient is a holder of the share), or (in any other case) to an address specified by the distribution recipient either in writing or as the directors may otherwise decide;

(c) sending a cheque made payable to such person by post to such person at such address as the distribution recipient has specified either in writing or as the directors may otherwise decide; or

(d) any other means of payment as the directors agree with the distribution recipient either in writing or by such other means as the directors decide.

(2) In the articles, "the distribution recipient" means, in respect of a share in respect of which a dividend or other sum is payable—

(a) the holder of the share; or

(b) if the share has two or more joint holders, whichever of them is named first in the register of members; or

(c) if the holder is no longer entitled to the share by reason of death or bankruptcy, or otherwise by operation of law, the transmittee.

No interest on distributions

32. The company may not pay interest on any dividend or other sum payable in respect of a share unless otherwise provided by—

(a) the terms on which the share was issued, or

(b) the provisions of another agreement between the holder of that share and the company.

Unclaimed distributions

33.—(1) All dividends or other sums which are—

    (a) payable in respect of shares, and

    (b) unclaimed after having been declared or become payable, may be invested or otherwise made use of by the directors for the benefit of the company until claimed.

  (2) The payment of any such dividend or other sum into a separate account does not make the company a trustee in respect of it.

  (3) If—

    (a) twelve years have passed from the date on which a dividend or other sum became due for payment, and

    (b) the distribution recipient has not claimed it, the distribution recipient is no longer entitled to that dividend or other sum and it ceases to remain owing by the company.

Non-cash distributions

34.—(1) Subject to the terms of issue of the share in question, the company may, by ordinary resolution on the recommendation of the directors, decide to pay all or part of a dividend or other distribution payable in respect of a share by transferring non-cash assets of equivalent value (including, without limitation, shares or other securities in any company).

  (2) For the purposes of paying a non-cash distribution, the directors may make whatever arrangements they think fit, including, where any difficulty arises regarding the distribution—

    (a) fixing the value of any assets;

    (b) paying cash to any distribution recipient on the basis of that value in order to adjust the rights of recipients; and

    (c) vesting any assets in trustees.

Waiver of distributions

35. Distribution recipients may waive their entitlement to a dividend or other distribution payable in respect of a share by giving the company notice in writing to that effect, but if—

(a) the share has more than one holder, or

(b) more than one person is entitled to the share, whether by reason of the death or bankruptcy of one or more joint holders, or otherwise, the notice is not effective unless it is expressed to be given, and signed, by all the holders or persons otherwise entitled to the share.

CAPITALISATION OF PROFITS

Authority to capitalise and appropriation of capitalised sums

36.—(1) Subject to the articles, the directors may, if they are so authorised by an ordinary resolution—

    (a)   decide to capitalise any profits of the company (whether or not they are available for distribution) which are not required for paying a preferential dividend, or any sum standing to the credit of the company's share premium account or capital redemption reserve; and

    (b)   appropriate any sum which they so decide to capitalise (a "capitalised sum") to the persons who would have been entitled to it if it were distributed by way of dividend (the "persons entitled") and in the same proportions.

(2)   Capitalised sums must be applied—

    (a)   on behalf of the persons entitled, and

    (b)   in the same proportions as a dividend would have been distributed to them.

(3)   Any capitalised sum may be applied in paying up new shares of a nominal amount equal to the capitalised sum which are then allotted credited as fully paid to the persons entitled or as they may direct.

(4)   A capitalised sum which was appropriated from profits available for distribution may be applied in paying up new debentures of the company which are then allotted credited as fully paid to the persons entitled or as they may direct.

(5)   Subject to the articles the directors may—

    (a)   apply capitalised sums in accordance with paragraphs (3) and (4) partly in one way and partly in another;

    (b)   make such arrangements as they think fit to deal with shares or debentures becoming distributable in fractions under this article (including the issuing of fractional certificates or the making of cash payments); and

    (c)   authorise any person to enter into an agreement with the company on behalf of all the persons entitled which is binding on them in respect of the allotment of shares and debentures to them under this article.

PART 4 DECISION-MAKING BY SHAREHOLDERS

ORGANISATION OF GENERAL MEETINGS

Attendance and speaking at general meetings

37.—(1)   A person is able to exercise the right to speak at a general meeting when that person is in a position to communicate to all those attending the meeting, during the meeting, any information or opinions which that person has on the business of the meeting.

(2)   A person is able to exercise the right to vote at a general meeting when—

    (a)   that person is able to vote, during the meeting, on resolutions put to the vote at the meeting, and

    (b)   that person's vote can be taken into account in determining whether or not such resolutions are passed at the same time as the votes of all the other persons attending the meeting.

(3)   The directors may make whatever arrangements they consider appropriate to enable those attending a general meeting to exercise their rights to speak or vote at it.

(4)   In determining attendance at a general meeting, it is immaterial whether any two or more members attending it are in the same place as each other.

(5)   Two or more persons who are not in the same place as each other attend a general meeting if their circumstances are such that if they have (or were to have) rights to speak and vote at that meeting, they are (or would be) able to exercise them.

Quorum for general meetings

38.   No business other than the appointment of the chairman of the meeting is to be transacted at a general meeting if the persons attending it do not constitute a quorum.

Chairing general meetings

39.—(1)   If the directors have appointed a chairman, the chairman shall chair general meetings if present and willing to do so.

(2)   If the directors have not appointed a chairman, or if the chairman is unwilling to chair the meeting or is not present within ten minutes of the time at which a meeting was due to start—

(a)   the directors present, or

(b)   (if no directors are present), the meeting, must appoint a director or shareholder to chair the meeting, and the appointment of the chairman of the meeting must be the first business of the meeting.

(3)   The person chairing a meeting in accordance with this article is referred to as "the chairman of the meeting".

Attendance and speaking by directors and non-shareholders

40.—(1)   Directors may attend and speak at general meetings, whether or not they are shareholders.

(2)   The chairman of the meeting may permit other persons who are not—

(a)   shareholders of the company, or

(b)   otherwise entitled to exercise the rights of shareholders in relation to general meetings, to attend and speak at a general meeting.

Adjournment

41.—(1)   If the persons attending a general meeting within half an hour of the time at which the meeting was due to start do not constitute a quorum, or if during a meeting a quorum ceases to be present, the chairman of the meeting must adjourn it.

(2)   The chairman of the meeting may adjourn a general meeting at which a quorum is present if—

(a)   the meeting consents to an adjournment, or

(b)   it appears to the chairman of the meeting that an adjournment is necessary to protect the safety of any person attending the meeting or ensure that the business of the meeting is conducted in an orderly manner.

(3)   The chairman of the meeting must adjourn a general meeting if directed to do so by the meeting.

(4)   When adjourning a general meeting, the chairman of the meeting must—

(a)   either specify the time and place to which it is adjourned or state that it is to continue at a time and place to be fixed by the directors, and

(b)   have regard to any directions as to the time and place of any adjournment which have been given by the meeting.

(5) If the continuation of an adjourned meeting is to take place more than 14 days after it was adjourned, the company must give at least 7 clear days' notice of it (that is, excluding the day of the adjourned meeting and the day on which the notice is given)—

(a) to the same persons to whom notice of the company's general meetings is required to be given, and

(b) containing the same information which such notice is required to contain.

(6) No business may be transacted at an adjourned general meeting which could not properly have been transacted at the meeting if the adjournment had not taken place.

VOTING AT GENERAL MEETINGS

Voting: general

42. A resolution put to the vote of a general meeting must be decided on a show of hands unless a poll is duly demanded in accordance with the articles.

Errors and disputes

43.—(1) No objection may be raised to the qualification of any person voting at a general meeting except at the meeting or adjourned meeting at which the vote objected to is tendered, and every vote not disallowed at the meeting is valid.

(2) Any such objection must be referred to the chairman of the meeting, whose decision is final.

Poll votes

44.—(1) A poll on a resolution may be demanded—

(a) in advance of the general meeting where it is to be put to the vote, or

(b) at a general meeting, either before a show of hands on that resolution or immediately after the result of a show of hands on that resolution is declared.

(2) A poll may be demanded by—

(a) the chairman of the meeting;

(b) the directors;

(c) two or more persons having the right to vote on the resolution; or

(d) a person or persons representing not less than one tenth of the total voting rights of all the shareholders having the right to vote on the resolution.

(3) A demand for a poll may be withdrawn if—

(a) the poll has not yet been taken, and

(b) the chairman of the meeting consents to the withdrawal.

(4) Polls must be taken immediately and in such manner as the chairman of the meeting directs.

Content of proxy notices

45.—(1) Proxies may only validly be appointed by a notice in writing (a "proxy notice") which—

(a) states the name and address of the shareholder appointing the proxy;

(b) identifies the person appointed to be that shareholder's proxy and the general meeting in relation to which that person is appointed;

      (c)   is signed by or on behalf of the shareholder appointing the proxy, or is authenticated in such manner as the directors may determine; and

      (d)   is delivered to the company in accordance with the articles and any instructions contained in the notice of the general meeting to which they relate.

(2)   The company may require proxy notices to be delivered in a particular form, and may specify different forms for different purposes.

(3)   Proxy notices may specify how the proxy appointed under them is to vote (or that the proxy is to abstain from voting) on one or more resolutions.

(4)   Unless a proxy notice indicates otherwise, it must be treated as—

      (a)   allowing the person appointed under it as a proxy discretion as to how to vote on any ancillary or procedural resolutions put to the meeting, and

      (b)   appointing that person as a proxy in relation to any adjournment of the general meeting to which it relates as well as the meeting itself.

Delivery of proxy notices

46.—(1)   A person who is entitled to attend, speak or vote (either on a show of hands or on a poll) at a general meeting remains so entitled in respect of that meeting or any adjournment of it, even though a valid proxy notice has been delivered to the company by or on behalf of that person.

(2)   An appointment under a proxy notice may be revoked by delivering to the company a notice in writing given by or on behalf of the person by whom or on whose behalf the proxy notice was given.

(3)   A notice revoking a proxy appointment only takes effect if it is delivered before the start of the meeting or adjourned meeting to which it relates.

(4)   If a proxy notice is not executed by the person appointing the proxy, it must be accompanied by written evidence of the authority of the person who executed it to execute it on the appointor's behalf.

Amendments to resolutions

47.—(1)   An ordinary resolution to be proposed at a general meeting may be amended by ordinary resolution if—

      (a)   notice of the proposed amendment is given to the company in writing by a person entitled to vote at the general meeting at which it is to be proposed not less than 48 hours before the meeting is to take place (or such later time as the chairman of the meeting may determine), and

      (b)   the proposed amendment does not, in the reasonable opinion of the chairman of the meeting, materially alter the scope of the resolution.

(2)   A special resolution to be proposed at a general meeting may be amended by ordinary resolution, if—

      (a)   the chairman of the meeting proposes the amendment at the general meeting at which the resolution is to be proposed, and

      (b)   the amendment does not go beyond what is necessary to correct a grammatical or other non-substantive error in the resolution.

(3)   If the chairman of the meeting, acting in good faith, wrongly decides that an amendment to a resolution is out of order, the chairman's error does not invalidate the vote on that resolution.

PART 5 ADMINISTRATIVE ARRANGEMENTS

Means of communication to be used

48.—(1)   Subject to the articles, anything sent or supplied by or to the company under the articles may be sent or supplied in any way in which the Companies Act 2006 provides for documents or information which are authorised or required by any provision of that Act to be sent or supplied by or to the company.

(2)   Subject to the articles, any notice or document to be sent or supplied to a director in connection with the taking of decisions by directors may also be sent or supplied by the means by which that director has asked to be sent or supplied with such notices or documents for the time being.

(3)   A director may agree with the company that notices or documents sent to that director in a particular way are to be deemed to have been received within a specified time of their being sent, and for the specified time to be less than 48 hours.

Company seals

49.—(1)   Any common seal may only be used by the authority of the directors.

(2)   The directors may decide by what means and in what form any common seal is to be used.

(3)   Unless otherwise decided by the directors, if the company has a common seal and it is affixed to a document, the document must also be signed by at least one authorised person in the presence of a witness who attests the signature.

(4)   For the purposes of this article, an authorised person is—

(a)   any director of the company;

(b)   the company secretary (if any); or

(c)   any person authorised by the directors for the purpose of signing documents to which the common seal is applied.

No right to inspect accounts and other records

50.   Except as provided by law or authorised by the directors or an ordinary resolution of the company, no person is entitled to inspect any of the company's accounting or other records or documents merely by virtue of being a shareholder.

Provision for employees on cessation of business

51.   The directors may decide to make provision for the benefit of persons employed or formerly employed by the company or any of its subsidiaries (other than a director or former director or shadow director) in connection with the cessation or transfer to any person of the whole or part of the undertaking of the company or that subsidiary.

DIRECTORS' INDEMNITY AND INSURANCE

Indemnity

52.—(1)   Subject to paragraph (2), a relevant director of the company or an associated company may be indemnified out of the company's assets against—

(a)   any liability incurred by that director in connection with any negligence, default, breach of duty or breach of trust in relation to the company or an associated company,

(b)   any liability incurred by that director in connection with the activities of the company or an associated company in its capacity as a trustee of an occupational pension scheme (as defined in section 235(6) of the Companies Act 2006),

(c)   any other liability incurred by that director as an officer of the company or an associated company.

(2)   This article does not authorise any indemnity which would be prohibited or rendered void by any provision of the Companies Acts or by any other provision of law.

(3)   In this article—

     (a)   companies are associated if one is a subsidiary of the other or both are subsidiaries of the same body corporate, and

     (b)   a "relevant director" means any director or former director of the company or an associated company.

Insurance

53.—(1)   The directors may decide to purchase and maintain insurance, at the expense of the company, for the benefit of any relevant director in respect of any relevant loss.

(2)   In this article—

     (a)   a "relevant director" means any director or former director of the company or an associated company,

     (b)   a "relevant loss" means any loss or liability which has been or may be incurred by a relevant director in connection with that director's duties or powers in relation to the company, any associated company or any pension fund or employees' share scheme of the company or associated company, and

     (c)   companies are associated if one is a subsidiary of the other or both are subsidiaries of the same body corporate.

Model Articles for a public company

Companies (Model Articles) Regulations 2008 Schedule 3 (SI 2008/3229)

PART I INTERPRETATION AND LIMITATION OF LIABILITY

Defined terms

1.   In the articles , unless the context requires otherwise—

"alternate" or "alternate director" has the meaning given in article 25;

"appointor" has the meaning given in article 25;

"articles" means the company's articles of association;

"bankruptcy" includes individual insolvency proceedings in a jurisdiction other than England and Wales or Northern Ireland which have an effect similar to that of bankruptcy;

"call" has the meaning given in article 54;

"call notice" has the meaning given in article 54;

"certificate" means a paper certificate (other than a share warrant) evidencing a person's title to specified shares or other securities;

"certificated" in relation to a share, means that it is not an uncertificated share or a share in respect of which a share warrant has been issued and is current;

"chairman" has the meaning given in article 12;

"chairman of the meeting" has the meaning given in article 31;

"Companies Acts" means the Companies Acts (as defined in section 2 of the Companies Act 2006), in so far as they apply to the company;

"company's lien" has the meaning given in article 52;

"director" means a director of the company, and includes any person occupying the position of director, by whatever name called;

"distribution recipient" has the meaning given in article 72;

"document" includes, unless otherwise specified, any document sent or supplied in electronic form;

"electronic form" has the meaning given in section 1168 of the Companies Act 2006;

"fully paid" in relation to a share, means that the nominal value and any premium to be paid to the company in respect of that share have been paid to the company;

"hard copy form" has the meaning given in section 1168 of the Companies Act 2006;

"holder" in relation to shares means the person whose name is entered in the register of members as the holder of the shares, or, in the case of a share in respect of which a share warrant has been issued (and not cancelled), the person in possession of that warrant;

"instrument" means a document in hard copy form;

"lien enforcement notice" has the meaning given in article 53;

"member" has the meaning given in section 112 of the Companies Act 2006;

"ordinary resolution" has the meaning given in section 282 of the Companies Act 2006;

"paid" means paid or credited as paid;

"participate", in relation to a directors' meeting, has the meaning given in article 9;

"partly paid" in relation to a share means that part of that share's nominal value or any premium at which it was issued has not been paid to the company;

"proxy notice" has the meaning given in article 38;

"securities seal" has the meaning given in article 47;

"shares" means shares in the company;

"special resolution" has the meaning given in section 283 of the Companies Act 2006;

"subsidiary" has the meaning given in section 1159 of the Companies Act 2006;

"transmittee" means a person entitled to a share by reason of the death or bankruptcy of a shareholder or otherwise by operation of law;

"uncertificated" in relation to a share means that, by virtue of legislation (other than section 778 of the Companies Act 2006) permitting title to shares to be evidenced and transferred without a certificate, title to that share is evidenced and may be transferred without a certificate; and

"writing" means the representation or reproduction of words, symbols or other information in a visible form by any method or combination of methods, whether sent or supplied in electronic form or otherwise.

Unless the context otherwise requires, other words or expressions contained in these articles bear the same meaning as in the Companies Act 2006 as in force on the date when these articles become binding on the company.

Liability of members

2.   The liability of the members is limited to the amount, if any, unpaid on the shares held by them.

PART 2 DIRECTORS

DIRECTORS' POWERS AND RESPONSIBILITIES

Directors' general authority

3.   Subject to the articles, the directors are responsible for the management of the company's business, for which purpose they may exercise all the powers of the company.

Members' reserve power

4.— (1)   The members may, by special resolution, direct the directors to take, or refrain from taking, specified action.

(2)   No such special resolution invalidates anything which the directors have done before the passing of the resolution.

Directors may delegate

5.— (1)   Subject to the articles, the directors may delegate any of the powers which are conferred on them under the articles—
   (a)   to such person or committee;
   (b)   by such means (including by power of attorney);
   (c)   to such an extent;
   (d)   in relation to such matters or territories; and
   (e)   on such terms and conditions;
   as they think fit.

(2)   If the directors so specify, any such delegation may authorise further delegation of the directors' powers by any person to whom they are delegated.

(3)   The directors may revoke any delegation in whole or part, or alter its terms and conditions.

Committees

6.— (1)   Committees to which the directors delegate any of their powers must follow procedures which are based as far as they are applicable on those provisions of the articles which govern the taking of decisions by directors.

(2)   The directors may make rules of procedure for all or any committees, which prevail over rules derived from the articles if they are not consistent with them.

DECISION-MAKING BY DIRECTORS

Directors to take decisions collectively

7.   Decisions of the directors may be taken—
   (a)   at a directors' meeting, or
   (b)   in the form of a directors' written resolution.

Calling a directors' meeting

8.— (1)   Any director may call a directors' meeting.

(2)   The company secretary must call a directors' meeting if a director so requests.

(3) A directors' meeting is called by giving notice of the meeting to the directors.

(4) Notice of any directors' meeting must indicate—

    (a) its proposed date and time;

    (b) where it is to take place; and

    (c) if it is anticipated that directors participating in the meeting will not be in the same place, how it is proposed that they should communicate with each other during the meeting.

(5) Notice of a directors' meeting must be given to each director, but need not be in writing.

(6) Notice of a directors' meeting need not be given to directors who waive their entitlement to notice of that meeting, by giving notice to that effect to the company not more than 7 days after the date on which the meeting is held. Where such notice is given after the meeting has been held, that does not affect the validity of the meeting, or of any business conducted at it.

Participation in directors' meetings

9.— (1) Subject to the articles, directors participate in a directors' meeting, or part of a directors' meeting, when—

    (a) the meeting has been called and takes place in accordance with the articles, and

    (b) they can each communicate to the others any information or opinions they have on any particular item of the business of the meeting.

(2) In determining whether directors are participating in a directors' meeting, it is irrelevant where any director is or how they communicate with each other.

(3) If all the directors participating in a meeting are not in the same place, they may decide that the meeting is to be treated as taking place wherever any of them is.

Quorum for directors' meetings

10.—(1) At a directors' meeting, unless a quorum is participating, no proposal is to be voted on, except a proposal to call another meeting.

(2) The quorum for directors' meetings may be fixed from time to time by a decision of the directors, but it must never be less than two, and unless otherwise fixed it is two.

Meetings where total number of directors less than quorum

11.—(1) This article applies where the total number of directors for the time being is less than the quorum for directors' meetings.

(2) If there is only one director, that director may appoint sufficient directors to make up a quorum or call a general meeting to do so.

(3) If there is more than one director—

    (a) a directors' meeting may take place, if it is called in accordance with the articles and at least two directors participate in it, with a view to appointing sufficient directors to make up a quorum or calling a general meeting to do so, and

    (b) if a directors' meeting is called but only one director attends at the appointed date and time to participate in it, that director may appoint sufficient directors to make up a quorum or call a general meeting to do so.

Chairing directors' meetings

12.—(1)   The directors may appoint a director to chair their meetings.

    (2)   The person so appointed for the time being is known as the chairman.

    (3)   The directors may appoint other directors as deputy or assistant chairmen to chair directors' meetings in the chairman's absence.

    (4)   The directors may terminate the appointment of the chairman, deputy or assistant chairman at any time.

    (5)   If neither the chairman nor any director appointed generally to chair directors' meetings in the chairman's absence is participating in a meeting within ten minutes of the time at which it was to start, the participating directors must appoint one of themselves to chair it.

Voting at directors' meetings: general rules

13.—(1)   Subject to the articles, a decision is taken at a directors' meeting by a majority of the votes of the participating directors.

    (2)   Subject to the articles, each director participating in a directors' meeting has one vote.

    (3)   Subject to the articles, if a director has an interest in an actual or proposed transaction or arrangement with the company—

        (a)   that director and that director's alternate may not vote on any proposal relating to it, but

        (b)   this does not preclude the alternate from voting in relation to that transaction or arrangement on behalf of another appointor who does not have such an interest.

Chairman's casting vote at directors' meetings

14.—(1)   If the numbers of votes for and against a proposal are equal, the chairman or other director chairing the meeting has a casting vote.

    (2)   But this does not apply if, in accordance with the articles, the chairman or other director is not to be counted as participating in the decision-making process for quorum or voting purposes.

Alternates voting at directors' meetings

15.   A director who is also an alternate director has an additional vote on behalf of each appointor who is—

    (a)   not participating in a directors' meeting, and

    (b)   would have been entitled to vote if they were participating in it.

Conflicts of interest

16.—(1)   If a directors' meeting, or part of a directors' meeting, is concerned with an actual or proposed transaction or arrangement with the company in which a director is interested, that director is not to be counted as participating in that meeting, or part of a meeting, for quorum or voting purposes.

    (2)   But if paragraph (3) applies, a director who is interested in an actual or proposed transaction or arrangement with the company is to be counted as participating in a decision at a directors' meeting, or part of a directors' meeting, relating to it for quorum and voting purposes.

    (3)   This paragraph applies when—

(a)   the company by ordinary resolution disapplies the provision of the articles which would otherwise prevent a director from being counted as participating in, or voting at, a directors' meeting;

(b)   the director's interest cannot reasonably be regarded as likely to give rise to a conflict of interest; or

(c)   the director's conflict of interest arises from a permitted cause.

(4)   For the purposes of this article, the following are permitted causes—

(a)   a guarantee given, or to be given, by or to a director in respect of an obligation incurred by or on behalf of the company or any of its subsidiaries;

(b)   subscription, or an agreement to subscribe, for shares or other securities of the company or any of its subsidiaries, or to underwrite, sub-underwrite, or guarantee subscription for any such shares or securities; and

(c)   arrangements pursuant to which benefits are made available to employees and directors or former employees and directors of the company or any of its subsidiaries which do not provide special benefits for directors or former directors.

(5)   Subject to paragraph (6), if a question arises at a meeting of directors or of a committee of directors as to the right of a director to participate in the meeting (or part of the meeting) for voting or quorum purposes, the question may, before the conclusion of the meeting, be referred to the chairman whose ruling in relation to any director other than the chairman is to be final and conclusive.

(6)   If any question as to the right to participate in the meeting (or part of the meeting) should arise in respect of the chairman, the question is to be decided by a decision of the directors at that meeting, for which purpose the chairman is not to be counted as participating in the meeting (or that part of the meeting) for voting or quorum purposes.

Proposing directors' written resolutions

17.—(1)   Any director may propose a directors' written resolution.

(2)   The company secretary must propose a directors' written resolution if a director so requests.

(3)   A directors' written resolution is proposed by giving notice of the proposed resolution to the directors.

(4)   Notice of a proposed directors' written resolution must indicate—

(a)   the proposed resolution, and

(b)   the time by which it is proposed that the directors should adopt it.

(5)   Notice of a proposed directors' written resolution must be given in writing to each director.

(6)   Any decision which a person giving notice of a proposed directors' written resolution takes regarding the process of adopting that resolution must be taken reasonably in good faith.

Adoption of directors' written resolutions

18.—(1)   A proposed directors' written resolution is adopted when all the directors who would have been entitled to vote on the resolution at a directors' meeting have signed one or more copies of it, provided that those directors would have formed a quorum at such a meeting.

(2)   It is immaterial whether any director signs the resolution before or after the time by which the notice proposed that it should be adopted.

(3) Once a directors' written resolution has been adopted, it must be treated as if it had been a decision taken at a directors' meeting in accordance with the articles.

(4) The company secretary must ensure that the company keeps a record, in writing, of all directors' written resolutions for at least ten years from the date of their adoption.

Directors' discretion to make further rules

19. Subject to the articles, the directors may make any rule which they think fit about how they take decisions, and about how such rules are to be recorded or communicated to directors.

APPOINTMENT OF DIRECTORS

Methods of appointing directors

20. Any person who is willing to act as a director, and is permitted by law to do so, may be appointed to be a director—

(a) by ordinary resolution, or

(b) by a decision of the directors.

Retirement of directors by rotation

21.—(1) At the first annual general meeting all the directors must retire from office.

(2) At every subsequent annual general meeting any directors—

(a) who have been appointed by the directors since the last annual general meeting, or

(b) who were not appointed or reappointed at one of the preceding two annual general meetings, must retire from office and may offer themselves for reappointment by the members.

Termination of director's appointment

22. A person ceases to be a director as soon as—

(a) that person ceases to be a director by virtue of any provision of the Companies Act 2006 or is prohibited from being a director by law;

(b) a bankruptcy order is made against that person;

(c) a composition is made with that person's creditors generally in satisfaction of that person's debts;

(d) a registered medical practitioner who is treating that person gives a written opinion to the company stating that that person has become physically or mentally incapable of acting as a director and may remain so for more than three months;

(e) by reason of that person's mental health, a court makes an order which wholly or partly prevents that person from personally exercising any powers or rights which that person would otherwise have;

(f) notification is received by the company from the director that the director is resigning from office as director, and such resignation has taken effect in accordance with its terms.

Directors' remuneration

23.—(1) Directors may undertake any services for the company that the directors decide.

(2) Directors are entitled to such remuneration as the directors determine—

    (a) for their services to the company as directors, and

    (b) for any other service which they undertake for the company.

(3) Subject to the articles, a director's remuneration may—

    (a) take any form, and

    (b) include any arrangements in connection with the payment of a pension, allowance or gratuity, or any death, sickness or disability benefits, to or in respect of that director.

(4) Unless the directors decide otherwise, directors' remuneration accrues from day to day.

(5) Unless the directors decide otherwise, directors are not accountable to the company for any remuneration which they receive as directors or other officers or employees of the company's subsidiaries or of any other body corporate in which the company is interested.

Directors' expenses

24. The company may pay any reasonable expenses which the directors properly incur in connection with their attendance at—

(a) meetings of directors or committees of directors,

(b) general meetings, or

(c) separate meetings of the holders of any class of shares or of debentures of the company, or otherwise in connection with the exercise of their powers and the discharge of their responsibilities in relation to the company.

ALTERNATE DIRECTORS

Appointment and removal of alternates

25.—(1) Any director (the "appointor") may appoint as an alternate any other director, or any other person approved by resolution of the directors, to—

    (a) exercise that director's powers, and

    (b) carry out that director's responsibilities, in relation to the taking of decisions by the directors in the absence of the alternate's appointor.

(2) Any appointment or removal of an alternate must be effected by notice in writing to the company signed by the appointor, or in any other manner approved by the directors.

(3) The notice must—

    (a) identify the proposed alternate, and

    (b) in the case of a notice of appointment, contain a statement signed by the proposed alternate that the proposed alternate is willing to act as the alternate of the director giving the notice.

Rights and responsibilities of alternate directors

26.—(1) An alternate director has the same rights, in relation to any directors' meeting or directors' written resolution, as the alternate's appointor.

(2) Except as the articles specify otherwise, alternate directors—

    (a) are deemed for all purposes to be directors;

    (b) are liable for their own acts and omissions;

    (c)   are subject to the same restrictions as their appointors; and

    (d)   are not deemed to be agents of or for their appointors.

(3)   A person who is an alternate director but not a director—

    (a)   may be counted as participating for the purposes of determining whether a quorum is participating (but only if that person's appointor is not participating), and

    (b)   may sign a written resolution (but only if it is not signed or to be signed by that person's appointor).

No alternate may be counted as more than one director for such purposes.

(4)   An alternate director is not entitled to receive any remuneration from the company for serving as an alternate director except such part of the alternate's appointor's remuneration as the appointor may direct by notice in writing made to the company.

Termination of alternate directorship

27.   An alternate director's appointment as an alternate terminates—

    (a)   when the alternate's appointor revokes the appointment by notice to the company in writing specifying when it is to terminate;

    (b)   on the occurrence in relation to the alternate of any event which, if it occurred in relation to the alternate's appointor, would result in the termination of the appointor's appointment as a director;

    (c)   on the death of the alternate's appointor; or

    (d)   when the alternate's appointor's appointment as a director terminates, except that an alternate's appointment as an alternate does not terminate when the appointor retires by rotation at a general meeting and is then re-appointed as a director at the same general meeting.

PART 3 DECISION-MAKING BY MEMBERS

ORGANISATION OF GENERAL MEETINGS

Members can call general meeting if not enough directors

28.   If—

    (a)   the company has fewer than two directors, and

    (b)   the director (if any) is unable or unwilling to appoint sufficient directors to make up a quorum or to call a general meeting to do so, then two or more members may call a general meeting (or instruct the company secretary to do so) for the purpose of appointing one or more directors.

Attendance and speaking at general meetings

29.—(1)   A person is able to exercise the right to speak at a general meeting when that person is in a position to communicate to all those attending the meeting, during the meeting, any information or opinions which that person has on the business of the meeting.

    (2)   A person is able to exercise the right to vote at a general meeting when—

        (a)   that person is able to vote, during the meeting, on resolutions put to the vote at the meeting, and

(b) that person's vote can be taken into account in determining whether or not such resolutions are passed at the same time as the votes of all the other persons attending the meeting.

(3) The directors may make whatever arrangements they consider appropriate to enable those attending a general meeting to exercise their rights to speak or vote at it.

(4) In determining attendance at a general meeting, it is immaterial whether any two or more members attending it are in the same place as each other.

(5) Two or more persons who are not in the same place as each other attend a general meeting if their circumstances are such that if they have (or were to have) rights to speak and vote at that meeting, they are (or would be) able to exercise them.

Quorum for general meetings

30. No business other than the appointment of the chairman of the meeting is to be transacted at a general meeting if the persons attending it do not constitute a quorum. Chairing general meetings

31.—(1) If the directors have appointed a chairman, the chairman shall chair general meetings if present and willing to do so.

(2) If the directors have not appointed a chairman, or if the chairman is unwilling to chair the meeting or is not present within ten minutes of the time at which a meeting was due to start—

    (a) the directors present, or

    (b) (if no directors are present), the meeting, must appoint a director or member to chair the meeting, and the appointment of the chairman of the meeting must be the first business of the meeting.

(3) The person chairing a meeting in accordance with this article is referred to as "the chairman of the meeting".

Attendance and speaking by directors and non-members

32.—(1) Directors may attend and speak at general meetings, whether or not they are members.

(2) The chairman of the meeting may permit other persons who are not—

    (a) members of the company, or

    (b) otherwise entitled to exercise the rights of members in relation to general meetings, to attend and speak at a general meeting.

Adjournment

33.—(1) If the persons attending a general meeting within half an hour of the time at which the meeting was due to start do not constitute a quorum, or if during a meeting a quorum ceases to be present, the chairman of the meeting must adjourn it.

(2) The chairman of the meeting may adjourn a general meeting at which a quorum is present if—

    (a) the meeting consents to an adjournment, or

    (b) it appears to the chairman of the meeting that an adjournment is necessary to protect the safety of any person attending the meeting or ensure that the business of the meeting is conducted in an orderly manner.

(3) The chairman of the meeting must adjourn a general meeting if directed to do so by the meeting.

(4) When adjourning a general meeting, the chairman of the meeting must—

    (a) either specify the time and place to which it is adjourned or state that it is to continue at a time and place to be fixed by the directors, and

    (b) have regard to any directions as to the time and place of any adjournment which have been given by the meeting.

(5) If the continuation of an adjourned meeting is to take place more than 14 days after it was adjourned, the company must give at least 7 clear days' notice of it (that is, excluding the day of the adjourned meeting and the day on which the notice is given)—

    (a) to the same persons to whom notice of the company's general meetings is required to be given, and

    (b) containing the same information which such notice is required to contain.

(6) No business may be transacted at an adjourned general meeting which could not properly have been transacted at the meeting if the adjournment had not taken place.

VOTING AT GENERAL MEETINGS

Voting: general

34. A resolution put to the vote of a general meeting must be decided on a show of hands unless a poll is duly demanded in accordance with the articles.

Errors and disputes

35.—(1) No objection may be raised to the qualification of any person voting at a general meeting except at the meeting or adjourned meeting at which the vote objected to is tendered, and every vote not disallowed at the meeting is valid.

(2) Any such objection must be referred to the chairman of the meeting whose decision is final.

Demanding a poll

36.—(1) A poll on a resolution may be demanded—

    (a) in advance of the general meeting where it is to be put to the vote, or

    (b) at a general meeting, either before a show of hands on that resolution or immediately after the result of a show of hands on that resolution is declared.

(2) A poll may be demanded by—

    (a) the chairman of the meeting;

    (b) the directors;

    (c) two or more persons having the right to vote on the resolution; or

    (d) a person or persons representing not less than one tenth of the total voting rights of all the members having the right to vote on the resolution.

(3) A demand for a poll may be withdrawn if—

    (a) the poll has not yet been taken, and

    (b) the chairman of the meeting consents to the withdrawal.

Procedure on a poll

37.—(1) Subject to the articles, polls at general meetings must be taken when, where and in such manner as the chairman of the meeting directs.

(2) The chairman of the meeting may appoint scrutineers (who need not be members) and decide how and when the result of the poll is to be declared.

(3) The result of a poll shall be the decision of the meeting in respect of the resolution on which the poll was demanded.

(4) A poll on—

(a) the election of the chairman of the meeting, or

(b) a question of adjournment, must be taken immediately.

(5) Other polls must be taken within 30 days of their being demanded.

(6) A demand for a poll does not prevent a general meeting from continuing, except as regards the question on which the poll was demanded.

(7) No notice need be given of a poll not taken immediately if the time and place at which it is to be taken are announced at the meeting at which it is demanded.

(8) In any other case, at least 7 days' notice must be given specifying the time and place at which the poll is to be taken.

Content of proxy notices

38.—(1) Proxies may only validly be appointed by a notice in writing (a "proxy notice") which—

(a) states the name and address of the member appointing the proxy;

(b) identifies the person appointed to be that member's proxy and the general meeting in relation to which that person is appointed;

(c) is signed by or on behalf of the member appointing the proxy, or is authenticated in such manner as the directors may determine; and

(d) is delivered to the company in accordance with the articles and any instructions contained in the notice of the general meeting to which they relate.

(2) The company may require proxy notices to be delivered in a particular form, and may specify different forms for different purposes.

(3) Proxy notices may specify how the proxy appointed under them is to vote (or that the proxy is to abstain from voting) on one or more resolutions.

(4) Unless a proxy notice indicates otherwise, it must be treated as—

(a) allowing the person appointed under it as a proxy discretion as to how to vote on any ancillary or procedural resolutions put to the meeting, and

(b) appointing that person as a proxy in relation to any adjournment of the general meeting to which it relates as well as the meeting itself.

Delivery of proxy notices

39.—(1) Any notice of a general meeting must specify the address or addresses ("proxy notification address") at which the company or its agents will receive proxy notices relating to that meeting, or any adjournment of it, delivered in hard copy or electronic form.

(2) A person who is entitled to attend, speak or vote (either on a show of hands or on a poll) at a general meeting remains so entitled in respect of that meeting or any adjournment of it, even though a valid proxy notice has been delivered to the company by or on behalf of that person.

(3) Subject to paragraphs (4) and (5), a proxy notice must be delivered to a proxy notification address not less than 48 hours before the general meeting or adjourned meeting to which it relates.

(4) In the case of a poll taken more than 48 hours after it is demanded, the notice must be delivered to a proxy notification address not less than 24 hours before the time appointed for the taking of the poll.

(5) In the case of a poll not taken during the meeting but taken not more than 48 hours after it was demanded, the proxy notice must be delivered—

    (a) in accordance with paragraph (3), or

    (b) at the meeting at which the poll was demanded to the chairman, secretary or any director.

(6) An appointment under a proxy notice may be revoked by delivering a notice in writing given by or on behalf of the person by whom or on whose behalf the proxy notice was given to a proxy notification address.

(7) A notice revoking a proxy appointment only takes effect if it is delivered before—

    (a) the start of the meeting or adjourned meeting to which it relates, or

    (b) (in the case of a poll not taken on the same day as the meeting or adjourned meeting) the time appointed for taking the poll to which it relates.

(8) If a proxy notice is not signed by the person appointing the proxy, it must be accompanied by written evidence of the authority of the person who executed it to execute it on the appointor's behalf.

Amendments to resolutions

40.—(1) An ordinary resolution to be proposed at a general meeting may be amended by ordinary resolution if—

    (a) notice of the proposed amendment is given to the company secretary in writing by a person entitled to vote at the general meeting at which it is to be proposed not less than 48 hours before the meeting is to take place (or such later time as the chairman of the meeting may determine), and

    (b) the proposed amendment does not, in the reasonable opinion of the chairman of the meeting, materially alter the scope of the resolution.

(2) A special resolution to be proposed at a general meeting may be amended by ordinary resolution, if—

    (a) the chairman of the meeting proposes the amendment at the general meeting at which the resolution is to be proposed, and

    (b) the amendment does not go beyond what is necessary to correct a grammatical or other non-substantive error in the resolution.

(3) If the chairman of the meeting, acting in good faith, wrongly decides that an amendment to a resolution is out of order, the chairman's error does not invalidate the vote on that resolution.

RESTRICTIONS ON MEMBERS' RIGHTS

No voting of shares on which money owed to company

41. No voting rights attached to a share may be exercised at any general meeting, at any adjournment of it, or on any poll called at or in relation to it, unless all amounts payable to the company in respect of that share have been paid.

APPLICATION OF RULES TO CLASS MEETINGS

Class meetings

42. The provisions of the articles relating to general meetings apply, with any necessary modifications, to meetings of the holders of any class of shares.

PART 4 SHARES AND DISTRIBUTIONS

ISSUE OF SHARES

Powers to issue different classes of share

43.—(1) Subject to the articles, but without prejudice to the rights attached to any existing share, the company may issue shares with such rights or restrictions as may be determined by ordinary resolution.

 (2) The company may issue shares which are to be redeemed, or are liable to be redeemed at the option of the company or the holder, and the directors may determine the terms, conditions and manner of redemption of any such shares.

Payment of commissions on subscription for shares

44.—(1) The company may pay any person a commission in consideration for that person—

  (a) subscribing, or agreeing to subscribe, for shares, or

  (b) procuring, or agreeing to procure, subscriptions for shares.

 (2) Any such commission may be paid—

  (a) in cash, or in fully paid or partly paid shares or other securities, or partly in one way and partly in the other, and

  (b) in respect of a conditional or an absolute subscription.

INTERESTS IN SHARES

Company not bound by less than absolute interests

45. Except as required by law, no person is to be recognised by the company as holding any share upon any trust, and except as otherwise required by law or the articles, the company is not in any way to be bound by or recognise any interest in a share other than the holder's absolute ownership of it and all the rights attaching to it.

SHARE CERTIFICATES

Certificates to be issued except in certain cases

46.—(1) The company must issue each member with one or more certificates in respect of the shares which that member holds.

 (2) This article does not apply to—

  (a) uncertificated shares;

  (b) shares in respect of which a share warrant has been issued; or

  (c) shares in respect of which the Companies Acts permit the company not to issue a certificate.

(3)   Except as otherwise specified in the articles, all certificates must be issued free of charge.

(4)   No certificate may be issued in respect of shares of more than one class.

(5)   If more than one person holds a share, only one certificate may be issued in respect of it.

Contents and execution of share certificates

47.—(1)   Every certificate must specify—

    (a)   in respect of how many shares, of what class, it is issued;

    (b)   the nominal value of those shares;

    (c)   the amount paid up on them; and

    (d)   any distinguishing numbers assigned to them.

(2)   Certificates must—

    (a)   have affixed to them the company's common seal or an official seal which is a facsimile of the company's common seal with the addition on its face of the word "Securities" (a "securities seal"), or

    (b)   be otherwise executed in accordance with the Companies Acts.

Consolidated share certificates

48.—(1)   When a member's holding of shares of a particular class increases, the company may issue that member with—

    (a)   a single, consolidated certificate in respect of all the shares of a particular class which that member holds, or

    (b)   a separate certificate in respect of only those shares by which that member's holding has increased.

(2)   When a member's holding of shares of a particular class is reduced, the company must ensure that the member is issued with one or more certificates in respect of the number of shares held by the member after that reduction. But the company need not (in the absence of a request from the member) issue any new certificate if—

    (a)   all the shares which the member no longer holds as a result of the reduction, and

    (b)   none of the shares which the member retains following the reduction, were, immediately before the reduction, represented by the same certificate.

(3)   A member may request the company, in writing, to replace—

    (a)   the member's separate certificates with a consolidated certificate, or

    (b)   the member's consolidated certificate with two or more separate certificates representing such proportion of the shares as the member may specify.

(4)   When the company complies with such a request it may charge such reasonable fee as the directors may decide for doing so.

(5)   A consolidated certificate must not be issued unless any certificates which it is to replace have first been returned to the company for cancellation.

Replacement share certificates

49.—(1)   If a certificate issued in respect of a member's shares is—

    (a)   damaged or defaced, or

    (b)   said to be lost, stolen or destroyed, that member is entitled to be issued with a replacement certificate in respect of the same shares.

(2)   A member exercising the right to be issued with such a replacement certificate—

    (a)   may at the same time exercise the right to be issued with a single certificate or separate certificates;

    (b)   must return the certificate which is to be replaced to the company if it is damaged or defaced; and

    (c)   must comply with such conditions as to evidence, indemnity and the payment of a reasonable fee as the directors decide.

SHARES NOT HELD IN CERTIFICATED FORM

Uncertificated shares

50.—(1)   In this article, "the relevant rules" means—

    (a)   any applicable provision of the Companies Acts about the holding, evidencing of title to, or transfer of shares other than in certificated form, and

    (b)   any applicable legislation, rules or other arrangements made under or by virtue of such provision.

(2)   The provisions of this article have effect subject to the relevant rules.

(3)   Any provision of the articles which is inconsistent with the relevant rules must be disregarded, to the extent that it is inconsistent, whenever the relevant rules apply.

(4)   Any share or class of shares of the company may be issued or held on such terms, or in such a way, that—

    (a)   title to it or them is not, or must not be, evidenced by a certificate, or

    (b)   it or they may or must be transferred wholly or partly without a certificate.

(5)   The directors have power to take such steps as they think fit in relation to—

    (a)   the evidencing of and transfer of title to uncertificated shares (including in connection with the issue of such shares);

    (b)   any records relating to the holding of uncertificated shares;

    (c)   the conversion of certificated shares into uncertificated shares; or

    (d)   the conversion of uncertificated shares into certificated shares.

(6)   The company may by notice to the holder of a share require that share—

    (a)   if it is uncertificated, to be converted into certificated form, and

    (b)   if it is certificated, to be converted into uncertificated form, to enable it to be dealt with in accordance with the articles.

(7)   If—

    (a)   the articles give the directors power to take action, or require other persons to take action, in order to sell, transfer or otherwise dispose of shares, and

    (b)   uncertificated shares are subject to that power, but the power is expressed in terms which assume the use of a certificate or other written instrument, the directors may take such action as is necessary or expedient to achieve the same results when exercising that power in relation to uncertificated shares.

(8)   In particular, the directors may take such action as they consider appropriate to achieve the sale, transfer, disposal, forfeiture, re-allotment or surrender of an uncertificated share or otherwise to enforce a lien in respect of it.

(9)   Unless the directors otherwise determine, shares which a member holds in uncertificated form must be treated as separate holdings from any shares which that member holds in certificated form.

(10)   A class of shares must not be treated as two classes simply because some shares of that class are held in certificated form and others are held in uncertificated form.

Share warrants

51.—(1)   The directors may issue a share warrant in respect of any fully paid share.

(2)   Share warrants must be—

(a)   issued in such form, and

(b)   executed in such manner, as the directors decide.

(3)   A share represented by a share warrant may be transferred by delivery of the warrant representing it.

(4)   The directors may make provision for the payment of dividends in respect of any share represented by a share warrant.

(5)   Subject to the articles, the directors may decide the conditions on which any share warrant is issued. In particular, they may—

(a)   decide the conditions on which new warrants are to be issued in place of warrants which are damaged or defaced, or said to have been lost, stolen or destroyed;

(b)   decide the conditions on which bearers of warrants are entitled to attend and vote at general meetings;

(c)   decide the conditions subject to which bearers of warrants may surrender their warrant so as to hold their shares in certificated or uncertificated form instead; and

(d)   vary the conditions of issue of any warrant from time to time, and the bearer of a warrant is subject to the conditions and procedures in force in relation to it, whether or not they were decided or specified before the warrant was issued.

(6)   Subject to the conditions on which the warrants are issued from time to time, bearers of share warrants have the same rights and privileges as they would if their names had been included in the register as holders of the shares represented by their warrants.

(7)   The company must not in any way be bound by or recognise any interest in a share represented by a share warrant other than the absolute right of the bearer of that warrant to that warrant.

PARTLY PAID SHARES

Company's lien over partly paid shares

52.—(1)   The company has a lien ("the company's lien") over every share which is partly paid for any part of—

(a)   that share's nominal value, and

(b)   any premium at which it was issued, which has not been paid to the company, and which is payable immediately or at some time in the future, whether or not a call notice has been sent in respect of it.

(2)   The company's lien over a share—

(a)   takes priority over any third party's interest in that share, and

(b)   extends to any dividend or other money payable by the company in respect of that share and (if the lien is enforced and the share is sold by the company) the proceeds of sale of that share.

(3)   The directors may at any time decide that a share which is or would otherwise be subject to the company's lien shall not be subject to it, either wholly or in part.

Enforcement of the company's lien

53.—(1)   Subject to the provisions of this article, if—
  (a)   a lien enforcement notice has been given in respect of a share, and
  (b)   the person to whom the notice was given has failed to comply with it, the company may sell that share in such manner as the directors decide.

(2)   A lien enforcement notice—
  (a)   may only be given in respect of a share which is subject to the company's lien, in respect of which a sum is payable and the due date for payment of that sum has passed;
  (b)   must specify the share concerned;
  (c)   must require payment of the sum payable within 14 days of the notice;
  (d)   must be addressed either to the holder of the share or to a person entitled to it by reason of the holder's death, bankruptcy or otherwise; and
  (e)   must state the company's intention to sell the share if the notice is not complied with.

(3)   Where shares are sold under this article—
  (a)   the directors may authorise any person to execute an instrument of transfer of the shares to the purchaser or a person nominated by the purchaser, and
  (b)   the transferee is not bound to see to the application of the consideration, and the transferee's title is not affected by any irregularity in or invalidity of the process leading to the sale.

(4)   The net proceeds of any such sale (after payment of the costs of sale and any other costs of enforcing the lien) must be applied—
  (a)   first, in payment of so much of the sum for which the lien exists as was payable at the date of the lien enforcement notice,
  (b)   second, to the person entitled to the shares at the date of the sale, but only after the certificate for the shares sold has been surrendered to the company for cancellation or a suitable indemnity has been given for any lost certificates, and subject to a lien equivalent to the company's lien over the shares before the sale for any money payable in respect of the shares after the date of the lien enforcement notice.

(5)   A statutory declaration by a director or the company secretary that the declarant is a director or the company secretary and that a share has been sold to satisfy the company's lien on a specified date—
  (a)   is conclusive evidence of the facts stated in it as against all persons claiming to be entitled to the share, and
  (b)   subject to compliance with any other formalities of transfer required by the articles or by law, constitutes a good title to the share.

Call notices

54.—(1)   Subject to the articles and the terms on which shares are allotted, the directors may send a notice (a "call notice") to a member requiring the member to pay the company a specified sum of money (a "call") which is payable in respect of shares which that member holds at the date when the directors decide to send the call notice.

    (2)   A call notice—
        (a)   may not require a member to pay a call which exceeds the total sum unpaid on that member's shares (whether as to the share's nominal value or any amount payable to the company by way of premium);
        (b)   must state when and how any call to which it relates it is to be paid; and
        (c)   may permit or require the call to be paid by instalments.
    (3)   A member must comply with the requirements of a call notice, but no member is obliged to pay any call before 14 days have passed since the notice was sent.
    (4)   Before the company has received any call due under a call notice the directors may—
        (a)   revoke it wholly or in part, or
        (b)   specify a later time for payment than is specified in the notice, by a further notice in writing to the member in respect of whose shares the call is made.

Liability to pay calls

55.—(1)   Liability to pay a call is not extinguished or transferred by transferring the shares in respect of which it is required to be paid.
    (2)   Joint holders of a share are jointly and severally liable to pay all calls in respect of that share.
    (3)   Subject to the terms on which shares are allotted, the directors may, when issuing shares, provide that call notices sent to the holders of those shares may require them—
        (a)   to pay calls which are not the same, or
        (b)   to pay calls at different times.
    When call notice need not be issued
56.—(1)   A call notice need not be issued in respect of sums which are specified, in the terms on which a share is issued, as being payable to the company in respect of that share (whether in respect of nominal value or premium)—
        (a)   on allotment;
        (b)   on the occurrence of a particular event; or
        (c)   on a date fixed by or in accordance with the terms of issue.
    (2)   But if the due date for payment of such a sum has passed and it has not been paid, the holder of the share concerned is treated in all respects as having failed to comply with a call notice in respect of that sum, and is liable to the same consequences as regards the payment of interest and forfeiture.

Failure to comply with call notice: automatic consequences

57.—(1)   If a person is liable to pay a call and fails to do so by the call payment date—
        (a)   the directors may issue a notice of intended forfeiture to that person, and
        (b)   until the call is paid, that person must pay the company interest on the call from the call payment date at the relevant rate.
    (2)   For the purposes of this article—
        (a)   the "call payment date" is the time when the call notice states that a call is payable, unless the directors give a notice specifying a later date, in which case the "call payment date" is that later date;
        (b)   the "relevant rate" is—
            (i)   the rate fixed by the terms on which the share in respect of which the call is due was allotted;

       (ii)   such other rate as was fixed in the call notice which required payment of the call, or has otherwise been determined by the directors; or

       (iii)   if no rate is fixed in either of these ways, 5 per cent per annum.

(3)   The relevant rate must not exceed by more than 5 percentage points the base lending rate most recently set by the Monetary Policy Committee of the Bank of England in connection with its responsibilities under Part 2 of the Bank of England Act 1998(1).

(4)   The directors may waive any obligation to pay interest on a call wholly or in part.

Notice of intended forfeiture

58. A notice of intended forfeiture—

    (a)   may be sent in respect of any share in respect of which a call has not been paid as required by a call notice;

    (b)   must be sent to the holder of that share or to a person entitled to it by reason of the holder's death, bankruptcy or otherwise;

    (c)   must require payment of the call and any accrued interest by a date which is not less than 14 days after the date of the notice;

    (d)   must state how the payment is to be made; and

    (e)   must state that if the notice is not complied with, the shares in respect of which the call is payable will be liable to be forfeited.

Directors' power to forfeit shares

59. If a notice of intended forfeiture is not complied with before the date by which payment of the call is required in the notice of intended forfeiture, the directors may decide that any share in respect of which it was given is forfeited, and the forfeiture is to include all dividends or other moneys payable in respect of the forfeited shares and not paid before the forfeiture.

Effect of forfeiture

60.—(1) Subject to the articles, the forfeiture of a share extinguishes—

    (a)   all interests in that share, and all claims and demands against the company in respect of it, and

    (b)   all other rights and liabilities incidental to the share as between the person whose share it was prior to the forfeiture and the company.

(2)   Any share which is forfeited in accordance with the articles—

    (a)   is deemed to have been forfeited when the directors decide that it is forfeited;

    (b)   is deemed to be the property of the company; and

    (c)   may be sold, re-allotted or otherwise disposed of as the directors think fit.

(3)   If a person's shares have been forfeited—

    (a)   the company must send that person notice that forfeiture has occurred and record it in the register of members;

    (b)   that person ceases to be a member in respect of those shares;

    (c)   that person must surrender the certificate for the shares forfeited to the company for cancellation;

    (d)   that person remains liable to the company for all sums payable by that person under the articles at the date of forfeiture in respect of those shares, including any interest (whether accrued before or after the date of forfeiture); and

    (e)   the directors may waive payment of such sums wholly or in part or enforce payment without any allowance for the value of the shares at the time of forfeiture or for any consideration received on their disposal.

    (4)   At any time before the company disposes of a forfeited share, the directors may decide to cancel the forfeiture on payment of all calls and interest due in respect of it and on such other terms as they think fit.

Procedure following forfeiture

61.—(1)   If a forfeited share is to be disposed of by being transferred, the company may receive the consideration for the transfer and the directors may authorise any person to execute the instrument of transfer.

    (2)   A statutory declaration by a director or the company secretary that the declarant is a director or the company secretary and that a share has been forfeited on a specified date—

        (a)   is conclusive evidence of the facts stated in it as against all persons claiming to be entitled to the share, and

        (b)   subject to compliance with any other formalities of transfer required by the articles or by law, constitutes a good title to the share.

    (3)   A person to whom a forfeited share is transferred is not bound to see to the application of the consideration (if any) nor is that person's title to the share affected by any irregularity in or invalidity of the process leading to the forfeiture or transfer of the share.

    (4)   If the company sells a forfeited share, the person who held it prior to its forfeiture is entitled to receive from the company the proceeds of such sale, net of any commission, and excluding any amount which—

        (a)   was, or would have become, payable, and

        (b)   had not, when that share was forfeited, been paid by that person in respect of that share, but no interest is payable to such a person in respect of such proceeds and the company is not required to account for any money earned on them.

Surrender of shares

62.—(1)   A member may surrender any share—

        (a)   in respect of which the directors may issue a notice of intended forfeiture;

        (b)   which the directors may forfeit; or

        (c)   which has been forfeited.

    (2)   The directors may accept the surrender of any such share.

    (3)   The effect of surrender on a share is the same as the effect of forfeiture on that share.

    (4)   A share which has been surrendered may be dealt with in the same way as a share which has been forfeited.

TRANSFER AND TRANSMISSION OF SHARES

Transfers of certificated shares

63.—(1)   Certificated shares may be transferred by means of an instrument of transfer in any usual form or any other form approved by the directors, which is executed by or on behalf of—

      (a)   the transferor, and

      (b)   (if any of the shares is partly paid) the transferee.

(2)   No fee may be charged for registering any instrument of transfer or other document relating to or affecting the title to any share.

(3)   The company may retain any instrument of transfer which is registered.

(4)   The transferor remains the holder of a certificated share until the transferee's name is entered in the register of members as holder of it.

(5)   The directors may refuse to register the transfer of a certificated share if—

      (a)   the share is not fully paid;

      (b)   the transfer is not lodged at the company's registered office or such other place as the directors have appointed;

      (c)   the transfer is not accompanied by the certificate for the shares to which it relates, or such other evidence as the directors may reasonably require to show the transferor's right to make the transfer, or evidence of the right of someone other than the transferor to make the transfer on the transferor's behalf;

      (d)   the transfer is in respect of more than one class of share; or

      (e)   the transfer is in favour of more than four transferees.

(6)   If the directors refuse to register the transfer of a share, the instrument of transfer must be returned to the transferee with the notice of refusal unless they suspect that the proposed transfer may be fraudulent.

Transfer of uncertificated shares

64. A transfer of an uncertificated share must not be registered if it is in favour of more than four transferees.

Transmission of shares

65.—(1)   If title to a share passes to a transmittee, the company may only recognise the transmittee as having any title to that share.

(2)   Nothing in these articles releases the estate of a deceased member from any liability in respect of a share solely or jointly held by that member.

Transmittees' rights

66.—(1)   A transmittee who produces such evidence of entitlement to shares as the directors may properly require—

      (a)   may, subject to the articles, choose either to become the holder of those shares or to have them transferred to another person, and

      (b)   subject to the articles, and pending any transfer of the shares to another person, has the same rights as the holder had.

(2)   But transmittees do not have the right to attend or vote at a general meeting in respect of shares to which they are entitled, by reason of the holder's death or bankruptcy or otherwise, unless they become the holders of those shares

Exercise of transmittees' rights

67.—(1)   Transmittees who wish to become the holders of shares to which they have become entitled must notify the company in writing of that wish.

(2)   If the share is a certificated share and a transmittee wishes to have it transferred to another person, the transmittee must execute an instrument of transfer in respect of it.

(3)   If the share is an uncertificated share and the transmittee wishes to have it transferred to another person, the transmittee must—
    (a)   procure that all appropriate instructions are given to effect the transfer, or
    (b)   procure that the uncertificated share is changed into certificated form and then execute an instrument of transfer in respect of it.

(4)   Any transfer made or executed under this article is to be treated as if it were made or executed by the person from whom the transmittee has derived rights in respect of the share, and as if the event which gave rise to the transmission had not occurred.

Transmittees bound by prior notices

68.   If a notice is given to a member in respect of shares and a transmittee is entitled to those shares, the transmittee is bound by the notice if it was given to the member before the transmittee's name has been entered in the register of members.

CONSOLIDATION OF SHARES

Procedure for disposing of fractions of shares

69.—(1)   This article applies where—
    (a)   there has been a consolidation or division of shares, and
    (b)   as a result, members are entitled to fractions of shares.

(2)   The directors may—
    (a)   sell the shares representing the fractions to any person including the company for the best price reasonably obtainable;
    (b)   in the case of a certificated share, authorise any person to execute an instrument of transfer of the shares to the purchaser or a person nominated by the purchaser; and
    (c)   distribute the net proceeds of sale in due proportion among the holders of the shares.

(3)   Where any holder's entitlement to a portion of the proceeds of sale amounts to less than a minimum figure determined by the directors, that member's portion may be distributed to an organisation which is a charity for the purposes of the law of England and Wales, Scotland or Northern Ireland.

(4)   The person to whom the shares are transferred is not obliged to ensure that any purchase money is received by the person entitled to the relevant fractions.

(5)   The transferee's title to the shares is not affected by any irregularity in or invalidity of the process leading to their sale.

DISTRIBUTIONS

Procedure for declaring dividends

70.—(1)   The company may by ordinary resolution declare dividends, and the directors may decide to pay interim dividends.

(2)   A dividend must not be declared unless the directors have made a recommendation as to its amount. Such a dividend must not exceed the amount recommended by the directors.

(3)   No dividend may be declared or paid unless it is in accordance with members' respective rights.

(4)   Unless the members' resolution to declare or directors' decision to pay a dividend, or the terms on which shares are issued, specify otherwise, it must be paid by reference to each member's holding of shares on the date of the resolution or decision to declare or pay it.

(5)   If the company's share capital is divided into different classes, no interim dividend may be paid on shares carrying deferred or non-preferred rights if, at the time of payment, any preferential dividend is in arrear.

(6)   The directors may pay at intervals any dividend payable at a fixed rate if it appears to them that the profits available for distribution justify the payment.

(7)   If the directors act in good faith, they do not incur any liability to the holders of shares conferring preferred rights for any loss they may suffer by the lawful payment of an interim dividend on shares with deferred or non-preferred rights.

Calculation of dividends

71.—(1)   Except as otherwise provided by the articles or the rights attached to shares, all dividends must be—

(a)   declared and paid according to the amounts paid up on the shares on which the dividend is paid, and

(b)   apportioned and paid proportionately to the amounts paid up on the shares during any portion or portions of the period in respect of which the dividend is paid.

(2)   If any share is issued on terms providing that it ranks for dividend as from a particular date, that share ranks for dividend accordingly.

(3)   For the purposes of calculating dividends, no account is to be taken of any amount which has been paid up on a share in advance of the due date for payment of that amount.

Payment of dividends and other distributions

72.—(1)   Where a dividend or other sum which is a distribution is payable in respect of a share, it must be paid by one or more of the following means—

(a)   transfer to a bank or building society account specified by the distribution recipient either in writing or as the directors may otherwise decide;

(b)   sending a cheque made payable to the distribution recipient by post to the distribution recipient at the distribution recipient's registered address (if the distribution recipient is a holder of the share), or (in any other case) to an address specified by the distribution recipient either in writing or as the directors may otherwise decide;

(c)   sending a cheque made payable to such person by post to such person at such address as the distribution recipient has specified either in writing or as the directors may otherwise decide; or

(d)   any other means of payment as the directors agree with the distribution recipient either in writing or by such other means as the directors decide.

(2)   In the articles, "the distribution recipient" means, in respect of a share in respect of which a dividend or other sum is payable—

(a)   the holder of the share; or

(b)   if the share has two or more joint holders, whichever of them is named first in the register of members; or

(c)   if the holder is no longer entitled to the share by reason of death or bankruptcy, or otherwise by operation of law, the transmittee.

Deductions from distributions in respect of sums owed to the company

73.—(1) If—

    (a)   a share is subject to the company's lien, and

    (b)   the directors are entitled to issue a lien enforcement notice in respect of it, they may, instead of issuing a lien enforcement notice, deduct from any dividend or other sum payable in respect of the share any sum of money which is payable to the company in respect of that share to the extent that they are entitled to require payment under a lien enforcement notice.

    (2)   Money so deducted must be used to pay any of the sums payable in respect of that share.

    (3)   The company must notify the distribution recipient in writing of—

        (a)   the fact and amount of any such deduction;

        (b)   any non-payment of a dividend or other sum payable in respect of a share resulting from any such deduction; and

        (c)   how the money deducted has been applied.

No interest on distributions

74. The company may not pay interest on any dividend or other sum payable in respect of a share unless otherwise provided by—

    (a)   the terms on which the share was issued, or

    (b)   the provisions of another agreement between the holder of that share and the company.

Unclaimed distributions

75.—(1) All dividends or other sums which are—

    (a)   payable in respect of shares, and

    (b)   unclaimed after having been declared or become payable, may be invested or otherwise made use of by the directors for the benefit of the company until claimed.

    (2)   The payment of any such dividend or other sum into a separate account does not make the company a trustee in respect of it.

    (3)   If—

        (a)   twelve years have passed from the date on which a dividend or other sum became due for payment, and

        (b)   the distribution recipient has not claimed it, the distribution recipient is no longer entitled to that dividend or other sum and it ceases to remain owing by the company.

Non-cash distributions

76.—(1) Subject to the terms of issue of the share in question, the company may, by ordinary resolution on the recommendation of the directors, decide to pay all or part of a dividend or other distribution payable in respect of a share by transferring non-cash assets of equivalent value (including, without limitation, shares or other securities in any company).

    (2)   If the shares in respect of which such a non-cash distribution is paid are uncertificated, any shares in the company which are issued as a non-cash distribution in respect of them must be uncertificated.

(3) For the purposes of paying a non-cash distribution, the directors may make whatever arrangements they think fit, including, where any difficulty arises regarding the distribution—

(a) fixing the value of any assets;

(b) paying cash to any distribution recipient on the basis of that value in order to adjust the rights of recipients; and

(c) vesting any assets in trustees.

Waiver of distributions

77. Distribution recipients may waive their entitlement to a dividend or other distribution payable in respect of a share by giving the company notice in writing to that effect, but if—

(a) the share has more than one holder, or

(b) more than one person is entitled to the share, whether by reason of the death or bankruptcy of one or more joint holders, or otherwise, the notice is not effective unless it is expressed to be given, and signed, by all the holders or persons otherwise entitled to the share.

CAPITALISATION OF PROFITS

Authority to capitalise and appropriation of capitalised sums

78.—(1) Subject to the articles, the directors may, if they are so authorised by an ordinary resolution—

(a) decide to capitalise any profits of the company (whether or not they are available for distribution) which are not required for paying a preferential dividend, or any sum standing to the credit of the company's share premium account or capital redemption reserve; and

(b) appropriate any sum which they so decide to capitalise (a "capitalised sum") to the persons who would have been entitled to it if it were distributed by way of dividend (the "persons entitled") and in the same proportions.

(2) Capitalised sums must be applied—

(a) on behalf of the persons entitled, and

(b) in the same proportions as a dividend would have been distributed to them.

(3) Any capitalised sum may be applied in paying up new shares of a nominal amount equal to the capitalised sum which are then allotted credited as fully paid to the persons entitled or as they may direct.

(4) A capitalised sum which was appropriated from profits available for distribution may be applied—

(a) in or towards paying up any amounts unpaid on existing shares held by the persons entitled, or

(b) in paying up new debentures of the company which are then allotted credited as fully paid to the persons entitled or as they may direct.

(5) Subject to the articles the directors may—

(a) apply capitalised sums in accordance with paragraphs (3) and (4) partly in one way and partly in another;

(b) make such arrangements as they think fit to deal with shares or debentures becoming distributable in fractions under this article (including the issuing of fractional certificates or the making of cash payments); and

(c) authorise any person to enter into an agreement with the company on behalf of all the persons entitled which is binding on them in respect of the allotment of shares and debentures to them under this article.

PART 5 MISCELLANEOUS PROVISIONS

COMMUNICATIONS

Means of communication to be used

79.—(1) Subject to the articles, anything sent or supplied by or to the company under the articles may be sent or supplied in any way in which the Companies Act 2006 provides for documents or information which are authorised or required by any provision of that Act to be sent or supplied by or to the company.

(2) Subject to the articles, any notice or document to be sent or supplied to a director in connection with the taking of decisions by directors may also be sent or supplied by the means by which that director has asked to be sent or supplied with such notices or documents for the time being.

(3) A director may agree with the company that notices or documents sent to that director in a particular way are to be deemed to have been received within a specified time of their being sent, and for the specified time to be less than 48 hours.

Failure to notify contact details

80.—(1) If—

(a) the company sends two consecutive documents to a member over a period of at least 12 months, and

(b) each of those documents is returned undelivered, or the company receives notification that it has not been delivered, that member ceases to be entitled to receive notices from the company.

(2) A member who has ceased to be entitled to receive notices from the company becomes entitled to receive such notices again by sending the company—

(a) a new address to be recorded in the register of members, or

(b) if the member has agreed that the company should use a means of communication other than sending things to such an address, the information that the company needs to use that means of communication effectively.

ADMINISTRATIVE ARRANGEMENTS

Company seals

81.—(1) Any common seal may only be used by the authority of the directors.

(2) The directors may decide by what means and in what form any common seal or securities seal is to be used.

(3) Unless otherwise decided by the directors, if the company has a common seal and it is affixed to a document, the document must also be signed by at least one authorised person in the presence of a witness who attests the signature.

(4)   For the purposes of this article, an authorised person is—
  (a)   any director of the company;
  (b)   the company secretary; or
  (c)   any person authorised by the directors for the purpose of signing documents to which the common seal is applied.
(5)   If the company has an official seal for use abroad, it may only be affixed to a document if its use on that document, or documents of a class to which it belongs, has been authorised by a decision of the directors.
(6)   If the company has a securities seal, it may only be affixed to securities by the company secretary or a person authorised to apply it to securities by the company secretary.
(7)   For the purposes of the articles, references to the securities seal being affixed to any document include the reproduction of the image of that seal on or in a document by any mechanical or electronic means which has been approved by the directors in relation to that document or documents of a class to which it belongs.

Destruction of documents

82.—(1)   The company is entitled to destroy—
  (a)   all instruments of transfer of shares which have been registered, and all other documents on the basis of which any entries are made in the register of members, from six years after the date of registration;
  (b)   all dividend mandates, variations or cancellations of dividend mandates, and notifications of change of address, from two years after they have been recorded;
  (c)   all share certificates which have been cancelled from one year after the date of the cancellation;
  (d)   all paid dividend warrants and cheques from one year after the date of actual payment; and
  (e)   all proxy notices from one year after the end of the meeting to which the proxy notice relates.
(2)   If the company destroys a document in good faith, in accordance with the articles, and without notice of any claim to which that document may be relevant, it is conclusively presumed in favour of the company that—
  (a)   entries in the register purporting to have been made on the basis of an instrument of transfer or other document so destroyed were duly and properly made;
  (b)   any instrument of transfer so destroyed was a valid and effective instrument duly and properly registered;
  (c)   any share certificate so destroyed was a valid and effective certificate duly and properly cancelled; and
  (d)   any other document so destroyed was a valid and effective document in accordance with its recorded particulars in the books or records of the company.
(3)   This article does not impose on the company any liability which it would not otherwise have if it destroys any document before the time at which this article permits it to do so.
(4)   In this article, references to the destruction of any document include a reference to its being disposed of in any manner.

No right to inspect accounts and other records

83. Except as provided by law or authorised by the directors or an ordinary resolution of the company, no person is entitled to inspect any of the company's accounting or other records or documents merely by virtue of being a member.
Provision for employees on cessation of business

84. The directors may decide to make provision for the benefit of persons employed or formerly employed by the company or any of its subsidiaries (other than a director or former director or shadow director) in connection with the cessation or transfer to any person of the whole or part of the undertaking of the company or that subsidiary.

DIRECTORS' INDEMNITY AND INSURANCE

Indemnity

85.—(1) Subject to paragraph (2), a relevant director of the company or an associated company may be indemnified out of the company's assets against—

    (a) any liability incurred by that director in connection with any negligence, default, breach of duty or breach of trust in relation to the company or an associated company,

    (b) any liability incurred by that director in connection with the activities of the company or an associated company in its capacity as a trustee of an occupational pension scheme (as defined in section 235(6) of the Companies Act 2006),

    (c) any other liability incurred by that director as an officer of the company or an associated company.

  (2) This article does not authorise any indemnity which would be prohibited or rendered void by any provision of the Companies Acts or by any other provision of law.

  (3) In this article—

    (a) companies are associated if one is a subsidiary of the other or both are subsidiaries of the same body corporate, and

    (b) a "relevant director" means any director or former director of the company or an associated company.

Insurance

86.—(1) The directors may decide to purchase and maintain insurance, at the expense of the company, for the benefit of any relevant director in respect of any relevant loss.

  (2) In this article—

    (a) a "relevant director" means any director or former director of the company or an associated company,

    (b) a "relevant loss" means any loss or liability which has been or may be incurred by a relevant director in connection with that director's duties or powers in relation to the company, any associated company or any pension fund or employees' share scheme of the company or associated company, and

    (c) companies are associated if one is a subsidiary of the other or both are subsidiaries of the same body corporate.

Web directory

Advisory, Conciliation and Arbitration Service
www.acas.org.uk

Bar Council
www.barcouncil.org.uk

British and Irish Legal Information Institute
www.bailii.org

Chartered Institute of Management Accountants
www.cimaglobal.com/

Chartered Institute of Legal Executives
www.cilex.org.uk

Companies House
www.gov.uk/government/organisations/companies-house

Company information
https://beta.companieshouse.gov.uk/

Company name checker
https://beta.companieshouse.gov.uk/company-name-availability

Competition & Markets Authority
www.gov.uk/government/organisations/competition-and-markets-authority

Confederation of British Industry
www.cbi.org.uk/

Court of Justice of the European Union
https://curia.europa.eu

Courts and Tribunals Judiciary
www.judiciary.gov.uk

Department for Business, Energy & Industrial Strategy
www.gov.uk/government/organisations/department-for-business-energy-and-industrial-strategy

Domain name registrars
ICANN
www.icann.org/

Nominet UK
www.nominet.uk/

Internic
www.internic.net/

European Business Register
www.ebr.org/

European Court of Human Rights
http://echr.coe.int

European Patent Office
www.epo.org/index.html

European Union
https://europa.eu

Financial Conduct Authority
FCA Handbook
www.handbook.fca.org.uk/handbook

Listing rules
www.handbook.fca.org.uk/handbook/LR/

Financial Services Register
https://register.fca.org.uk/

Mutuals Public Register
www.fca.org.uk/firms/mutuals-public-register

Financial Reporting Council
www.frc.org.uk/

Audit resources
www.frc.org.uk/auditors

Corporate governance
www.frc.org.uk/directors/corporate-governance-and-stewardship
www.frc.org.uk/

HM Courts & Tribunals Service
www.gov.uk/government/organisations/hm-courts-and-tribunals-service

HM Land Registry
www.gov.uk/government/organisations/land-registry

HM Revenue & Customs
www.gov.uk/government/organisations/hm-revenue-customs

Stamp duty
www.gov.uk/topic/business-tax/stamp-taxes

Information Commissioner's Office
www.ico.org.uk

Institute of Chartered Accountants in England and Wales
www.icaew.com/

Institute of Chartered Accountants in Ireland
www.charteredaccountants.ie/

Institute of Chartered Accountants in Scotland
www.icas.com/

Institute of Directors
www.iod.com/

International Corporate Governance Network
www.icgn.org/

Judicial Committee of the Privy Council
www.jcpc.uk

Law society
www.lawsociety.org.uk/

London Stock Exchange
www.londonstockexchange.com/home/homepage.htm

Admission and disclosure standards
www.londonstockexchange.com/companies-and-advisors/main-market/
documents/admission-and-disclosure-standards.pdf

AIM rules
www.londonstockexchange.com/companies-and-advisors/aim/advisers/rules/aim-rules-
for-companies-updated-october-2018.pdf

Dividend timetable
www.londonstockexchange.com/traders-and-brokers/rules-regulations/dividend-
procedure-timetable-2019.pdf

Panel on Takeovers and Mergers
www.thetakeoverpanel.org.uk/

Patent/Trademark Office
www.gov.uk/government/organisations/intellectual-property-office

Prudential Regulation Authority
www.bankofengland.co.uk/prudential-regulation

Supreme Court of the United Kingdom
www.supremecourt.uk

The Chartered Governance Institute
www.icsa.org.uk/

Guidance material
www.icsa.org.uk/knowledge

Publications
www.icsa.org.uk/shop

Trade Union Congress
www.tuc.org.uk/

UK Legislation
www.legislation.gov.uk/

UK Listing Authority
www.fca.org.uk/markets/ukla

UK Parliament
www.parliament.uk

Index

Lightning Source UK Ltd.
Milton Keynes UK
UKHW021309180221
378950UK00004B/257